To Ca

Love, ~nonya

see page 151

4-15-2011

MW01007694

DAILY DEVOTIONS FOR WRITERS

By members of
The Writing Academy
and other Christian writers

Compiled and edited by Patricia Lorenz

Copyright © 2008 by The Writing Academy

ISBN 0-7414-4594-8

Cover design by Chris A. Master

Compiled and edited by Patricia Lorenz; copy edited and interior formatted by Melanie Rigney

The writers celebrate the diversity in God's written word. Versions of the Bible used in this book are abbreviated in this way: Contemporary English Version (CEV); English Standard Version (ESV); King James Version (KJV); The Living Bible (TLB); The Message (MSG); New American Bible (NAB); New American Standard Bible (NASB); New Century Version (NCV); New International Revised Standard (NIRV); New International Version (NIV); New King James Version (NKJV); New Living Translation (NLT); New Revised Standard Version (NRSV); and Revised Standard Version (RSV)

Published by:

PUBLISHING.COM

1094 New DeHaven Street, Suite 100
West Conshohocken, PA 19428-2713
Info@buybooksontheweb.com
www.buybooksontheweb.com
Toll-free (877) BUY BOOK
Local Phone (610) 941-9999
Fax (610) 941-9959

Printed in the United States of America
Printed on Recycled Paper
Published March 2008

History of
The Writing Academy

The Writing Academy is a worldwide community of Christian writers whose mission is to encourage excellence in writing through correspondence courses, annual seminars and personal nurturing. Of its sixty-plus-person roster, twenty-two are charter members.

The Academy is Wisconsin-born, the offspring of the Bethel Bible series. Rev. Harley Swiggum of Madison, the series' author, envisioned a cadre of people who could elevate the standards of Christian writing. So in 1978, he organized sixty aspiring writers nationwide who had survived a series of tests he conducted over a five-day period at the Yahara Center in Madison, then home of the Adult Christian Education Foundation (Bethel's parent organization).

Swiggum's dream was to have The Writing Academy grow and flourish, with members participating in seminars and group projects. Out of this desire emerged an instructional program that included courses in basic writing skills, fiction, myth and metaphor.

The Writing Academy incorporated in 1982 and continues today as an independent, nonprofit organization. The academy met in Madison, Wisconsin, through 1990, then in New Harmony, Indiana; Des Moines, Iowa; Nashville, Tennessee; Minneapolis, Minnesota; Snow Mountain Ranch, Colorado; back in

Madison; then St. Louis, Missouri. In 2000, the group settled at the Mount Olivet Retreat Center south of Minneapolis and has been there ever since, meeting once a year.

The academy is volunteer-powered; only professional tutors and speakers are paid. Friendships are born and relationships nourished by a common spirit, strengthened by a common struggle, bonded by a common goal.

Pastor-writer Tom Mullen of Richmond says, "The Writing Academy is set apart from other short-term workshops that nurture writers seeking to improve their skills and cross over into the promised land of publication. The academy encourages community, not competition. The outside resource leaders understand and appreciate the fears and anxieties of aspiring writers and identify with their labors to write and rewrite. Participants quickly catch the spirit of all-for-each-other as they provide and seek feedback on written work."

At The Writing Academy's twenty-fifth anniversary in 2003, Harley Swiggum said, "I think the reason you (members) have stayed together is that you see Christ in one another's faces."

Foreword

This book of devotions has been written by people just like you. As you read these stories, you may laugh, cry, sigh, remember, and dream. We hope you'll be inspired to continue to strengthen your life as a writer. As writers, we know that ideas are everywhere. But just as a farmer's seeds will never grow and produce a crop unless the seeds are sown, we must take our ideas and put them into words. The words become sentences, then paragraphs, then stories.

We needed a project to help The Writing Academy accomplish three goals: encourage the members to write more, help raise money to keep The Writing Academy in existence, and bring in new members.

I called everyone together to discuss a group project. Our 2007 conference's keynote speaker, Patricia Lorenz, was so inspired by the group's camaraderie and warmth that she became involved with all the activities and our concerns. She suggested we write a daily devotional book for writers.

It has been amazing to watch God bless this book. From that first hour as we shared ideas to the miracle you hold in your hands, God has opened heart after heart and provided just the right person we needed, each step of the way. Patricia is a treasure. For three months full time, she gathered, selected, and edited the devotions as they poured in from all over the country. She called her friends, who called their friends, to help. Her gift of leadership, time, and talent from concept to publication was invaluable.

It has been a blessing to watch as the devotions poured in from The Writing Academy members and from so many other Christian writers from all over the country. This book represents two hundred writers from thirty-five states, Canada, Australia, and Japan.

The Writing Academy desires to use the talents with which God blessed us to inspire, encourage, educate, and entertain others. It has been a safe, comfortable place to express ideas and share our work. We hope you will be as inspired to read this book each day and become a better writer because of it.

Through our personal stories, you will get to know the contributors to this book. Most have provided their e-mail addresses at the end. Some are speakers and teachers and would love to participate in your conferences.

Perhaps you are looking for a safe place to enhance your writing. Consider joining The Writing Academy and attending our annual conference. You can always stay informed by going to www.wams.org.

Lonni L. Docter
President of The Writing Academy

Thank You

When I suggested to The Writing Academy members that a book of daily devotions about writing would encourage them to do more writing, bring in much-needed financial help, and draw in new members, I had no idea that I was about to volunteer to coordinate the project and pull the book together.

I remember standing in that room in Minnesota in the summer of 2007, my brain saying, "No, no, don't volunteer. This could take the best part of a year out of your writing life." But my heart, oh dear, that was another matter. My heart felt the love in that room. I saw people who had grown so close to each other over the years. My heart answered quickly. "Yes, I'll do it."

Back home in Florida, I put all other projects on hold and worked seven days a week. I couldn't wait to get up in the morning to see what was waiting in my e-mail. Thanks to the all the people below and to the power of e-mail, this book was born in record time. I am forever grateful for your help, talent and generosity in making this book a 100 percent donation for a good cause and for helping to make the birthing of this book such a fun, challenging, and delightful experience.

Thank you to all the talented writers who opened their minds, their hearts, and their writing experiences and then wrote splendid devotions for every day of the year.

Thank you to the board of directors of The Writing Academy for your faith in this project and for being so cooperative and helpful in making every step a joyful one.

To my dear friend Melanie Rigney, www.editorforyou.com, thank you for donating your skillful final editing and formatting of this book to make it look and read as professional as all the contributors dreamed it would.

To Tom Gregory, president of Infinity Publishing, www.infinitypublishing.com, who encourages all writers to write their passion and get it published, thank you for your generosity with the contract terms and for believing in this nonprofit group. Thanks also to the Infinity employees who worked so hard to turn the work of two hundred writers into a book that is so helpful for all writers the world over.

Thank you to Cec Murphey, www.cecilmurphey.com, whose generous donation from the Cecil Murphey Scholarship Fund made the publication of this book possible and help launch the fund-raising aspect of this project.

Many blessings to you all.

Patricia Lorenz

January 1

Empty page. Blank screen. Dread and sometimes panic. A writing rite of passage that never ends. Sometimes, I'm able to set aside self-absorption to rejoice in the notion of community. Maybe "rejoice" is too strong a word. Let's say I'm comforted by knowing other writers are feeling nauseated at the exact same moments, for the exact same reasons.

Frankly, I'm suspicious of anyone claiming to love writing all the time. I love it, too. Except when I don't. And I do not love writing when I'm staring into the abyss of getting started. I don't love it when project shape shifts. I definitely don't like it after I've finished whatever I once dreaded beginning.

My precious rituals for getting past panic have changed over the years. I used to reread my published oeuvre. I used to reread a folder of kudos. I used to lay supine on my office floor until all three cats purred me into calm.

Then, I added prayers to the mix. These too have changed over the years. Prayers of supplication have given way to prayers of gratitude. Worrying about what to write is, after all, such a high-class problem. Not that I've stopped whimpering. At least the cats answer. So does God. Eventually.

Lord, you've created me to be creative. Please come to my assistance Lord, make haste to help me.

In returning and rest you shall be saved; in quietness and in trust shall be your strength. Isaiah 30:15 RSV
—Meredith Gould, Ph.D

January 2

When Harley Swiggum announced tryouts for The Writing Academy, "crude" described my essays. No one ever said, "Jim, you should be a writer."

But my wife, Vivian, a Bethel Bible Study Series teacher, saw the printed notice for the trials and said, "You can do it."

After the Academy selected me, I met writers who could tell me what was wrong with my efforts. I did not want to critique their work because it all looked better than mine.

For almost thirty years, every teacher and member of our fellowship has strengthened me. Two years ago, Shirley Stevens introduced me to short story writing, teaching me to develop characters and build crises. She made me feel I could do it.

During the years when Vivian and I lived on the shore of Lake Michigan, we could see Manitou Island eight miles away. In the 1850s, immigrants landed there. I wrote historical fiction about Kevin from Ireland and Anna from Bavaria.

When I arranged for that book, *Tales of Manitou,* to be sent to The Writing Academy in 2006, it was one of the most satisfying moments of my life.

Lord, thank you for the gift of writing and for giving me courage to keep trying.

With God all things are possible. Matthew 19:26 RSV
—James R. Tozer

January 3

When my daughter Julia was five years old, she put a note under her pillow. *Dear Tooth Fary. Heres my toooth. It dint bleed. I love you. Julia*

The tooth fairy responded with fifty cents and a longer note thanking Julia for the tooth, about the importance of brushing her teeth every day and smiling often because it would make people happy.

Julia loved the note so much she took it to school to show her teacher and friends. Thus began a long habit:

Jeanne, good luck on that spelling test today! I think you're a spelling whiz. Love, Mom
Michael, don't forget to take out the garbage. By the way, you did a great job cleaning your room. I love you, Mom
Andrew, I am so proud of you! I heard you helped Mrs. Cook rake her leaves. Way to go, son. Love, Mom

As my four children entered high school and college and then went out on their own, I began to write longer pieces about how their antics inspired or confounded me. Before long, some of my stories were getting published; in a few years, I was writing whole books. And to think it all began with a simple note from the tooth fairy.

Lord, thank you for the gift of writing and for so many amazing things in your world that keep inspiring me to write.

A little child will lead them. Isaiah 11:6 TLB
—Patricia Lorenz

3

January 4

Over twenty years ago, I wrote a short tribute to my parents for Mother's Day and Father's Day. I outlined each tribute with an oval shape and mounted them in one frame, separating them with calico printed material.

Upon completion, I almost threw them out. Having no confidence in my writing ability, I thought they were terrible. But, instead, I swallowed my pride and thought, "I went through all this work, and I may as well give it to them."

My parents loved my tributes. Tears swelled up in my mother's eyes and my father beamed. Mother proudly displayed the frame on their bedroom dresser.

I realize now that it would have been a shame if I had thrown out the tributes. My father is deceased, and my mother still enjoys reading them. Even I enjoy the tributes now.

We never know when our written words will brighten someone's day or entire life. That's why we need to keep writing.

Thank you, Lord, for giving me ability to show my love in this special way.

Write things worth reading or do things worth writing. Benjamin Franklin

—Sally Devine

January 5

I stared at the rejection slip. The half sheet of paper held more power than the editor realized. The article had been hatched in a moment, grew to momentous length on paper, and flew onto the editor's desk. Two months passed, and the pages returned instead of the anticipated check.

The typewriter came out of the case for one last try, but I sat stymied at the blank paper. I wept, arose, and cleared the desk. Other duties called. Often I would read a magazine and think, I could have written that, but I didn't try.

Many years later I faced the empty nest syndrome. The paper came out of the drawer. My fingers flew across the computer keys and I knew the exhilaration of a new challenge, a new game. Experiences with my children, their pets, and their father turned into print, but still I was afraid to submit to an editor.

I shared the best with friends and family.

"These should be published," they said.

"No, I tried. I failed."

"Nonsense. Try again."

I prepared the manuscript. The envelope lay on my desk for days. Then in a brash moment of reaching out, I marched to the post office. Weeks passed.

Then the check came with a note. "Do you have more manuscripts?"

Dear Father, help me realize that writing is a ministry I cannot give up no matter how many times I'm rejected.

Your faith has healed you. Go in peace and [write some more]. Luke 8:48 NIV

—Rose Goble

January 6

Mother often said, "I want to write a book about your dad's experiences in World War II, about when he was a POW in Stalag XIII-C in Hammelburg, Germany, for six months."

At age seventy-five, her dream still had not been accomplished, but she had lots of small writings and poems in an old stationery box tied shut with a sheer purple ribbon. Her five-year bout with Alzheimer's was in its early stages when, with a friend's help, she compiled Maxine's Musings.

Mother's project inspired me to start writing. In high school, my writings had never been considered exceptional. I could get a B, not an A. I didn't know how to get started on a productive path of writing. So, I started searching for training opportunities on the Web.

The year Mom died, I found The Writing Academy and attended its seminar at Mount Olivet Retreat Center south of Minneapolis, Minnesota. I soon realized it was not too late to awaken my dreams and find fulfillment in writing. The fellowship, friends, and knowledge I have gained each year since then have been immeasurable.

Lord, I can't thank you enough for allowing me the privilege of finding The Writing Academy, this superb group of writers who encourage one another in so many ways.

Your vision will become clear only when you look into your heart. Who looks outside, dreams. Who looks inside, awakens. Carl Jung

—Margaret Steinacker

January 7

My college lit teacher was reading my paper to the class and I was thrilled. My profile of the schemer Iago had a uniqueness she hadn't seen in any student's appraisal of Shakespeare's *Othello*.

Then she put the essay in my hands. B-plus, it said.

B-plus! With rhapsodizing on that scale, why hadn't that young graduate assistant given me an A?

"Well, I'm not sure you wrote it," she explained after class. "It looks professional."

"Look," I answered, voice quivering half in anger, half in nervousness. "If I didn't write that paper—I mean, if I lifted it from somewhere—I deserve an F. But if I wrote it, which I certainly did, then I deserve an A. No B-plus about it."

Appeal denied. The paper went into my file, turned yellow and eventually disappeared.

But what I took away from the encounter stayed with me: I had stood up for my writing. For the first time, I had stood up. Unwittingly, that literature instructor had done me a big favor.

Lord, grant me the grit it takes to defend my work.

Anxiety is…an unreasoning dread…Full faith in God puts it to rest. Horace Bushnell

—Jerry Elsea

January 8

Bone weary, I came home from my job to care for my loving husband. His recent diagnosis of esophageal cancer had put our lives in a tailspin.

Neither of us could have survived those months of treatment and surgery without the daily love, prayers and care of our church family. Each night, someone would knock on the door and deliver whole-grain bread, a crispy garden salad, and a bowl of piping hot soup.

As my Christian friends fed me, I realized that, as a freelance writer, I needed to be nourished daily with stimulating reading material, time to listen to the quiet whisper of God, and an uncluttered place to compose. Just as I set aside time to eat three meals a day, I needed time for writing.

Between 6:30 and 7:30 each morning I began to meditate in silence or with my keyboard. I learned that listening and being still is hard in the midst of the blaring TV, ringing phone, and knocking at the door. So I snapped off the TV, read the paper instead of listening to the news, shut off the ringer on the phone, and put a "do not disturb" sign on the door. Thanks to my early-morning plan, writing became just as much a discipline as brushing my teeth.

Dear Lord, help me write what you want me to say.

Inch by inch, life is a cinch. Yard by yard, life is hard. Author unknown

—Sheryl Van Weelden

January 9

I didn't want to write my last book. My plan was to retire to Arizona, do some part-time work for a hospice organization, enjoy my woodshop and play tennis and golf. After thirty-five years of pastoral ministry, I thought it was a good plan. The plan was right on schedule for about eighteen months. I worked weekends as a hospice chaplain, and during the week played with my shop toys, tennis racquet and golf clubs. What a plan.

But then it happened. It wasn't a burning bush experience, only a statement from a friend about the stories I was sharing with him regarding my hospice work. They were stories of dying people's spiritual journeys, and what I was learning from them.

He said, "You ought to write a book."

I said, "No thank you, I'm content to be a one-book author."

Others began echoing his suggestion, so I finally gave in and the next four years did not go according to my plan. The book was published, not because I planned it but because a voice in the desert was listened to.

It makes me think of Moses, in retirement, at eighty years of age fulfilling his plan to just be a shepherd but hearing the voice from the burning bush suggest another plan.

Gracious God, help me hear your still small voice again today.

If you want to make God laugh, tell him your plans. Author unknown

—William H. Griffith

January 10

After receiving two devastating rejections one spring, I wanted to quit. Just give up the whole thing. One morning with my Bible open, I considered what writing had already cost me. A lot.

It cost time, lots of it. I barely had time for my friends anymore. Most of my hobbies were long gone. It cost self-discipline, making myself work long hours and do things I hated, like paperwork and taxes. Once, I worked all day on my birthday.

Why on earth did I ever want to write? I could make more money selling real estate.

That's when God whispered, reminding me how much I'd been paid. Had I forgotten how my articles were circulated to remote churches in Australia's outback? How about others reprinted around the world? Words are missionaries. Did I not value the ministry of words?

Writing for Christian markets forced me to study the Scriptures regularly. Was that not priceless, not to mention the joy of obedience? Would I dump my calling over two rejections? I sat ashamed, looking at the Bible on my lap.

Where did this little verse come from? "Complete the work you have received in the Lord." (Col. 4:17)

That's it? Just get it done? I guessed I could do that. In fact, I couldn't imagine doing anything else.

Why was I surprised when both rejected pieces sold the following month?

Lord, keep me faithful to you.

"My food," said Jesus, "is to do the will of him who sent me." John 4:34 NIV

—Virelle Kidder

January 11

The journaling course instructor said, "If you have unresolved issues with someone, write a dialogue between yourself and the person about the issue."
I wondered how that would resolve anything. I had unresolved issues with my father who had died several years before. The instructor assured me the person did not have to be present, or even alive, for this exercise.
I wrote my true feelings, saying things I never would have said directly to my father. I was happy to vent my feelings and then write my father's response. What a great way to have him say things I wished he had said when he was alive.
As the exercise continued, I found my father's responses surprising, unexpected. Could I be gaining new insight into who my father was and why he behaved as he did? Could I be discovering things as an adult that I simply could not have understood as a child?
Dialoguing may not resolve issues, but it begins the journey to forgiveness and compassion. I learned a valuable lesson that day about the power of writing.

Lord, help me to speak, think, reason, and, most of all, write, in ways that bring glory to you.

When I was a child, I spoke like a child, I thought like a child, I reasoned like a child; when I became an (adult), I gave up childish ways. 1 Corinthians 13:11 RSV
—Nancy Remmert

January 12

"Rick," I shouted. "What in the world are you doing?"
Rick, a high school sophomore, had slit the end of the middle finger of his right hand, and it began to bleed. To fill his time while I worked with two other students, he began squeezing the blood from his finger with his left hand and writing his name in his textbook. I came upon him in time to watch him begin the k.

As a new teacher, I was outraged. I grabbed a tissue, mopped the blood, and scolded him.

"But Mrs. Clark," he whined, "I weren't doin' nothing, just writin' my name." He slammed the book closed.

Over the years when I've written poetry, essays, or devotions and have struggled to find just the correct word, the right phrase, or the best style, a picture of Rick pops into my head. I can see his blood dripping onto the page. He demonstrated in a physical way the whole process of writing for me. It's just like squeezing my life blood right out the ends of my fingers.

Dear Lord, thank you for your promise written in Revelation 3:5 that you will not blot my name out of the book of life.

Writing is easy. You just sit down at the typewriter and open a vein. Red Smith

—Kay J. Clark

January 13

Today I write on the yellow pad, on my couch at 3:00 a.m. On three recent days I wrote on the computer in my office at 2:00 p.m.; then, not at all; and finally, in the notebook in a restaurant at noon. Most books on writing advise that we writers find a time to write every day and be consistent. But I can't tell you how many times I've tried and failed to be consistent at writing. "Self, you MUST get up at 5:00 a.m. every day and write for three hours before the phone starts to ring," I think. But it doesn't work; I'm still tired.

One reason I'm tired is that I am often awake at 3:00 in the morning and it can take an hour or more to get back to sleep. With no ringing telephones or impending chores I don't call it insomnia, I call it reading heaven. It could just as well be writing heaven when it happens, but that is not consistent either.

Therefore, I have given up on consistent and given myself permission to change my schedule as needed, to write when I am able and to not feel guilty about it. Now I find myself writing more than ever. Who knew?

Dear God, thank you for giving me the freedom to find my own way. Give me wisdom and courage to follow my own path.

This above all, to thine own self be true. William Shakespeare

—Connie Scharlau

January 14

When I was young, mother tied my shoes. My stubby fingers could not control the unruly laces. Finally, the day came when I tied my shoes myself, and took a growing step forward.

In 1979, I joined The Writing Academy. Building friendships with other Christian writers thrilled me. I sat in awe of Harley Swiggum, founder of the Academy. Harley didn't want awe. I came to love his sense of humor, his warmth, his gift for storytelling.

At home, I wrote, wrote, wrote. Assignments in every genre were scrutinized by professional editors and returned bloodstained with red ink. Wondering why my creations weren't recognized as perfection, I grumbled while I rewrote, rewrote, rewrote. Finally, I came to savor the red ink. I took another growing step forward.

For nearly thirty years, the Academy has helped me put shoes on my dreams. Summer seminars energized me with inspiring speakers, opportunities to explore my thoughts, critiques to hone my craft, devotional services to feed my faith.

One summer, realizing how much I had learned, still had to learn, I wrote: "I brought him my accomplishments that he might see only my success. He showed me my weaknesses, tempered with gentle judgment that I might see myself."

Lord, thank you for guiding my steps to The Writing Academy, and for editors who help me grow as a writer.

Let the wise listen and add to their learning, and let the discerning get guidance. Proverbs 1:5 NIV
—Tommie Lenox

January 15

"I can't stand being stuck one more minute!" I screamed on a quiet morning after the boys had left for school. I wanted to write children's stories, but fear of failure kept me from trying.

Slumped on the couch, I slammed my coffee cup down on the table, closed my eyes, and breathed deeply.

Lord, take away this fear! I don't want it anymore!

I sank into a deep and peaceful meditation. Twenty minutes later, I opened my eyes. In the instant it took to focus on the oriental carpet in front of the couch, an entire story formed in my mind. A story about the beautiful bird in the carpet's center, and his relationship with a mischievous boy named Matthew McCallister.

I hopped off the couch and ran for notebook and pen. The story gushed forth like a geyser, unstoppable. My arm ached after a solid hour of writing, but my spirit sang. You've heard of runner's high? This was writer's high!

I was given that story twenty-five years ago. While it was never published, it unstopped the dam. I've since written and published two books, as well as numerous magazine, journal, and newspaper articles. Writer's block? Never again.

Lord, your unfailing love bought me a ticket for a magic carpet ride into the land of my dreams. My heart (and pen!) overflows.

There is no fear in love, but perfect love casts out fear. 1 John 4:18a RSV

—Kathleen Deyer Bolduc

January 16

In one of my first years as a writing professor at Taylor University in Fort Wayne, Indiana, I had a young man named Sean in my class. He was a champion weight lifter and wrestler.

One day Sean came into my office, closed the door, and began to cry. He lifted a paper I had returned to him the previous day. On it, along with an A grade, I had written, "Excellent work, son. Well done."

He looked at me and said, "My father deserted our family when I was only four. All my life, I've wanted a man I respect to call me son. That means more to me than my grade, Dr. Hensley. I promise you, I'll never let you down."

Sean went on to be a teacher in the inner city of a major metropolis, where most kids never knew a dad. He became their surrogate father.

I've never forgotten, as a teacher and as a writer, that one word has the potential to alter a life.

Father, let me be sensitive to the fact that I am involved in a ministry when I am writing.

Is not a word better than a gift? Ecclesiastes 18:17 KJV
—Dennis E. Hensley, Ph.D.

January 17

Encouraged by my pastor, I queried Augsburg Publishing for the guidelines to *Christ in our Home* devotions book. I received them and was asked to submit three devotionals. Augsburg then sent me an assignment for twenty, which were all accepted. And, I was paid. Wow! I thought. I'm now a writer!

My addiction to alcohol then led me to a month's treatment, followed by a three-month residence in a halfway house for chemically dependent women. When visiting me one evening in February, my husband said he had a surprise for me. He reached into his pocket and presented me with a copy of the February through March *Christ in our Home*.

I opened the cover and on the first page, where the credits were, I saw it: Marlys A. Korman, Writer. I was mortified. How on earth could I have written these devotionals at a time my alcoholism had escalated?

The next night in the large-group setting, I shared how embarrassed I was to have my works published at this time. The group responded by saying, "It's OK, Mar, not everything you did prior to treatment was bad." What comfort that brought.

The next night I introduced myself in the group by saying, "I'm Mar, and I'm chemically dependent." To myself I added, And, I'm a writer!

Gracious God, strengthen my faith and grant me the confidence to write well and often.

Write the vision; make it plain on tablets. Habakkuk 2:2a NRSV

—Rev. Marlys Korman

January 18

Junk, toss it. Bill, stack it. I systematically sorted my mail. And then...an intriguing postcard advertised a Southampton College, Long Island, summer course on memoir writing. I signed up.

Southampton's summer residents added panache to our class—a sophisticated soap opera veteran, a Trieste socialite, a still-gorgeous sixtyish model with stage and screen experience, and other quasi-famous folks. In addition, we had a Hell's Kitchen survivor and a very intimidated me.

Edith, our no-nonsense Swiss instructor, was like a mother bird. She flapped her arms and twittered as she taught, her sharp black eyes calculating when to shove us from the nest.

The day came to read our work. The determined Hell's Kitchen woman went first. Her riveting introduction detailed abuses she'd overcome.

"Next," Edith chirped, head cocked. "Annette."

My hands shook. I looked down and read.

Edith led the critique—positive feedback first, then constructive criticism. After her pointers she said, "Good! We want more." It was unanimous! These fascinating people wanted more of my story.

The others discussed what they could write, would write, should write. Only Ms. Hell's Kitchen and I wrote. Writing and reading for critique has become easier, but when fears grip me, I remember the alternative is a story that's never told.

Jesus, thank you for helping me overcome fear.

I command you—be strong and courageous. Joshua 1:9 NLT

—Annette M. Eckart

January 19

Recently, I told an aunt about my latest book. She chuckled. "Honey, I wish I could just sit down and write." I wish I could too. Even with seventeen books and five-hundred-plus articles to my credit, I find writing hard work. And if that isn't enough, life has a way of interrupting publishing plans. Years ago, while writing my first book, I cared for a young husband with brain cancer, grieved his death, raised two young children, and switched careers from teaching to editing. Today, those children are grown and married, and have given me two adorable grandsons. I still have excuses I could use if I wanted a more routine life. But writing isn't for quitters.

My son Jay graduated with a friend who planned to write the Great American Novel. Instead, he took an entry-level job. When Jay asked about the book, his friend shrugged, "I'm waiting for the muse."

Jay looked at him. "Come to my mom's house some night when she's on deadline and she's typing through tears because she's so tired. Then I'll show you the muse."

When Jay reported the scene, I hugged him for his understanding. No, I'm not the most talented writer this world has ever seen, but I persevere. And that allows me to smile instead of murmuring, "I wish."

Lord, thank you for writing opportunities—and for your encouragement to persevere.

Great works are performed not by strength, but perseverance. Samuel Johnson

—Sandra P. Aldrich

January 20

"Who do you think you're fooling?"

"What?"

"You can't be serious."

"Oh, you again. Shhhh. I'm writing."

"Oh yes, your little hobby. But is that the best use of your time? You didn't sort the socks yet. The lint trap needs cleaning. Your library books are overdue. Do you have any idea what you're making for dinner tonight?"

"Not listening to you. Let's see, where was I?"

"You really aren't qualified to write a devotional piece, you know. Your prayer life hasn't been that great lately..."

"I...I prayed in the car on the way to Wal-Mart."

"Well, I guess you could call that praying, but you weren't really focused. Remember? You were still seething about what your husband said this morning. If you can't get your own act together, how will you ever help somebody else?"

"Maybe that's why I need to write about prayer—to let the reader know I struggle too."

"Perhaps...but um—how can I say this delicately? This prose is swill. There's no cadence, no content. The more you write, the worse you get. Do us all a favor and quit now. And another thing..."

"Arrrrrrr wrrrrrr errrrrrr..."

Lord, help me to take those unsorted socks and stuff them in the mouths of all the negative voices. Give me ears to hear you only and the courage to put one word after another.

His sheep follow him because they know his voice.
John 10:3 NIV

—Patty Kyrlach

January 21

"Julia, the piece you submitted lies within the real story." Suzanne Clauser gazed from me to the manuscript.

Although she didn't understand the vulnerabilities writing my story would unleash, that encounter set me on the journey to my destiny. She introduced me to authors and screenwriters at the Antioch Writers' Workshop who encouraged me.

Lianne Spidel, a poet in my dorm, and I became good friends. "Revealing a life after memory loss could help readers who have dealt with similar situations," she said. After spending eighteen years wishing someone would tell his or her story and give me guidelines on how to survive, I was being asked to do that for others.

Tears flowed as I wrote what I knew, searched for what I didn't, and filled gaps to cover what I may never recall. I began telling my story as Suzanne had suggested in 1988 and started climbing a treacherous path. Each victory strengthened me for the next challenge. Now, I live rather than survive.

I believed Hebrews 11:1: "Faith is the substance of things hoped for, the evidence of things not seen." I completed several writing courses and had the manuscript professionally edited. Sometimes I send letters or stories to people who are hurting and answer their questions about faith through the struggle. Writing heals.

Lord, thank you for the gift of writing and the vision to be a writer.

There are no secrets to success. It is the result of preparation, hard work, and learning from failure. Colin Powell

—Julia F. Bell

January 22

Our eighth-grade English teacher read us "The Lady or the Tiger" by Frank Stockton. In the story, a young man is forced to choose between two doors in punishment for having fallen in love with the king's daughter. A ravaging tiger lurks behind one door and behind the other a beautiful woman. The king's justice was either death or marriage to someone other than his daughter. The king's daughter, knowing which door held which, pointed to a door—and the young man chose it.

"Did a lady or a tiger come out of the door?" we demanded to know. Our teacher only said, "What do you think?"

I learned that day another dimension to writing. I learned that fiction writing could be not only entertaining but also could create dialogue between author and reader. Could I learn to write in such a way that people would feel compelled to enter into a mental dialogue with me?

In search of an answer, I started writing. I longed only to develop enough skills to trigger a response in another person. How far along am I? I don't know. But it is a fantastic journey.

Creator God help me develop the gifts so freely given.

Excellence is a journey, not a place to be. Author unknown

—Gerald Ebelt

January 23

I find delight where stories meet one another.

I enjoy stories—hearing them, writing them. After a lifetime of writing, much of it professionally, I am still humbled when, as managing editor of *The Lutheran* magazine, I interview people and they trustingly share their stories with me. They lay open large chunks of their lives or shine a spotlight on small pieces, trusting that I will take what they've given me and shape it into something honest and meaningful that others will want to read because it somehow touches their own stories.

I take seriously the trust that's placed in me to take heartfelt sharings and retell them with faithfulness and integrity. I'm especially aware of this when I interview people who have been abused. It was front and center in my mind in May 1991 when I spent three weeks in Liberia hearing the faith stories of Lutherans who had experienced incredible brutality during the civil war.

What's really delightful is when a person's story joins with the story of God's activity in that person's life—and that connects with the stories of those who read it. A sweet mix indeed.

Loving God, you call each of us by name. Each of us is unique. Each has a story. May we lovingly call out each other's stories.

I have called you by name, you are mine. …you are precious in my sight, and honored, and I love you. Isaiah 43:1, 4 NRSV

—Sonia C. Solomonson

January 24

Educated and active in painting and design, I was invited to help expand the arts program of our retirement center. The executive director, holding a red marker, stood by a large tablet.

"Let's brainstorm. Anything that might motivate our residents," she said.

Suggestions flowed. Painting...drawing...weaving...ceramics...sculpting...

Finally I raised my hand.

"What about writing? Writing is an art, you know."

I learned to write after I returned to college at fifty-five. I graduated with an English literature degree, minoring in art. I soon joined The Writing Academy and, benefiting from many courses and seminars, became published.

Then in retirement, the Passavant Writers and Passavant Poets were born. Two wonderful retired teacher friends agreed to head the workshops.

When I approached my neighbors, they protested, "I can't write!" But I persisted, and our workshops got going. We shared life experiences. We scribbled our memoirs without the worry of good grammar and spelling. We learned and read new and classic forms of poetry. We created our own. After two years, we even published a journal called *Once Upon a Memory*. And we're still going strong.

Thank you, Lord, for helping me fill my senior years with learning so I can share my life in new ways.

There is no old age. There is, as there always was, just you. Carol Matthau

—Mary A. Koepke

January 25

"Sometimes I think I live in a madhouse!" I complained to my writing partner, Joan. "I don't have time to even think about writing, let alone actually do any."

I'd been reeling from the hectic life I'd led since the birth of my son's twins, Zane and Anna, who had just turned eighteen months. Since both parents worked nights, grandparents were called upon to baby-sit. They're lovable kids and lots of fun, but they don't merely walk; they run, jump, climb, especially climb. There isn't a drawer or cupboard they haven't opened.

To that chaotic situation add the two kittens we had recently adopted. I'd lost count of the plants, pots, and figurines they'd destroyed.

"Zane crawled into the fireplace, opened the flue, and let in a bat. The kids and cats had a great time," I told Joan, describing the pandemonium that followed. "I have two sets of baby twins running rampant, wreaking havoc, and you want me to write? About what?"

"Sounds more like a fun house than a madhouse," she said, laughing. "But to answer your question, start with the story about the bat."

Lord, help me recognize that what I see as problems are really gifts. Thank you for so many subjects to write about right under my nose.

Great opportunities come to all, but many do not know they have met them. A. E. Dunning

—Fran Elsea

January 26

My first foray into writing fiction was a laughable failure. Though I had written nonfiction articles, I longed to release my imagination. Inspired by Isaac Asimov, I quickly created a science fiction story and sent it off. My story was quickly rejected. But I was not daunted. I tried suspense writing, fantasy, adventure, homespun tales of old men at the coffee shop, and more. Every good book I read by someone else inspired me to try my hand at a new genre.

Every attempt failed.

But then a new book inspired me: *The Courage to Write* by Ralph Keyes. In it he wrote, "I prefer a man who is unskillful, who is an awkward writer, but who has something to say, who is dealing with himself one time on every page."

An unskillful, awkward writer? Perhaps that's me. But looking upon my writing, I agree with Mr. Keyes. Those stories I wrote that were an imitation of another's were malodorous. The stories I write in which my life intertwines with the characters' lives, in which the ink is mixed with a measure of blood, these stories far excel all my others.

Lord, grant me the courage to write from my heart, using my own voice.

Write what you know. Author unknown
—Drew Zahn

January 27

Over the years, I've paid the bills with my proofreading, not my writing. I was born with an excruciating attention to detail, and proofreading seemed the only way to use that dubious skill without annoying people. My children had grown tired of me proofreading the news crawl at the bottom of the television, and nobody likes a know-it-all who corrects grammar during conversations at parties.

I've seen every type of spelling and punctuation mistake ever made—probably twice. I'm good at what I do. But I'd often wondered if my nitpicking was a worthy use of my time. It seemed so trivial a thing in God's glorious world. As long as people were communicating, did it really matter if they misspelled a word or two along the way?

Then I heard a sermon in which the preacher quoted the first chapter of John: "In the beginning was the Word, and the Word was with God, and the Word was God." This simple, profound truth suddenly leapt at me: God considers words so important that Christ is the Word. God communicates his offer of salvation using words so that we can understand and be saved. It gives meaning to my mundane work to know God loved words long before I did.

Lord, thank you for the gift of words. Help me to use them wisely and well, always for your glory.

And the word became flesh and dwelt among us, and we beheld his glory. John 1:14 NKJV

—Linda M. Au

January 28

"It's snowing," my husband said, "You might want to cancel plans to go to the convention."

I can't! I'm a delegate! I thought. But after seeing how bad it was outside and making several calls, I decided to stay home.

When I woke up that morning, I never expected to have six hours for writing projects, prepare a home-cooked meal, and relax with family. The day had been preprogrammed for another event.

But God sent a snowstorm.

There were times when I didn't consider acts of God a gift, nor did I have a thankful attitude. To me they were intrusions rather than a welcome unscheduled opportunity.

The previous year, I had allowed time to slip by rather than complete a writing project. Even that was due to choices. When asked to do this or that, I agreed, instead of making time to write.

When our writers' group shared New Year goals, I said mine would be to devote more time to writing. Along with that I selected a verse: "Not slothful in business; fervent in spirit; serving the Lord (Romans 12:11)."

Thank you, Lord, for the gift of time. Help me remember that if I don't use it, I'll lose it.

Instead you ought to say, If it is the Lord's will, we will live, and do this or that. James 4:15 NIV

—Kathy Scott

January 29

Many years ago I began correspondence with Esther L. Vogt, a Christian author whom I admired. She was known for her children's novel *Turkey Red* and its sequels. She captured readers with the 1877 story of Mennonites from the Ukraine. They brought their faith and Turkey Red wheat seed to Kansas.

One weekend, I went to Esther's home in Hillsboro, Kansas, and interviewed her for an article. Soon we became close friends. She mentored me and planted motivating seeds.

"Always pray before you write, and love your reader," she said. To my surprise she dedicated one of her books: "To my friend Charlotte, whose love and encouragement I cherish."

In 1994, I phoned Esther on her seventy-ninth birthday. I scribbled down her sharing: "I've told the Lord: as long as you have a job for me to do in writing, give me the grace and I'll do it. And he has!" That year, she released another novel.

Esther is in heaven now. I miss her. She inspired me to plant words deeply from the soil of the faith. And God has given the growth.

Lord, thank you for empowering those who write for you—at any age.

Even in old age they will still produce fruit; they will remain vital and green. Psalms 92:14 NLT
—Charlotte Adelsperger

January 30

After sending articles to numerous editors, I anxiously waited for answers. Rejections arrived. "I'm no good." I ripped the envelope in half. "I'm wasting my time. Why did I ever think I could write?"

Weeks later, I received my first acceptance letter and a fifty-dollar check. "Hot dog! God must want me to be a writer."

But the following weeks brought only disappointment. "No one will ever buy my writing again. I have no talent. God must want me to do something else with my life." Then I received another acceptance letter.

My life became a frightening roller coaster ride, controlled by editors' responses. Brief highs were followed by deep despair. At the computer, my mood would swing from, "I can do this," to "Why bother?" Then, a verse I read in my daily devotion put me on the right track: "Write, rejoice, reflect on man's comments, but rely on God's divine plan."

Thank you, God, for being with me during the good times and the bad. Teach me not to question and worry about my future, but to seek and trust only you.

When times are good, be happy; but when times are bad, consider: God has made the one as well as the other. Therefore, a man cannot discover anything about his future. Ecclesiastes 7:14 NIV

—Rebecca Willman Gernon

January 31

When I was five years old, my parents gave me *The Cat in the Hat Comes Back*, the first book that was my very own. I giggled in delight at the cat's antics, and the pages became tattered from countless readings. I dreamed that someday I would write like Dr. Seuss.

At nine years of age, I read my first Nancy Drew mystery. My heart pounded each time Nancy, Bess, and George found themselves in a hopeless predicament, and I sighed with relief at their deliverance. I devoured that series in two years—twice. I dreamed that someday I would write like Carolyn Keene.

When I was fourteen, I solved the first of scores of murders with Miss Marple and Hercule Poirot. I fell in love with English cottages and tiny villages, and I longed to sip tea and nibble on cucumber sandwiches; and, oh, the delight of discovering whodunit before the final page. I dreamed that someday I would write like Agatha Christie.

Now, as an adult, I read nearly fifty books a year—Max Lucado, John Grisham, Chuck Swindoll, Mary Higgins Clark, and more; well-known authors, great authors, best-selling authors.

And, after reading hundreds of books, I dream only that I will write like—me!

Lord, thank you for the gift of being me.

Think left and think right and think low and think high. Oh, the things you can think up if only you try!
Theodor Seuss Geisel

—Mary Englund Murphy

February 1

The February I was in second grade, I had frequent colds that kept me home—and not only from school. I usually accompanied my parents to their Thursday night choir rehearsal and sit in the robe room, reading or playing with toys. But during my illness, a woman came to sit with me. Millie was white-haired, heavyset, and talcum-scented, and she read me stories from my books.

After several weeks, I tired of hearing the same old stories in Millie's singsong voice. During the next week, I sat up in bed and wrote a new story entitled "My Dolls." I printed it in a composition notebook and illustrated it with stick figures in the margin at the top of each page. "This is my story-of-the-week," it began, and it chronicled seven pretend-days in the life of Nancy and four of her dolls.

When Millie arrived on Thursday, I handed her the notebook and said, "Here. Read me this one."

I soon recovered and returned to school. But I continued to pencil words on blue lines. My second story, "Working Hard," imagined what the four dolls did when Nancy went away for a day and assigned them household chores. Other stories followed. By next February, the notebook was full.

As school homework became more challenging, I had less time for extracurricular writing. But I never forgot the fun of hearing my own story read.

Lord, may I always write with childlike enthusiasm.

Teach us delight in simple things. Rudyard Kipling
　　　　　　　　　　　　　　　　—Nancy E. James

February 2

I enjoy sewing, but sometimes it can be frustrating. I sit down at the machine with visions of making wonderful gifts, only to find I spend most of my time pulling stitches and starting over again.

This reminds me of writing. The frustration of not finding the perfect word or having to rewrite several times, sends many of my essays to the "later" file or the garbage.

At seminars, the instructors tell us, "Rewrite, rewrite, rewrite." This is a valuable part of writing. Even professional authors do not turn out a perfect manuscript the first time.

After from one seminar, I went to my "later" file and looked at the essays I had started. One was about being an identical twin, titled "Shared Identity." "Misguided Trust" was about my cousin's camping experience. I even tried writing poems. "Road Trip" was about when we were driving on snow-packed roads; "Reflection" was written while looking at a calm lake.

With hard work and determination, I know I can become a published writer. Who knows? It might even be something from my "later" file.

Lord, give me the ability to believe in myself and the courage to continue writing.

Every writer is a frustrated actor who recites his lines in the hidden auditorium of his skull. Rod Serling

—Sally Devine

February 3

It was the lowest time in my life. I came down with environmental illness, reacting to foods, medications, and things in the environment with frightening and painful symptoms. As the illness progressed, I became housebound and was forced to leave my career as a nurse. I was dealing not only with my feelings of isolation from being housebound, but also with the deaths of my oldest sister and my father. Feeling hopeless, I started getting up before the crack of dawn to pray.

One morning, I sensed God directing me to write. This can't be, I thought...after all I was a nurse, not a writer. Still, I decided to follow that lead and found it to be a life-changing experience.

I started by writing devotions on beautiful angel stationery and sending them to friends. With their encouraging words and the leading of the Holy Spirit, I approached my local paper and began writing a weekly religion column. My writings now appear in my own books, newspaper columns, several anthologies, magazines, and devotional books—all because I took a step of faith.

Faithful Father, thank you for your plan for my life.

For I know the plans I have for you. Jeremiah 29:11 NIV

—Annettee Budzban

February 4

I surveyed the books recently placed in the small bookshelf in my spare bedroom. I had already filled one bookshelf and borrowed one from my mother. It had been my bookshelf as a child and fittingly, I placed those books in it that I'd acquired as a young person. Each title represented an early influence: *The Black Stallion, Black Beauty,* and *Benji* to name a few.

Growing up on a farm in rural West Virginia, my imagination flourished. In reality, I led a simple life, but in my mind were dreams and worlds unknown to others. But I had failed to connect my love of reading and my gift of imagination with the wonder of writing. Not until I entered a mandatory writing contest in my ninth-grade English class did I realize the power writing would hold over my life.

I experienced my first rejection slip as other stories passed mine in the contest. But something wonderful happened as I wrote that story; my soul shivered with excitement at finally putting those things in my imagination down on paper. I became a writer that day.

Lord, thank you for helping me find my way to writing.

I am a writer, and I'm going to be a writer, and I'll die believing that! Gilbert Morris

—Shannon Wine

February 5

No deep-sea fisherman ever worked harder than I did to land an agent. I read every book on the subject, attended workshops, and then pestered an author in a certain agent's stable for a sure-fire approach. And it worked.

But I worried that my agent wasn't a true visionary. She explained that a book could take fourteen months or more to travel from acceptance to the shelf, especially for a new author. She totally snuffed out my dreams of a bidding war among publishers, but at least she was gentle about it. I hung in there because she was kind. She even paid the postage on my mailings.

Some thought my book funny, some well written, but the demand for humorous memoirs by total unknowns had crashed and burned while I was researching how to get an agent. That was in 2002, and I still think about the irony when I read my favorite authors.

But should I ever finish my humorous-cozy mystery-suspense-chick-lit novel, I won't adapt it to any existing genre or polish it till I die a wizened old woman curled over the computer. I'll mail copies of that sucker, still warm from the printer, to every agent in the world, cold turkey.

So there.

Oh Lord, help me finish this novel I have kept on the back burner, and give me courage to turn it loose.

God provides the wind, but man must raise the sails.
St. Augustine

—Betsy Dill

February 6

Several years ago I completed the Stephen Ministry training. This Christian caregiving program for laypeople taught me the importance of reaching out to those who are hurting. I learned that just a short visit, a listening ear, or taking the time to write a handwritten message on a card can mean a lot.

When I need to show my support and concern to someone, I often find it is easier to write a card. Rarely do I send a card and just sign my name. Writing words of comfort or sharing special memories of a loved one only takes a few minutes, but is something that can be read many times.

At the end of my note, I write a sentence prayer for God's love to surround the person and include a quote from scripture. Writing gives me the opportunity to express my compassion and love to a hurting friend.

Gracious God, help me remember that a written note can mean so much. Give me the words to share your love and forgiveness.

Whenever I open my mouth, words may be given me so that I will fearlessly make known the mystery of the gospel. Ephesians 6:19 NIV

—Louise Glimm

February 7

A hand-torn slip of paper clings by aging cellophane tape to the top edge of my monitor. The message is just one line in watery blue ink. The day I printed it, my printer had run out of black, and I couldn't afford to buy more.

The economic recession that gripped the nation in the early nineties hit the Puget Sound hard. It hit my new writing business even harder. Every time I contacted a client or publisher, I was rejected. The reason most often given was, "With the recession on, we have to write this ourselves."

One morning, I stared out my window. Gray storm clouds rolled in a slow, endless boil across the sky. For the hundredth time, I asked myself, "What made me think I could start a writing business? Did I answer God's call—or imagine it? Should I change my direction?"

Eventually, I opened my Bible to the day's reading—a brief psalm about a mighty struggle and the temptation to second-guess. Buried neatly in the middle of the passage, several plain words reminded me that God was still with me: "The Lord... will not change his mind."

Those are the words I read every day as I start work in my writing studio.

Lord, thank you for your staying power.

The Lord has sworn and will not change his mind.
Psalms 110:4a NIV

—Paulette B. Henderson

February 8

In 2003, I was due for minor surgery. Following the example of a friend, I wrote a letter to each of my two kids and to my husband. You know, just in case. What would I want my daughter to know, should I suddenly be torn from her life? What would my young son need to hear from me if I left him unexpectedly? What would encourage my husband to carry on in my absence?

The exercise made me cry. I tucked the letters away for enterprising survivors to find. God's will was otherwise, though. My surgery was uneventful, and I forgot about the letters.

Four years later, I found them. My daughter had married and had a child of her own. My son had become an independent teenager. And my husband had walked out on us months earlier. Had I not documented my feelings for my loved ones when I did, how unaware might I be now to the slow metamorphosis that had taken place over time. Especially surprising was that circumstantial changes did little to alter the emotions I felt in 2003. That revelation gave me a peace I didn't even know I needed.

Thank you, Lord, for leading me to write with assurance about unconditional, enduring love.

My aim is to put down on paper what I see and what I feel in the best and simplest way. Ernest Hemingway
—Trish Perry

39

February 9

I had studied hard. I knew the material well. So I felt mystified when my essay exam in sociology came back with a poor grade. So, I did what I normally would be too timid to do. I paid a visit to my professor in his office to protest.

I believe I convinced this gracious man that I knew the material. All the same, he insisted that I'd written around the answers.

We reviewed my essays together, and I had to admit he was right. If the exam had been two hours longer, perhaps I might have gotten to the point.

He upped my grade a bit, simply because I had come to speak with him. But as I left his office he said, "Just remember this: If you put enough monkeys at enough typewriters, eventually one of them will write the complete works of Shakespeare."

Today when I write, I narrow my focus, and strive to hit that proverbial nail on the head.

Lord, give me the words I need to share nuggets of truth.

Let thy speech be short, comprehending much in a few words. Apocrypha
— Helene Clare Kuoni

February 10

I was in the seventh grade when the teacher asked us to memorize a poem of our choice and recite it before the class. Growing up on a farm in the early fifties, there was little money for extras. The few books in my house consisted of the Bible, a hymnbook and my sister's country and western songbook.

However, my grandmother was a poet so she wrote a poem just for me. I memorized it and shared it with my class, feeling extremely special that my poem had been written especially for me. From that time on, I began writing my own poems.

In high school, I wrote about my boyfriends and the pain of failed relationships. In the years that followed, I wrote poems about my husband overseas, the births of my children, and even the death of my son. I poured out my heart on paper.

Eventually, I turned to writing magazine articles, devotions, and even books, but poems always lived in my soul and would be born though tears when my heart was overwhelmed. I believe God used my grandmother and her remarkable gift of poetry to help guide me into a life of writing for him.

Lord, thank you for giving me words of love and encouragement to share with others.

Therefore encourage one another and build each other up. 1 Thessalonians 5:11 NIV

—Louise Tucker Jones

February 11

I still remember it...the power of a classmate's essay to transport me out of fifth-period English into an enchanted autumn glen, dappled with sunlight and brilliant with majesty. In seventh grade, I knew I would be a writer.

I organized a writing group with two friends. We spent hours pouring all the hopes and dreams about our future lives into an action/adventure/fantasy that was published only at slumber parties. My handwritten saga weighed in at five pounds, 259 pages. Today it has a place of honor—somewhere under a pile of papers in the bottom of a very deep drawer.

But real dreams are not so easily buried. I studied writing in college and worked for a couple of newspapers. With marriage and family, I shifted to freelance efforts for greater flexibility and much less pay. Even if no one wanted my stories, the wonder of everyday events begged to be birthed into words. My wallet was empty, but my journal was full.

Now, in the autumn of my life, I'm in a golden place again. Time and experience make wonderful editors. Those rejected stories are now finding homes. The God who planted the dream is witnessing a harvest. And his timing is so much better than mine.

Lord, help me remember it's never too late to begin again.

He has made everything beautiful in its time. Ecclesiastes 3:11a NKJV

—Marcia Swearingen

February 12

I have been writing for years, and seeing my words in print always brings fulfillment. But my greatest writer's moment came not from winning an award but from an unexpected accolade from my husband.

Valentine's Day was fast approaching. Married almost thirty years, I wrote an article about my husband, titled, "He's a Keeper." The words spoke of a faithful love in a committed Christian marriage. I sent it to the local newspaper for review and, hopefully, publication in the paper.

February 14 arrived and, opening the paper, I was thrilled to see that it had made the front page of the family section. Perhaps my words would encourage others to appreciate the wonder of a strong, devoted, day-to-day relationship. I thought my joy was complete.

Still basking in the afterglow of publication, I was even more surprised when my husband came home from work the next day and told me his coworkers liked my story. A very private person, he had never before shared my stories with his friends. The fact that he took it to work with him and said, "Look, my wife wrote this" was the greatest gift of affirmation I have known.

Thank you, Father, for treasured moments of absolute joy.

Joy is a net of love by which you catch souls. Mother Teresa

—Dorissa J. "Prissy" Vanover

February 13

Years ago, a friend gave me a Clivia plant. She told me to be patient because it would be a long time before it bloomed. Year after year I watered this plant, fed it with plant food, wiped the dust and pests from the leaves, and examined it for buds, but there were none.

After seven years of tending the plant, I went to the window very early in the morning to read the outdoor thermometer. The light from my flashlight fell on a stem in the center of the Clivia; clustered at the top were eleven buds.

My writing also grew for many years before it bloomed. Sometimes I watered my manuscripts with tears and sometimes I had to remove dust and pests. Critiques from more skilled writers enabled me to shape my writing into something more graceful.

The Clivia was healthy and the promise of flowers lay within it even when the buds could not be seen. My writing talent was always there, but it, too, took years of care and nourishment—many times from other writers—before it bloomed.

Father, I acknowledge that you are the giver of talent, but I have work to do. Teach me to accept the instruction of others.

Listen to advice and accept instruction, and in the end you will be wise. Proverbs 19:20 NIV

—Anne Siegrist

February 14

As expressions of love for other people, we give cards, chocolate and flowers, especially on Valentine's Day. I get valentines throughout the year, yet sometimes fail to recognize them as such.

I remember the first acceptance letter I received. It said, "You've been accepted into The Writing Academy." "Hooray!" I shouted. What a wonderful valentine that was.

I received another when my teacher said my devotions were publishable. I appreciated her verbal valentine more than any card.

I can think of ways to send written valentines to many people throughout the year, not just on Valentine's Day. I can write an encouraging note to my pastor or a heartfelt poem to a hurting friend when she's experienced disappointment. I can write the story of an event that happened to my husband because of something my great-aunt did, send it to a magazine, and, when it's published, send a copy to her with a heartfelt note. I've done these things. The thank-yous from the recipients are immeasurable.

Valentine's Day for a writer can be any day of the year. Perhaps every day of the year.

Remind me, Lord, of all the ways I can use my gifts as a writer to write valentines to all those I love throughout the year.

Give someone a smile, express a word of kindness, lend a helping hand, write a note of gratitude, give a word of encouragement, share your material possessions with others. William Arthur Ward

—Margaret Steinacker

February 15

My expressive forte has always been song. No happy-go-lucky serenades for me; give me a creative master-piece that reaches into the human soul, grabbing hold and making an impact in a matter of well-orchestrated minutes. Each precious word, shaped, colored and enlivened by the music that paints its meaning. Words sung so tenderly that attention to anything else is eclipsed and the essence of the soul is revealed. Words sung with gusto and strength, enlivening the body and causing the spirit to soar.

How am I to write words without music? How do I capture the stimulating essence of a crescendo when there is no accompaniment? How do I soothe and comfort the entire being with nothing but shapes of black on white? How do I express a feeling that resonates through body, soul and spirit with no actual resonance? I write under the inspiration of the same spirit by which Moses, Miriam, David, and Mary sang.

Under the spirit's power, words pulse and vibrate in synch with each individual reader, unlimited by time or changes in musical style. Words breathed from God's spirit into mine are alive as no other words will ever be.

Lord, may my words be your words, my thoughts your thoughts and my ways your ways.

Let my teaching fall on you like rain; let my speech settle like dew. Let my words fall like rain on tender grass, like gentle showers on young plants. Deuteronomy 32:2 NLT

—Lea Mack

February 16

It was simple advice: if you want to be a writer, you have to write. Sometimes, it was easier said than done. How many times did I sit at a blank computer screen when my column was past due?

I'd been so elated when not one but three newspapers picked up my column. Things were going fine until it hit: writer's block, that big black space where my ideas should have been.

But then just when I thought my writing days were over, an idea would spring forth and the process would start all over again.

I used to think that writing would bring a certain amount of success and prestige. But I've been at it long enough now to know that success is achieved from within. When I complete a story or column that I'm content with, it brings me joy that no amount of money can buy.

I know that writing won't make me financially wealthy. But when my words touch the hearts of others I feel as though I've struck gold, for deep within my being I know I am using my worth as a writer.

Lord, thank you for the wealth of words that keep me rich in thought.

Writing is the only thing that, when I do it, I don't feel I should be doing anything else. Gloria Steinem
—Kathy Whirity

February 17

In August 2005 after attending a Christian writers' conference, I met with my pastor to discuss writing an Advent devotional for the families of our church.

Within one month, my life began to unravel. First, my only sibling was hospitalized and diagnosed with bipolar disorder. Then, Hurricane Rita slammed into the Texas Gulf Coast and nearly destroyed my home. Two weeks later, my husband had an emergency appendectomy.

It was then that my pastor called and asked if the devotional guide I was supposed to write could be completed by the next Friday, only six days away. My first thought was: Don't you know what I am going through? I can't do this!

Instead, I began writing. I wrote beginning at 4:00 a.m. I wrote during the day at work. I wrote so late into the evening that my fingers and wrists were sore from typing.

The only way I can describe that experience is that I was sure the Lord knew what was happening in my life. I felt him speak to me: I know you are hurting. I'll give you the words and the time. We'll do it together.

By the time I finished the project I'd learned that God does, indeed, give gifts to be used. I'd received inexplicable joy in the midst of difficult circumstances.

Lord, I know that I am never closer to you, than when we are writing together.

For the gifts and calling of God are without repentance. Romans 11:29 KJV

—Brook Dwyer

February 18

My husband and I worked in Houston. We kept a one-room apartment there, but returned to our home in Louisiana every Friday evening. Most of the time I looked like a bag lady, hauling my laptop, reference books, and manuscripts back and forth.

One evening, I was horribly discouraged. We were rushing to attend a banquet for those involved in prison ministry, and I didn't want to go. I'd received several rejection slips with no encouraging notes from the editors.

As my husband drove toward the Louisiana line, I moped in the passenger seat. This is it, Lord, I grumbled. I'm giving up writing. No one's encouraging me.

We reached the restaurant and socialized with our ministry friends. Toward the end of the evening, announcements were made. "We need someone to be editor of a newsletter that will inform and encourage our volunteers."

Could I do this? I crammed my hands inside my jacket pocket and was surprised to find my business card: Jessica Ferguson ~ Writing as a Ministry. Who better to encourage than someone who needs encouragement?

Lord, thank you for caring about every thing in my life. Thank you for letting me know that quitting is unacceptable.

Correction does much, but encouragement does more. Johann Wolfgang von Goethe
—Jessica Roach Ferguson

February 19

The *New York Times* best-selling author of *Where Angels Walk, True Stories of Heavenly Visitors* and other books sat down in the studio. Joan Wester Anderson was being interviewed on Chicago Irish radio, and so was I. Together, we chatted with the lively hosts.

Afterward, I asked Joan if she would meet me for coffee. Graciously, she agreed. Two words stand out from our visit: keep writing.

When Joan was doing a local book signing, I went. She asked if anyone had had an angelic experience. Surprisingly, I stood up.

Twenty years earlier, I had been without money and food. I closed my empty cabinet, left my home saying, "God provides." Minutes later, a man appeared and asked to buy a chair that I was donating to a rummage sale. He gave me enough money for food and then vanished. For years, I thought he was the strangest person.

That day with Joan Wester Anderson, I learned differently: First, God knows when to send an angel. Second, a well-known author who takes time for an unknown author is an angel too.

Father, as I keep on writing, thank you for providing for me, sometimes in amazing ways.

Do not forget to entertain strangers, for by so doing some have unwittingly entertained angels. Hebrews 13:2 NKJV

—Audrey Marie Hessler

February 20

My coauthor and I never doubted our book, *A Match Made in Heaven,* would sell a million copies. Oh, how naïve we were. Disappointed by our sales, I questioned the Lord's call on my life to write.

Then my doubts were removed when I received a letter from a reader. "Your book saved my life," she wrote. Before Christmas, her third husband had walked out on her. Friends and family tried to comfort her, but the humiliation was devastating in her small town. So, she made a decision to kill herself.

Although the woman's mother was worried, she hadn't known the extent of her daughter's depression. Standing in line at Wal-Mart on Christmas Eve to purchase last minute gifts, her mother noticed a turnstile of books. The title of our book intrigued her. "This will be the perfect stocking stuffer for my hurting daughter," she thought.

That Christmas Eve, a young woman found hope on the pages of our book. And I found hope as a writer. Who doesn't want to make the best-seller list? But I've learned not to lose sight of my true purpose as a Christian writer—God's best-seller list…where angels rejoice when one life is saved.

Heavenly Father, may my books inspire readers.

For we are God's workmanship, created in Christ Jesus to do good works, which God prepared in advance for us to do. Ephesians 2:10 NIV

—Susan Huey Wales

February 21

Editors at the magazine for junior high age kids were thrilled by the poetry contest results. The winner had submitted a virtually flawless tribute to the sixteenth U.S. president:

> Young Abe Lincoln was a poor man's son
> Toiled all day till his work was done...

Having seen that very poem in a book of verse, I was jolted. Should I say something? Surely, I thought, someone has blown the whistle on that kid. Also, I was too shy a seventh grader to relish complaining. But as an aspiring writer, I was so offended that I wrote to the editors anyway.

Within a week came their reply. It turned out I was alone in pointing out the prize-winning entry had been lifted word for word. Thanks to my singular alertness, the young plagiarist had been stripped of his prize.

The twelve-year-old me influenced the sixty-two-year-old me. "What's the big idea of lifting entire paragraphs from another newspaper?" I fumed at a would-be guest columnist turned Internet thief. Nice symmetry to a career in writing and editing, I thought later. Mild-mannered except when defending the integrity of the writing craft.

Lord, may I never assume that others will speak in my place.

It is wonderful what strength of purpose and boldness and energy of will are roused by the assurance that we are doing our duty. Sir Walter Scott

—Jerry Elsea

February 22

"I just want to come home," I pleaded with my husband with six hours of highway and a cell phone between us. This feeling brought back memories of junior high camp and calling my parents in tears to come get me.

"You can do this, honey," he offered lovingly.

I was attending my first writers' conference. Carefully I'd filled out the form to have an appointment with an editor at the very end of the conference. I needed as much time as I could find to learn what I would need for that meeting.

Unfortunately, they had me scheduled with an editor at the first meeting of the conference. I asked questions, shared my dreams for writing, and survived.

Over the next few days I was surprised to see my passions surface. After meeting with four more editors, I had a clear vision, fresh inspiration, and a renewed sense of confidence. They were interested in my writing, and that was just what I needed to know to take action. I knew I had been given skills and would choose to put them to good use.

Lord, in my weak moments give me confidence and remind me of the reward that's waiting.

So do not throw away your confidence; it will be richly rewarded. Hebrews 10:35 NIV

—Jami Kirkbride

February 23

When I finally decided to take up writing, words surged from my heart like an overflowing river. Writing poetry became a daily journaling.

I joined a writers' group and found amazement in words that stirred me. Soon my writing skills increased and my poetry expanded into prose. Submissions, rejections, rejections and more rejections, then, finally, acceptances. Eventually, I was published.

I wrote for the Internet; wrote a book; became a newspaper lifestyle and devotional columnist and a speaker; then penned three more books.

Now, disabled with multiple sclerosis, I see how God was preparing me not only to be a witness with my inspirational and devotional writing, but also giving me strength through rejection to meet the adversities and hard times that lay ahead.

I've learned that the talent God has given me has become a life-saving gift, an avenue that keeps me feeling useful in this body that is defective.

Thank you, God, for the gift of writing you gave me and for strength and purpose and the ability to witness in spite of this disease.

I have discovered the secret that after climbing a great hill, one only finds that there are many more hills to climb. Nelson Mandela

—Betty King

February 24

Sunday mornings I attend an early traditional church service and go home inspired, ready to face my weekly ritual of putting ideas down on paper via the computer. I am full of thoughts and musings, ready to shock and awe an audience out there in the world. I put on a mesmerizing song by Dolly Parton, "Hello God."

I sit at the computer and stare into the vast emptiness of the screen and wonder inwardly as to the best way to place my vocabulary on that white screen.

I've done all the mechanics of preparing my mind and physical body. Now my fingers can fly over the keyboard. I type something inane like "It was a dark and stormy night." Then I remember it isn't me writing, it's God through me, and I backspace through my first line and type, "The day dawned magnificently, full of hope and glory, and I saw the sun from a new perspective."

Now, I am ready to write.

God, grant me wisdom, insight and love as I write.

The preacher sought to find out acceptable words; and that which was written was upright, even words of truth… be admonished: of making many books there is no end; and much study is a weariness of the flesh. Ecclesiastes 12:10-12 KJV

—Scott Williams

February 25

After years of submissions, I finally had an acceptance from a widely circulated devotional guide. The editors liked how I described God staying near when trouble makes us feel all alone.

Someday, hundreds of thousands around the world would read my words in various translated editions. I tried to imagine who would find inspiration in my little story. An office worker in Bolivia? A nurse in South Africa? Maybe a baker in Australia?

My author's copy arrived several weeks before the official publication date. I glanced through it, and then filed it.

A few weeks later, a friend called from Alaska, where she was helping her daughter and new baby. The daughter's mental illness had worsened with the stress of childbirth.

"We were reading her devotional guide today," my friend said. "Today's selection really spoke to where we are in her recovery. I couldn't believe it when I saw your name at the bottom. Thank you!"

I hung up, amazed. God knew just who would need that encouraging word I offered in a little devotional. People around the globe would read it. But most important, it ministered to my friend.

I praise you for being the omniscient God, who can place what I write in the hands of those who need your touch.

For the eyes of the Lord range throughout the earth to strengthen those who hearts are fully committed to him. 2 Chronicles 16:8 NIV

—Jeanne Zornes

February 26

A few years ago, my wife and I were enjoying a relaxing vacation at a cabin on a lake in Maine. I had just been studying a form of medieval poetry developed in France called the triolet (pronounced tree-o-lay). The simple eight-line form seemed a perfect way to capture the serenity and peace of the moment. So I sat down and wrote my first triolet:

> She reads, I write and all is still
> For nothing breaks our quietude.
> Disturb the other, neither will.
> She reads, I write and all is still.
> The turning page, the flowing quill:
> The only sounds that dare intrude.
> She reads, I write and all is still
> For nothing breaks our quietude.

God saw fit to bless this simple poem. It was published in *Time of Singing*, a magazine of contemporary Christian poetry. And it was a finalist in the Miracles contest sponsored by the Walt Whitman Birthplace Association. The message of peaceful quietude seems to strike a chord with people in today's busy world.

Lord, certainly quiet, solitude, companionship, mutual respect, and purpose must also be fruits of the Spirit.

But the fruit of the Spirit is love, joy, peace, patience, kindness, goodness, faithfulness, gentleness and self-control. Galatians 5:22-23 NIV

Bill Batcher

February 27

As one of the leaders in an outreach group, I was encouraged to write the story of my spiritual journey. Steps included writing a rough draft and presenting my story before those who would critique me.

Somewhere between "I was born" and "I grew up," my ego crept into my thinking and appeared blatantly on my written page. I penned many words with haste and excitement. I came home from my presentation with my papers full of red-inked comments. Tossing them aside I decided I would never be a speaker, much less a writer.

One February in Wisconsin, the phone rang. Due to a snowstorm, our scheduled speaker would not be at our outreach luncheon the following day. Our area representative said I should share my story.

I dug out my papers and prayed with great passion. We had to cancel our luncheon, but God used that experience to let me know I was an appropriate speaker and perhaps even a writer. I've now had the privilege of sharing that story before 187 groups, and God has used it to change lives.

Lord, thank you for never giving up on me. Your ways are always best.

Let the words of my mouth and the meditation of my heart be acceptable in thy sight, O Lord, my strength and my redeemer. Psalms 19:14 KJV

—Ethel Jensen Stenzel

February 28

I was nervous when the teacher asked the class at a writers' conference: "What is your purpose in writing?"

As a Christian writer, I believed my purpose was to glorify God. My ability came from God, and he would give me the words. Though I felt guided as to content, I needed instruction in the proper fundamentals for submitting. My writing didn't always come out the way I intended. Rejection letters flooded my mailbox.

I continued attending conferences and seminars, and reading instructional books. I even set up a writers' group in our area. And, I persisted in submitting my work.

At a St. Davids writers' conference, I met Lisa Crayton, editor of *Spirit-Led Writer*. I pitched an idea for an article, and she told me to send it to her. She accepted the article and it was published online. At last, I was a published author. This encouraged me to continue on my journey as a writer.

Father, help me to always know your purpose in my writing.

All things work together for good to them that love God, to them who are the called according to his purpose. Romans 8:28 KJV

—Jan Sady

February 29

Happy Leap Year! Today is nothing more than a bit of a correction. An edit. And yet if we didn't stick this extra day into the calendar every four years, pandemonium would break out and our entire world would be in chronological chaos. As a writer, I've learned that if I put a manuscript in a drawer for a few days and look at it later, a small tweaking can change the meaning, create a whole new takeaway message, liven up the language, or make the subjects in my story sizzle with new descriptions. Like leap year, often all it takes is a little tweaking here and there to make things right.

Today, I'm going to treat this leap year day as a gift. I'm going to get out there and enjoy the world. I want to smell bacon frying, notice the bright red Florida hibiscus in full bloom in my backyard, take a swim in the heated pool across the street, and jump on my bike and sail through the park's paved bike path inhaling the delicious aroma of stately pine trees.

Today is a gift. An extra day. I'm going to use it to jumpstart all my senses. Then later, refreshed and ready to go, I'll start writing something new.

Lord, give me the wisdom to grab onto this day with gusto and write something amazing.

It is not enough simply to relate your observations or experiences; you, the author, must point and shape them to some fresh lesson or purpose. Marjorie Holmes

—Patricia Lorenz

March 1

As our van cruised down the highway, my friends decided to play a game. It works like this: someone poses a hypothetical situation. On that day, the question was: "You find out that you have only one month to live. What is one thing you want to do before then?"

When my turn came, I talked about a song I had written about a high school friend. I hadn't seen her in the two or three years since graduation. If I had a month to live, I would track her down and play her song for her. Then she could give it a name because I couldn't come up with one I liked. It was the only song I'd ever written that was any good.

Soon afterward, I tried to make this happen. I recorded the song in my dorm room and burned it onto a CD. I got her college address from her parents and mailed it off.

As the months went by with no reply, I became discouraged. Maybe she never got it? Maybe she hated it?

Instead of giving up, I improved it—a new intro, a new guitar solo. I still don't know what she thinks of it, and the song is still nameless. But I think it's pretty rocking.

Lord, help me to persevere in the face of indifference and rejection.

A thing of beauty is a joy for ever. John Keats
—Paul Forsyth

March 2

Chess is one of my hobbies. I like the opportunity to find a winning combination, the attack that leads to checkmate or a winning advantage. There are many books that can help me with chess combinations. However, the best way for me to learn is to sit down with a chess expert and ask him questions.

Writing is a lot like chess. There is a sense of excitement when I find the right combinations of words. Sure, there are books about writing that can help me, but it's better for me to sit down with an expert writer and have him or her give me feedback about my sentence construction or the way I've organized a paragraph.

Father, thank you for the many ways to improve my writing.

Daring ideas are like chessmen moved forward. They may be beaten, but they may start a winning game. Johann Wolfgang von Goethe

—Danny Woodall

March 3

When I attended a writers' seminar a couple years ago, I did not think of myself as a writer, simply because I was not published in magazines or the author of books. But all of a sudden, my pen was meeting the paper, and creativity I never knew I had was flowing across the page.

I've learned over the years that I am a creative writer whenever I've written a letter, an article for a newsletter or newspaper, a book review, or an excuse for school.

I find myself writing all the time. I write about the weather, traveling, vacations, childhood memories; anything that comes to mind. Sometimes I share my writings; other times I tuck them away in my notebook.

"Should I? Could I?" These are words asked by new writers. Thank you to those who have boldly replied, "Yes, you should, and yes, you can. Get a pen and paper and let your creative juices flow."

Thank you, Lord, for friends who encourage me to continue writing.

Writing is no trouble: you just jot down ideas as they occur to you. The jotting is simplicity itself—it is the occurring which is difficult. Stephen Leacock

—Sally Devine

March 4

I plodded along with my book report while my friend Jeff surged ahead with his. This was puzzling, because I was the honor roll student—a budding writer no less—while he struggled for Bs and Cs. What's more, I had chosen *Run Silent, Run Deep*, a high schooler's safe favorite, while Jeff had picked the daunting *Uncle Tom's Cabin*.

When Jeff read his report in class, the mystery was solved. "That brutal slave owner Simon Legree," he read, "was a big, menacing guy in a plaid shirt."

Plaid? Legree's shirt was blood-red. Several giggling kids knew it. So did Miss Banks. Jeff had bypassed the 636-page classic and jogged the easy route through No. 15 in the comic book adaptation.

I can't recall the penalty he drew, but surely it involved a flat-out flunk and a report to his parents.

I do recall the lesson I took from it: an effective writer shuns the shortcut no matter how tempting.

Lord, grant me the strength to meet challenges, not sidestep them.

God has so made the mind of man that a peculiar deliciousness resides in the fruit of personal industry.
William Wilberforce

—Jerry Elsea

March 5

Twenty-three years of marriage had been good to me. We had two great boys who sang with us in churches, fulfilling a call from the Lord my husband and I both felt we needed to obey. But the stress of job, family, practicing our music, packing, performing, and pleasing a perfectionist husband had taken its toll on my mental stability.

I had been visiting my doctor for physical help, but I needed more. My husband was against counseling. One night, I sat down and wrote for half an hour or so through tearful sobbing. When my husband read what I had spilled out, he realized I had to have some professional help.

Writing is cathartic, cleansing and purifying. If used as a type of journaling where structure, spelling, and grammar are not the main focus, one can begin to work through problems and find healing.

Lord, help those of us who are troubled to use our writing to define our woes and anxieties.

Be strong. Take courage. Don't be intimidated. Don't give them a second thought because God, your God, is striding ahead of you. He's right there with you. He won't let you down; he won't leave. Deuteronomy 31:6 MSG

—Margaret Steinacker

March 6

Hiland Presbyterian Church in Pittsburgh prints an annual Lenten devotional. It's not easy, convincing forty or so members of the congregation who by profession are not writers to pen a meaningful devotion, but it always comes together in the end.

Since joining this church in 1998, I've always contributed to the Lenten devotional. Unlike some of the others, whose arms are fairly twisted, I enjoy writing. But the true joy, even for those still rubbing their biceps, is when people comment how much they appreciated a devotion or how it helped them in some way.

As a Christian writer, I occasionally struggle with knowing what God desires for me to write. Will my words speak to someone in need? Will they help someone in their walk with Christ? What does God want me to say? My hope is that the words I write will glorify the one who gave me the desire and talent to write in the first place.

Hiland Pastor Larry Ruby often begins his sermons with this prayer quoting Psalms 19:14 (NIV) "May the words of my mouth and the meditation of my heart be pleasing in your sight, O Lord." Without changing the meaning, I've paraphrased the verse into this little ditty I use for my writing life: May the words that I write be pleasing in your sight.

Lord, please use the words I write to inspire, encourage, and help others.

A writer ought to comfort the afflicted, and afflict the comfortable. Mark Twain

—Angie Kay Dilmore

March 7

The Bulgarian student sat beside me, her eight-page journalism paper spread out on my dining room table. English was her third language, Spanish her second. She sought help on grammar, punctuation, and spelling. Before editing her college paper, I read it again.

Behind all the mistakes and bad word usage was a brilliant mind. She just needed a little more training to be able to express it.

During the past few years, I've learned to offer advice sparingly. Students need encouragement to keep writing, to not give up when they get a bad grade or can't say exactly what they want. I tell young people that God gives talents to be used, not hidden away. The sky is the limit.

You see, I was there once. As a teenager, words flowed from my pen to express emotions from joy to anger to despair. Not brave enough to show anyone, I continued to write for decades. When I finally read my essays to another, negative words would have halted my creativity and I never would have gone on to publish articles or Bible studies.

The Bulgarian student? She was accepted into a prestigious graduate program for journalism. I like to think I helped her along a bit.

Lord, help me continue to share this love of writing with others.

The Lord is good to all. Psalms 145:8 NIV
—Kathryn A. Spurgeon

March 8

A high school classmate and I had a disagreement. She attacked me in my vulnerable spot—the newspaper that I edited and my writing. I felt that what she did was unforgivable, and I hated her.

I had joined the church, committing my life to Christ, a year earlier. In my darkness and despair, I begin praying, asking God to deal with my feelings. A few days later, this person came to me and apologized, saying she should not have said these hurtful things. I can still feel the burden of hate and resentment as it left me, and the light of love and forgiveness as it washed over me. We stood there in the school hall, embracing, crying, and rejoicing in our feelings of forgiveness.

I have never hesitated to take the initiative in obtaining forgiveness since then. I know the cleansing feeling it brings. I know that it makes my words flow smoother.

Thank you, Lord for teaching me how to forgive.

Anyone who claims to be in the light but hates his brother is still in the darkness. 1 John 2:9 NIV

—Ivie Bozeman

March 9

In my memory, he ripped the pages into irretrievable bits. In reality, he may have simply set them aside. He may have simply said, "Take another crack at it." But that's not what I remember. I remember him snarling, "This will teach you not to leave things until the last minute."

Did I cry? Did I roll yet another piece of paper into the Royal typewriter? Did I haul out yet more composition paper and start rewriting? Whatever happened to the pictures I'd cut out, pasted, and captioned? Did I manage to hand in my report about the blue whale on time? I don't remember anything but the lesson taught. Taught hard. Fifth grade may have been tough, but my father was tougher. My first copy chief.

Decades later, I would cry. I was about to blow a deadline. The interviewee, old enough to be my father, wanted perfection. I wanted good enough. I wanted to hand in my feature story on deadline. I fought with him until out of the depths of memory, the blue whale burst through to the surface of consciousness. Completely intact. Later, I became completely intact after setting the blue whale free to swim away in a sea of tears.

I asked my editor for a little more time, which she graciously conferred.

Lord, help me transform life's hard lessons into opportunities for revelation and growth.

Every writer I know has trouble writing. Joseph Heller
—Meredith Gould, Ph.D.

March 10

"Do you know what the boys are doing?" My husband yelled.

"No," I stammered. "They've been quiet all day."

After he came into the house, he took me by the hand and led me outside. I starred at the twenty-five-foot evergreen. The tree's middle branches all were missing. I burst out laughing. It was not the response my normally patient husband expected.

Our seven- and eight-year-old sons were inseparable. One had climbed up the tree, sawed off a branch with Dad's bow saw, and then dropped it below, continuing the process over and over. His brother piled the branches on their red coaster wagon and hauled them into the backyard.

The boys had forced my husband to do then what he would have had to do later. The tree's roots reached well beyond its base and were pressing against the basement wall.

Recording the boys' antics provided sanity for me, once a classroom teacher and now a stay-at-home mom. I wrote my frustrations, my joys, and my anger so that when I arose the next morning, I would have the strength to meet new challenges.

Father, thank you for giving me wisdom and insight through my daily journal writing.

A writer is not someone who is published, or someone who is famous. A writer is someone who writes. Pat Schneider

—Sheryl Van Weelden

March 11

"I wonder if you'd help me with a story," my pastor said. I was shocked.

While I was on good terms with my parish's other priests, being around the man who had absolved me of sin after thirty-five years away from Catholicism made me uncomfortable. I either stayed away from him or argued publicly with him.

But I couldn't turn away a writer who wanted help, and he agreed to leave the story about his missionary days for me at the parish office. He accidentally also left a poem written during the same period.

"I have some thoughts about how to improve the article," I told him later, "but the poem is haunting. I'd send it to *The New Yorker*."

He didn't do that, but a Catholic publication bought the poem and it placed third in a contest. At first, he seemed to discount his achievements.

"I take it all with a grain of salt," my pastor said, then added: "I've written one now that's even better than that poem."

"I look forward to seeing it," I said. I could now look beyond the collar and view him as part of a tribe I understood and loved—the tribe of writers.

Lord, help me use our shared connection to understand my brothers and sisters who write.

Only connect the prose and the passion, and both will be exalted, and human love will be seen at its highest. E. M. Forster

—Melanie Rigney

March 12

When my contributor's copy arrived, I quickly tore the envelope open. My story in *Chicken Soup for the Soul in Menopause: Living and Laughing through Hot Flashes and Hormones* immortalized my wife Lisa's struggles with perimenopause. And since the family was taking my father-in-law out for an early Father's Day dinner, the timing was perfect.

As we arrived at the restaurant, we sat out front with the other groups of families who obviously had the same idea of avoiding the holiday crowd. As we waited to be paged, I pulled out the book and everyone took a turn reading the story.

Then, it was my father-in-law's turn. "God, I'm Shvitzing!" he recited the title with a chuckle. (Shvitzing being a Yiddish term for sweating.)

As he finished, we could see his eyes were filling with water. I wondered what he was thinking. He could have been thinking about how much I loved his daughter. Or he could have been thinking of how his little girl was entering a new phase of womanhood. Or he could have been wishing his wife was still here to share this moment.

Watching them together, I wished for all three.

God, thank you for the ability to touch others with my words.

To a father growing old nothing is dearer than a daughter. Euripides

—Lawrence D. Elliott

March 13

It was four weeks and the concussion wasn't getting better. The doctor now cautioned it could be months. Wracking pains and all the symptoms made thinking difficult. I was wrestling with God: How can I care for my family? Will I get better? How can I write? I can't even think.

Then I heard these words in my head: Do not fear. I am with you. Rest in me.

I stopped fighting. Thank you, Lord. OK. You have allowed this place. Tears dripped slowly down. What do you have for me here? I'm looking. Gradually I drifted to sleep.

Suddenly, my mind cleared and thoughts of a poem came flowing through. I reached out for a pen and paper to quickly write till it was done. The pain came back, and I rested. But somehow, it was OK. I knew that God was in control. He would bring me through and he was not limited by my circumstance.

Seven poems came from that time and I learned that sometimes words are found in strange and unusual places. But no matter where they are found, God is there and he will bring me through.

Lord, thank you for taking the painful places and creating a rich valley.

Water will gush forth in the wilderness and streams in the desert. Isaiah 35:6b NIV

—Elizabeth Sebek

March 14

When Doris and I founded a writers' group, The First Word, in Sewickley, Pennsylvania, each prospective member brought a piece of writing to share. The next week, Marjie announced that she wanted to read a letter to the group:

"If you all do what you did last meeting, I am not coming back. Each of you trotted out your best piece of writing. Many of you made copies of something that had already been published. You challenged us to find anything wrong with your polished writing. We need to bring pieces we're currently working on, pieces that need help. Of course, you don't have to accept our suggestions unless you choose to."

We followed her lead and took risks. Our group has been meeting for over thirty years. It gives us a chance to try new techniques at each stage of the process: thinking, reporting, structuring and writing. We have learned to start with a positive comment before we make suggestions for improvements. It is easier to take constructive criticism after we receive a compliment.

Members grow as writers, win prizes, and get published. We chuckled when the local paper did an article on our group and called us The Last Word. We know that we are not.

Lord, help us to remember to be gracious both in giving and accepting criticism.

Taking a risk is something that I recommend. Great writing comes from a willingness to take a risk. Tom Hallman Jr.

—Shirley Stevens

March 15

Sometimes I find it helpful to put on paper the words I hear in my head. It seems to work best when I let Grandmother be my advocate.

VOICE: Who are you fooling, anyway? You will never write. You are not a writer. Why not just give up? You are a failure. You are a lazy good-for-nothing.

ME: Wow, who are you?

VOICE: I am you. I live deep inside.

ME: You are making me cry. Who are you?

VOICE: It doesn't matter what you name me. I speak truth. You will never be a writer. Writers write. You are not writing.

ME: Maybe you are right.

GRANDMOTHER: Say more, sweetheart. Write what's in your mind.

ME: I feel like that voice may be right, but in my heart I know the voice is wrong. I know I am better than that. I know I am loved. I know I can write.

GRANDMOTHER: All right then, let's take this a little bit at a time.

I continue this conversation with Grandmother for many more pages in my journal. Together, we devise plans that give me time, place and permission to write. I'm doing it. And best of all, I haven't heard that voice for a long while.

I thank you, God, for advocates, real and imagined.

I am reminded of your sincere faith, a faith that lived first in your grandmother. 1 Timothy 1:5a NRSV
—Connie Scharlau

March 16

Not long ago, I received the following e-mail from a man named Joe. His writing was simple, but I'll never forget the profound impact it had on me.

Ms. Shockley, you wrote a small article in the *Dallas Morning News*, "Faith Comforting in Troubling Times" a short time after 9-11. I was so impressed with it I cut it out and placed it in my billfold. Two years ago my wife kicked me out because of my drinking. Later that night agonizing over the loss of my family I came across your article in my billfold. After reading it, a renewed hope began to build up in me. I knew God was going to see me through. Today, my marriage has been restored and I belong to a Christian- based 12 step program called "Celebrate Recovery." I shall forever be grateful for your article because I felt the presence of God. Joe

When I read Joe's e-mail, I wept. Joe made me realize all over again why I write—to encourage, to change, to motivate, to offer a glimmer of hope when all seems lost.

Precious Lord, may the words you graciously give me help a troubled soul today.

Whatever your hand finds to do, do it with all your might. Ecclesiastes 9:10 NIV

—Dayle Allen Shockley

March 17

Although I was only four when he died, I cherish the family history that Great-Uncle Eldo Swayne Long wrote. He captured more than the names of his relations; he revealed their personalities and their character. I marvel at how many personality traits have carried down generation after generation and appreciate his inventive grammar and opinions.

I'm a product of how my ancestors chose to parent, earn a living, and worship. As a writer, I enjoy romanticizing their personalities. Writing their stories allows my ancestors to live on for my kids.

I've begun writing a family history for my own children. Although I might not describe each person perfectly, the stories will bring them to life. Besides, I know my children will fill any gaps with their own embellishments. Perhaps in my simple words about the people who have shaped my life and, in turn, theirs, they'll recognize a part of themselves. They might even gain an appreciation for the things Mom finds humorous.

I smile when I think that perhaps someday my great-granddaughter might read those words and romanticize these ancestors and their quirky traits. Especially when she realizes the possible source of her own children's peculiar sense of humor.

Lord, thank you for encouraging me to record our family's history for my children.

We write to taste life twice. Anaïs Nin
— Amy J. Harrelson

March 18

Ever since I was little, I have loved to write. My teddy bear would sit on my lap listening to every single word, his awed silence speaking volumes about my work. Later, I would write stories for my brothers and sister; although less reverent, they still listened eagerly.

In high school, I won an award for a poem and short story I wrote. When I read my work in front of the class, my legs shook so badly that the front row of students laughed. I was mortified; no amount of cajoling could get me back up there.

Still, the urge to write never left me. Through job changes, a divorce, illness, and a new marriage, it was there like a friend to comfort me. Characters floated around my mind, telling me their stories, urging me to put pen to paper. Yet still I ran from it.

It was at my husband's advice that I finally yielded to that urge. His love had given me back my self-worth, and I was finally able to listen to that small, still voice of God calling me to write.

I finally realized it's easier to just submit to the Lord's will than to run from it. And far more fun too.

Thank you, Lord, for the gifts you've given me. Help me to be faithful to your calling.

One of the greatest moments in anybody's developing experience is when he no longer tries to hide from himself but determines to get acquainted with himself as he really is. Norman Vincent Peale

—Lee Franklin

March 19

While driving to a shopping trip, I prayed and whined about a publisher for my books. Why, I wondered, couldn't I get published more often?

Suddenly, in my peripheral vision, I spotted a church marquee. The sign read, "Is your name written in the Lamb's Book of Life?"

I got excited. What better place can one's name be written? I asked myself. My name on books, articles, poems, or anywhere else pales in comparison.

When my cell phone rang, I could hardly wait to tell my husband about this revelation.

"My name is written in the Lamb's Book of Life, and that's better than anywhere else. Isn't that wonderful?"

"Yeah, that's great!" he agreed, but I knew he didn't get my message in full. When God reveals something to me, sometimes it's hard to explain it in detail.

After this encounter, knowing that my faith has already placed me in the Book of Life which certainly outshines any best seller, I was able to forge ahead as a writer.

Lord, thank you for the privilege of being in your book of life and for encouraging me to write for other books.

Nothing impure will ever enter it, nor will anyone who does what is shameful or deceitful, but only those whose names are written in the Lamb's book of life. Revelation 21:27 NIV

—Charlotte Holt

March 20

One of the reasons I write is that I think we sleepwalk through much of our lives, not noticing the beauty around us. My son, who has autism, notices everything, and in one of my poems, I praise him for this with the words: "You have made me pay attention to the world's smallest minutia."

Part of my job as a writer is to wake up, be present in the moment, and use my senses to navigate the world. Sensory details make my writing come alive for others, as well. When I open my eyes, I also open my heart, and as Talmud says, God wants the heart.

Every time I take a walk, there are things to notice: the way the hills turn lavender, with the sun's last light pink and gold behind them, the drone of bees, how twilight covers the earth like a blanket. Matthew wrote that the eye is the lamp of the body, and I am trying to keep mine open.

There's a famous saying that God is in the details, and I think this is true for all good writing. I believe I touch my readers most when I bring them into a world alive with the richness of the senses.

Lord, help me to wake up, open my eyes, and write.

Attention is the natural prayer of the soul. Charles Wright

—Barbara Crooker

March 21

Thousands of writers draw inspiration from the captivating words of J. R. R. Tolkien and C. S. Lewis. When I was in college, I got it from their desks instead. The year was 2003 and I was taking a weekend to hang out with friends in West Chicago. We visited a library that displayed letters, books, and the very writing desks of Lewis and Tolkien.

Since I was anything but the rising star of the English department, and juggling modern poetry, Biblical Greek, and Socratic philosophy in one semester, you could say inspiration wasn't left on my doorstep every morning. I'd run dry, and it was only October. Having turned to the usual resources—venting to other students, venting to my mom, rolling my eyes and claiming writer's block, begging God for oh-please-just-500-words—I went on vacation. I must say I didn't expect inanimate objects to resuscitate me.

But these were their *writing desks*! I let my fingers smudge up the polished surfaces just a little, while no one was looking. In my silly way I felt I was connecting to some soul of writing, or maybe the souls of Gandalf or Lucy. The moment was quite romanticized, but I have pictures to remember that day. In fact, I've smudged the corners a bit.

Thank you, God, for being my answer and for providing inspiration for my writing in the strangest places.

I know now, Lord, why you utter no answer. You are yourself the answer. C. S. Lewis

—Christy A. Davis

March 22

My father worked as a mechanic and wrote *Motor West* magazine's monthly Care of Your Car column. I knew he preferred writing songs and stories because our Model A disintegrated while he rode the streetcar, scribbling notes about passengers to make his characters believable.

Daddy kept a Dictaphone beside his bed. On sleepless nights, he rolled over, flipped the switch, and grumbled insights to save until morning.

I listened eagerly to tales of enough rejection slips to paper a room before his first story was published. His song "Take Care of My Boy Over There" performed at the Orpheum the day the Armistice was signed.

Daddy nurtured my writing. The warm July night I accepted my first poetry prize, this twelve-year-old rode in a taxi for the first time.

The following October, Daddy died. I poured my pain into words, trying to make sense out of chaos.

Shortly after my mother's death in 1970, I found a battered tin box filled with Daddy's writings, and a worn *Argosy All-Story* featuring "The Hairpin Turn," his first published work.

Daddy's life taught me to treasure my passion for writing. He wrote about personal experiences, triumphs and tragedies. So do I. He accepted rejection slips and kept writing. So do I.

Lord, thank you for my father's writing spirit, reborn in me.

There is a time for everything. Ecclesiastes 3:1 NIV
—Tommie Lenox

March 23

After major surgery, I was recuperating at home all alone and was eager to write. I'd longed for that time of solitude.

Physically, I was held captive. No stairs, no driving. I couldn't even put the dog out in the backyard. So, why was I unable to sit down and put into words what was in my heart? I tried silence. I sat on my porch and listened to the traffic. I found myself looking for anything to do but write.

In the past I'd often replied to deadline pressure. When I was asked to get my Bible study in print and ready to sell on a book table for a women's conference, I got the job done.

One day, I sat at my desk determined to write something. Then I noticed after many dark and rainy days, the sun was shining on my face. I started thinking about how God is light and in him there is no darkness. I thought about how words have the power to brighten the lives of others.

Before I knew it the Son as well as the sun had turned my writer's block into inspiration.

Thank you, Lord, that your word gives light and helps me to write.

The unfolding of your words gives light; it gives understanding to the simple. Psalms 119:130 NIV
—Cheri L. Dedman

March 24

I could scarcely contain my excitement as I listened to my voice mail. "The publication committee loves your book proposal and wants to publish it," said the acquisitions editor. A year later, I received a second phone call from the same publisher with the same message.

My third book proposal was submitted to a different publisher. When I received the e-mail communicating the committee's decision, the results were different. While affirming the book's content, the publisher did not feel that it was a good fit for its publication goals.

Knowing the importance of responding to a no decision as graciously as I would a yes, I sent a small gift and note to the editorial administrator who had served as my liaison throughout the review process.

A year later, another proposal was ready for submission. Though I knew the publisher who had passed on my third book no longer accepted unsolicited manuscripts, I contacted the editorial administrator. Within minutes of my e-mail query, she wrote that she would process my proposal because the publisher knew me. Less than a month later, I had a contract. As I signed it I thanked my heavenly Father for providing me with the strength to model his character and graciously accept a no response.

Gracious heavenly Father, help me to accept that "yes," "no," and "wait" are all responses to my prayers.

No good thing does he withhold from those who walk uprightly. Psalms 84:11b ESV

—Pat Ennis

March 25

I was in overdrive: writing my novel, critiquing several screenplays, and editing writers' group submissions.

One morning I was engrossed in the story of Moses leading the Israelites from captivity. But when my overworked writer's brain encountered the sudden shift in Exodus 6:14 from Moses's adventure to those long passages of the Israelites' family tree, I looked up to heaven exasperated.

"Lord, you stopped the action of the story to give me more begats?"

The outburst shocked me. I had the audacity to offer editing advice to my creator—whose book has sold an estimated six billion copies?

Worse, I forgot why I read his word.

So shaken by this event, I wrote nothing for two months. But the long-term effects have been powerful. There was a brief disconnect in my writing circuitry, but that wake-up call proved my need for more time with God. He showed me writing had become my idol, that I needed a more balanced life. In the process he made my writing responsibilities more manageable—and fun. Since then God has never failed to make time for my writing— as long as I keep my focus on him.

Lord, when I study your word, check my internal editor at the door. Open me to the joys of knowing you. Renew all areas of my life, including my writing.

But seek ye first the kingdom of God and his righteousness; and all these things shall be added unto you. Matthew 6:33 KJV

—Brenda Kay Jackson

March 26

I was home from first grade with a sore throat. I sat on the warm floor in the kitchen, filling my toy blackboard with words. I scribbled happily, the words tumbling quickly onto the board. When the front was filled, I flipped the board over and continued.

"What are you writing?" Mother asked. She was ironing one of my father's starched shirts, shaking water from a Coke sprinkler bottle to keep the garment damp.

"It's a story," I said. I made careful strokes with my chalk.

"Read it to me." I heard the smile in Mother's voice.

"It's not very good," I protested. I grabbed my eraser and began rubbing. I erased the other side as well.

Mother flipped the shirt around to work on a new sleeve. "Sometimes our best words are the ones we throw away," she said quietly.

Through the years, I've repeated those wise words to my college English students. "Save those drafts," I've advised them. "Often your first thoughts are the freshest. Don't throw them out in self-doubt or frustration."

Fortunately, computer technology allows us to save revisions with ease. As writers, we find joy in the editing process. After all, that's when early nuggets of creative thought can be stitched like scraps into a beautiful quilt of words.

Lord, help me remember that your gifts often come in small steps. Let me rise above discouragements by surrendering my blunders to you.

The Spirit helps us in our weakness. Romans 8:26 NIV
—Margaret W. Garrison

March 27

I entered the Atlanta airport Starbucks, headed for the Mount Hermon Christian Writers' Conference in California. At the condiment counter I stirred skim milk into my decaf, my belongings sprawled around me.

Several men approached. "I'm sorry, I'm hogging the area," I said.

"No," one said with a smile. "You go ahead. You're right where you're supposed to be."

"Thank you," I said.

Zing. His words zapped my bubbles of doubt. Should I, a mere baby writer at age fifty-five, attend a writers' conference the caliber of Mount Hermon? Why hadn't I begun writing years ago, propelling my skills and experience to a higher level by now?

God had opened the top of that man's head and poured those gracious words out through his mouth. How he had put me at ease—not about taking up Starbucks' counter space, but about God's will and my writing.

Those simple words have reminded me often: I'm where God wants me at this moment, in my writing and my life.

Lord, when I doubt your lead, reassure me. Remind me that if I desire to follow you and demonstrate faith by obedience, you will make the path searchlight-clear and the timing perfect.

When I'm really working, really writing, I have the feeling it's coming from outside of me, through me. An absolute submission, absolute surrender. William Goyen

—Karen H. Phillips

March 28

"Another rejection?" I blubbered under my breath as I stood beside the mailbox that morning, clutching my third no thank-you letter in a row. The confidence I'd gained through receiving many acceptances of my greeting card verses in the past had begun to crumble. So, with bruised ego and broken heart, I said with a sigh, "Lord, if writing greeting cards isn't what you want me to do, then I'll quit today. I don't know if writing these is making a difference in anyone's life anyway."

That night, I accompanied my husband to a pastors' conference. Much to my surprise, as the keynote speaker took the podium that evening, he began by reciting his top ten favorite birthday cards he'd received that year and the crowd responded in uproarious cheer.

With each verse he quoted, I sensed a heavenly nudge prodding, "How do you feel about writing greeting cards now?"

Lord, thank you for the methods you use and the people you choose to encourage me to keep on writing.

Publish his glorious deeds among the nations. Tell everyone about the amazing things he does. 1 Chronicles 16:24 NLT

—Peggy Morris

March 29

I scratched with my fingernail at the spelling words I'd penciled, but they glared back at me—racing willfully uphill instead of marching obediently along the ruled line. I rubbed the paper with my finger and, having a bit of luck, wet my thumb with the tip of my tongue and pressed harder. But the lead only smeared, darker and uglier.

Tears welled in my eyes at the sight of the ragged smudge on the crisp page of my spanking new Big Chief tablet. I rubbed again.

Miss Townsley's plump hand stilled mine. "Carol," she leaned down to whisper, "that's what erasers are for."

"But ... now I've ruined it."

"Mistakes aren't worth worrying about." Kneeling beside my desk, my first-grade teacher reached for the gum eraser in my pencil box and demonstrated. With a few flicks of her wrist, the spot disappeared.

"See? Now you can start fresh and try again." She smiled and tousled my penny red hair. "That's what erasers are for."

Even today, those words calm my spirit and ease my mind.

When I'm faced with rewriting an awkward passage or reworking a chapter that stalls the storyline, I think back on Miss Townsley's wise counsel. And, with a few flicks of my wrist, I delete and start fresh. That is what erasers are for.

Thank you, Father, for fresh starts and second chances.

You always pass failure on your way to success.
Mickey Rooney

—Carol McAdoo Rehme

March 30

While my childhood friends dreamed of becoming astronauts and nurses, I longed to be an author. I carried that passion with me throughout the years, but always had a reason as to why I didn't write. My class load was too heavy. All my time went to my young children.

Still, the desire kept growing until I could no longer contain it and began writing. My soul came to life. Everything once bottled danced across the screen, creating a magnificent collage of words.

Magnificent in my mind, that is. Once I completed the manuscript, excuses ran rampant again. I didn't have a publication history. Who would sign a novice writer like me?

I recently heard we must pass our freak-out point to embrace our passions. Mine is that dreaded "r" word. Do you know it too? "Thank you for your submission, but we regret to inform you it doesn't meet our editorial needs." Oh, the sting of rejection.

My goal this year is to receive an unprecedented number of form letters. Yes, it's a bizarre resolution, yet one that quite probably will bring about a greater amount of positive feedback too. Fear turned the king of the jungle into a cowardly lion. Dare I let it do the same to me?

Lord, give me the courage to be the writer you want me to be.

None but a coward dares to boast that he has never known fear. Ferdinand Foch

—Stacy Voss

March 31

"So Kathy, what's new?"

"Well, I'm writing a book," I answered tentatively.

The response was generally the same: head cocked to the side, lips curled in amusement, and a raised eyebrow accompanied by, "I didn't know you were a writer or English major."

The person with whom I was having the conversation usually knew I hadn't studied English in college, but had a degree in community health. Not to be dissuaded, however, I typically responded this way: "If you're wondering if I studied English in college, the answer is no. But if you're wondering if I have a story to tell, the answer is yes."

For many of us, that is what keeps us going.

Lord, your words are inside me. I am the scribe.

I wrote because I had to. I couldn't stop. There wasn't anything else I could do. Tennessee Williams

—Kathy Pride

April 1

I'll never forget that day almost twenty years ago when a policeman stopped me as I was on the way to the school where I taught. It seemed as if millions of little eyes were staring at me as the school buses drove past my parked car. My cheeks were red with embarrassment and shame.

How could I, a woman who had driven safely for many years, get a speeding ticket? How foolish I felt.

Hours later, I was still trying to turn it over to God. But what appeared to be one of the most embarrassing moments of my life turned around a few years later when I wrote about it. When that little piece was published, I received more comments from folks who related more to my feelings of foolishness than any other article I had written.

I learned that it's not my moments of being strong that bless others the most. In my moments of weakness, God's strength is even more evident.

Lord, thank you for using even my moments of feeling foolish to honor and glorify your name.

He is no fool who gives what he cannot keep to gain what he cannot lose. Jim Elliot

—Sharon Beth Brani

April 2

It might be a stretch to say that I am a writer, although I have written for a local journal and a short publication for the writing center at the college where I work. I became an English teacher partly because I was a decent writer. But mostly, I appreciated the ability of the spoken or written word to touch the heart, encourage the weary, or give hope to the despairing.

After college, I taught high school English for four years. Years later, I found myself teaching developmental English at a community college. Every class period I put a quote on the board, usually something encouraging, always beginning with "There is no substitute for hard work" (Thomas Jefferson). Frequently, I noticed students copying the quotes in their notebooks. They were hungry for the morsels of encouragement those few words presented.

My mission became convincing students that becoming better writers was about much more than passing classes. I shared stories about the importance and power of writing something well, even just a few heartfelt words added to a sympathy card. And I tried to make the point that good writing required time and effort. Abraham Lincoln, I told them, revised the Gettysburg Address at least five times.

Inspire me, O Lord, to share words that bless others.

Your word is a lamp to my feet and a light to my path. Psalms 119:105 NKJV

—Kay Laughlin

April 3

When a friend gave me a book with blank pages except for nature drawings in a corner of each page, I decided to use it to write about what was happening in the garden. That was in 2001 and I am now writing in my seventh garden journal recording my planting, tending and appreciation of God's good earth.

Writing in my journal also inspires me to write poems connecting nature and life. I have recalled the seasons of life from a cold wintry separation to the renewal of life in seeing the first crocus, being a caretaker, and seeing grandchildren blossom and mature just as I have. I showed this in the poem "Married":

Married thirty-two years
And as many years alone.
The time of forgive and forget
lived; no longer mired in regrets.
And now married to all
I can be a part of humanity
I say, *pass the peas please.*

I get on my knees to garden and to pray and then write about it. All three—gardening and writing and prayer—help me confront cancer and continue to see the joy and beauty in life.

Dear Lord, I thank you for all of life.

One ought, every day at least, to hear a little song, read a good poem, see a fine picture, and if it were possible, to speak a few reasonable words. Johann Wolfgang von Goethe

—Dorothy Holley

April 4

While sitting in my college library one afternoon, I received a shocking e-mail from an editor with an attached letter. He informed me that someone named Mary had seen my photo along with an article I'd recently written. She claimed she knew me way back when, but that we'd lost contact.

Tears came as my memory jumped back ten years. Mary was my elementary school best friend. Due to some difficult family circumstances, Mary had been temporarily placed in my family's care before being relocated overseas by one of her parents. Mary and I never got to say good-bye.

I clicked on Mary's e-mail and learned she was well and living in Asia. She expressed how much she had missed me and how thankful she was that my family had been there to care for her when her family couldn't.

I have never been to Asia, but God allowed my article to travel eight thousand miles and heal not one but two hearts.

Lord, thank you for being the God of first, second, and third chances.

I waited patiently for the Lord; he turned to me and heard my cry. Psalms 40:1 NIV

—Kate E. Schmelzer

April 5

I was sitting in the waiting room at the ophthalmologist, thinking about my next writing assignment. Dreading it would be a more apt description.

My last assignment had been about Chile, where we lived for three years as missionaries. I loved writing about Chile—the majestic Andes Mountains; the three thousand miles of rugged Pacific coast; the well-educated, genial, and self-assured people.

Then, abruptly, we had been reassigned to Paraguay—that little peanut-shaped country in the center of South America where most roads were dirt, streets were cobblestone, and many people went barefoot and were ignorant of the larger world. And that was my current assignment.

I had done my research, had my outline and notes, but I didn't know how to portray the country without diminishing it or how to describe the people without demeaning them.

In the waiting room to my right sat an elderly gentleman with his middle-aged daughter. The old man mumbled and complained, mumbled and complained. Finally the daughter said sternly, "Can you see out of one eye?"

"Yeah," he mumbled.

"Then you can see!" she scolded.

It didn't hit me until I arrived home. I was grumbling just like the old man. I hadn't been able to see clearly how to begin to describe Paraguayan life, but…I could see out of one eye.

Today, Lord, let me be thankful for what I can see, can perceive, with your help.

Open my eyes that I may see. Psalms 119:18 NIV
—Margaret "Maggie" Arnold Register

96

April 6

Ideas for stories and articles are sometimes dumped into my writer's brain like a bag of old clothes or a raging dust storm or dust mites floating through the kitchen window. Sometimes, I jot those thoughts down on scraps and toss them into a box or file. Sometimes, I carry a three-by-five card.

Every idea has potential, but a major sort and organizational party must take place before it's a story or publishable article. A card file is most efficient, but ideas also can be grouped in piles on a large table. Stapled or taped in order, they form rough copy to type into the computer. It doesn't look pretty, but now there's something to cut and paste.

God may have given us the genius, but we still have to press and hang our thoughts neatly in a closet of sentences and paragraphs. I find myself reading and editing until others understand my message and, I hope, appreciate the lesson learned.

Jesus, help me to collect my ideas, organize them, and present them in a manner worthy of a Christian writer.

Let us not be weary in well-doing: for in due season we shall reap, if we faint not. Galatians 6:9 KJV
—Rose Goble

April 7

At the age of fifty-five, my company's merger had a domino effect on everything that was important to me. Because I needed the medical coverage and pension that my many years of service would provide, I had to move from my home of thirty-three years to Pittsburgh, four hundred miles away. I went from a challenging career to a job that paid considerably less. Most of all, I had to leave my sister, who was my best friend, and nieces and nephews whom I adored. I had to make new friends and find a church. Wasn't I too old to be making such drastic changes?

I was frightened about my future. Because of my pride, I did not want to reveal my anxieties to my family and close friends.

I had kept a journal sporadically in the past. With a little more time in my new life, I wrote about my feelings and experiences. Some of those entries developed into meditations for publication. Writing brought me comfort. Since my move, I have become a regular contributor to the devotional *Penned from the Heart* and my church's quarterly magazine, *Calvary's Mailbox*.

Father, without you, I could never have turned the despair in my life into hope.

You can make many plans, but the Lord's purpose will prevail. Proverbs 19:21 NLT

—Elizabeth Mary Van Hook

April 8

"I sold my article for kids," I called into the bright morning sky from the balcony overlooking our backyard, waving the publisher's check with excitement.

It was a solemn moment—and a grateful one. This was the gold star I had sought ever since I left the tender care of Sister Mary Pius, my fourth-grade teacher. "This is a gold-star story," she had said aloud, as she licked the small glittery sticker and placed it above the title line for all to see before pinning my story to the bulletin board.

After school that day she called me to her desk. "Karen, you're going to be a professional writer someday. Reach for those stars. Write the words God gives you."

Today, some thirty-five years after my first sale and sixty years since I sat in that classroom, I continue to write—despite the rejections and the revisions—even despite the awards and the acclaim. For I have learned something important in all of this. I am a writer. Sister Mary Pius said I would be.

When I feel scared or shaken, uncertain or unworthy, I sense her presence and hear her encouraging words. "Reach for those stars. Write the words God gives you."

And so I do.

Lord, help me to write the words you give me.

Let love and faithfulness never leave you; bind them around your neck, write them on the tablet of your heart. Proverbs 3:3 NIV

—Karen O'Connor

April 9

In a box on my desk are envelopes from editors of magazines and book publishers. Inside the envelopes are the reasons why the work I presented wasn't what they were looking for.

The first few times I read a rejection slip, it stung. My face burned with embarrassment. I took it personally, became depressed and doubtful, and wanted to quit.

I went to the library and studied the finer points of writing. I read books about editing, query letters, and polishing prose. I set a few goals. I wrote a query, sent it to an editor, and wrote more essays to forget about it. When the rejection letter came a week later, I noticed certain word combinations immobilized me. Editor and query letter. I took a writing class.

Ten months later, two classes from graduation, I enlisted my friend to hold me accountable. At the top of the page I stated my reverse psychology goal of one hundred rejections.

I also listed weekly and year-end goals and checked in every week. Now I smile when rejections show up in the mail, because I'm still on track.

Last week, however, I received a contract, a check, and a lot more courage.

Lord, inspire my words and give me the determination to persevere in the face of adversity.

Writing is easy. All you do is stare at a blank sheet of paper until drops of blood form on your forehead. Gene Fowler

—Julie Morrison

April 10

Every eye in the room was on me as I stood by the chalkboard. I felt so stupid.

"Why," the teacher said aloud.

I stammered. All I could see in my mind was a large, capital Y. I suddenly felt hot. Time was running out. It was boys against the girls and we were down to the wire. The girls were complaining the word was too easy. This was one of those moments that would forever define who I was to the guys, a hero or a heel.

"Time," the teacher said, "The correct spelling is W. H. Y." My ship was sunk. I knew that word, but the pressure to perform had caused my mind to go blank.

That experience taught me that I'm human and I may drop the ball. When it feels like everyone is watching me, maybe they are. All I can do is give it my best shot. Golfers miss putts. Bowlers miss strikes. Businesspeople miss airplanes. Writers miss deadlines. But we don't quit. We putt again. Throw another ball. Find another flight. Go to the next story.

I've stopped beating myself up. Now, I just get busy and do the next one and tell myself to never, never quit.

My chance came later that year. I spelled it perfectly. "V.A.C.U.U.M."

Heavenly Father, thank you for your grace and the opportunity to improve.

Forgetting what is behind and straining toward what is ahead, I press on toward the goal. Philippians 3:13-14 NIV

—Lonni L. Docter

April 11

After attending a home prayer meeting, I said to my husband, "I feel like it's time to write a book about my Christian life. But isn't that ridiculous? You and I know my Christian life isn't that great. Who am I to tell the world how to walk with God?"

I felt rather daunted, expecting him to agree with me, for he knows my faults and failings better than anyone. But his attitude was one of concern, "Hey, wait a minute," he said, "You're missing the boat."

"OK, what's the boat?"

"You're not supposed to tell how great a Christian you are. You don't have to convince anyone of that. Just tell them if God could take someone like you and make something of you, just look at what he could do with someone who had something to begin with."

Fortunately for him, he laughed as he said it. And fortunately, too, there was nothing handy to throw at him. But he's right. If I use the talent God has given me, God will make something good of it and enable me in turn to write what will inspire and encourage others.

God, may your written word, through me, reach into the lives of others to encourage and inspire them.

My word. I send it out and it always produces fruit. It will accomplish all I want it to, and it will prosper everywhere I send it. Isaiah 55:11 NLT

—Yvonne Lehman

April 12

The church was packed for the Easter sermon that Reverend Pat was about to deliver.

That morning, I was full of doubt for many reasons. Mostly it was because as a writer my creative confidence was on the wane. I hadn't penned anything productive in days, only a jumble of stirrings that had no focus.

For years whenever I felt that way, I had asked God for a sign and he never had disappointed me. That morning, Reverend Pat's sermon consisted of four little words that spoke volumes to my sagging spirit. With outstretched arms he stood in the center aisle and simply said, "Blossom where you are!"

The Lord chose the day we celebrate Jesus's rising from the dead to compel me to rise above my own stale set of circumstances.

Blossom where you are! Those words of wisdom gave me reason to look in the mirror and see the potential that God has placed in me. I went home, organized my thoughts, and began to write.

Thank you, Lord, for the gift of writing. When my faith falters, guide me in the direction you want me to go.

The act of writing is the act of discovering what you believe. David Hare

—Kathy Whirity

April 13

Jim and I were enjoying a working lunch, with manuscripts of poetry and prose spread out among the dessert plates and coffee cups. We were English teacher colleagues and coeditors of a small, independent, semiannual literary magazine.

"Have you noticed," I said, "that the best material comes in right on top of the deadline? But the manuscripts that arrive weeks ahead...."

Jim nodded and pantomimed dropping something into a wastebasket.

"Why do you think that is?" I asked. "Is it because most writers are natural procrastinators?"

Jim leaned back in his chair. "I can think of more flattering explanations," he said. "Serious writers are always revising. They have trouble letting go of a manuscript because they keep trying for clearer word choice, stronger images. Finally, they mail the piece exactly on the postmark deadline."

I nodded. I could identify with compulsive revising.

"The other thing," Jim said, "is that serious writers are always submitting. They get a story back from one publication, check the deadlines of other magazines, see that ours is tomorrow—and turn their manuscript around in the mail!"

I nodded again, but my smile dimmed. I knew I could do better when it came to persistence in submissions.

Thanks for reminding me, Jim.

Thank you, Lord, for friends who give us words in good season.

Let us run with perseverance the race that is set before us. Hebrews 12:1 NRSV

—Nancy E. James

April 14

For the first twenty years of my writing life, my poetry wound up under my bed in a dark and dusty box. I rarely shared my work with anyone. Occasionally, if a friend needed encouragement, I hauled the box out, dug through the pile, and timidly shared a poem.

One day, I read in our church bulletin about a new writers' group. I finally stirred up the courage to attend.

"Bring some of your pieces. We'd like to hear your work," the leader said.

The next week I brought some poems and read aloud to the others. They liked them. Later, we held a poetry reading and they included me in the program.

As I listened to others' work, I was encouraged to expand my writing to inspirational short stories and devotionals. My fellow writers encouraged me to send pieces out for publication. To my surprise, in spite of rejections, there were a few acceptances.

"Why don't you publish your work in a book? This is good stuff," the leader suggested. As a result, my book *Sonflower Seeds* was born. The next year I entered it in a large writers' conference contest and won first place. God is full of surprises.

Father, allow me to let you expand my horizons.

Though thy beginning was small, yet thy latter end should greatly increase. Job 8:7 KJV

—Sally Jadlow

April 15

The night my neighbor passed away was the first time I remember experiencing the death of someone close to me. It was at this time that I first experienced a need to write.

After watching paramedics drive away with her body, I sought solace in my bedroom. I was only in the fifth grade and didn't quite know how to handle the overwhelming emptiness that comes with death. I needed to do something, so I wrote a poem of comfort to give to her family the next morning. I remember the daughter reading my poem aloud to everyone in the room when I handed it to her.

Writing that poem was the beginning of what would become a lifelong habit. I began to write poems and letters to those who had touched me in some special way. It was a gift to them, and an emotional release for me.

Through the changes life has brought, my need to write has continued to flourish. It is a gift I cannot imagine being without.

Thank you Lord for the gift you have given me, allowing me to pour out my love, emotion and thanks, so that others might benefit.

The writer must write what he has to say, not speak it.
Ernest Hemingway

—Linda Strong

April 16

When I was halfway through the first draft of my memoir, *Eleanor's Story: An American Girl in Hitler's Germany,* I reached a low that took away all the enthusiasm and creative joy in the writing process.

I wrote in my journal: "With the daily writing and mundane attention to detail, I'm losing focus of the book. Nobody will be interested in the story of an ordinary child. I wasn't heroic or beautiful or brilliant. Will the story have an effect on readers? Does it have a message? Will it be interesting?"

One night during this uncreative period, I dreamed I was standing on the roof of a tall building. I needed to jump across a dark abyss to the opposite building. I was afraid to leap. I would always stop just before jumping, thus losing the speed I needed to vault the space.

Suddenly, a little boy showed up, "Look at me! It's easy!" he shouted, running past me and playfully jumping to the other side. "Just do it! Don't be afraid, and you'll be carried across."

Finally I overcame fear of failure and found the courage to take that leap. I felt myself lifted up soaring effortlessly to the other side.

After it was published, my memoir won nine awards.

Lord, when self-doubt keeps me from being creative, help me take a leap of faith.

Faith is the realization of what is hoped for and the evidence of things not seen. Hebrews 11:1 NAB
—Eleanor Ramrath Garner

April 17

For years I attended writers' conferences and accumulated a wealth of information. But I never did much with it, except pray for ways to use this library of information. Then at a mission fair I investigated prison ministries. The chaplain at the local jail learned I was a writer and invited me to teach creative writing to male offenders. This was a leap of faith as it was uncharted waters.

Teaching troubled men behind four sets of locked doors was not something I had given thought to until I felt God's leading. People discouraged me, especially since I was already busy with my life. But God had other ideas. I accepted the challenge and now enter the jail with no fear and leave with an enriched heart.

It breaks my heart to read the men's stories, but I rejoice to see them lifted up by improving their writing skills. We pray for each other and recognize that we share the same heavenly Father. When one of them stands before the class to share, we often cry but sometimes we laugh, which is also healing.

Now I know that those years invested in the skill of writing were preparing me for this place of service. My writing library is in full use and I have borrowed exercises learned from past Christian writers' conferences.

Lord, thank you for encouraging me to teach writing skills to those in prison for I am the one who is blessed.

I was in prison and you came to visit me. Matthew 25:36 NIV

—Joy C. Bradford

April 18

One summer afternoon, I sat on the patio and shelled peas for dinner—pop, scoop, dump. I felt as drained of energy as an empty pea pod after working all day on an article that just wouldn't jell.

Still mulling, I watched my husband John and our three-year-old son open a box that arrived in the mail. Kenny ripped off the wrappings and pulled out a red helicopter. "Look, Mom!" he shouted.

Daddy read the directions and tried to show Kenny how to operate his new toy.

But the toddler wouldn't listen. "I want to do it!" he whined. Stubbornly, he pulled the string again and again, but nothing happened. "I can't do it! This dumb thing won't work." He threw down the toy in disgust.

"Now will you let me show you how?" Daddy asked. When Kenny reluctantly agreed, John guided the chubby fingers in winding the string the right way. Soon, father and son ran across the lawn after the soaring helicopter.

I smiled sheepishly. How like Kenny I am, I thought. I had plunged into my work that morning but had forgotten to pray for help. I wanted to do it my way. And then I grew frustrated when it didn't go right.

As I shelled the last pea pod, I vowed to ask God for help before I started the next day's work.

Lord, please be my teacher as I write.

More things are wrought by prayer than this world dreams of. Alfred Lord Tennyson

—Agnes C. Lawless

April 19

I'd researched diligently for an article on the ministry of encouragement, but didn't use all my notes. I could have written five thousand words, but the editor only wanted twelve hundred. As I scanned the unused information in my article file, I wished I didn't have to throw it all away.

Then I realized I didn't have to waste it. Facts and anecdotes were like the bags of sewing scraps people often brought me, knowing I made patchwork quilts. How many times had I sat at my kitchen table cutting five-inch squares out of odd-sized scraps? And how many blankets had they become?

I riffled through my research and interview notes.

Maybe I could do separate articles on ways to encourage, I thought, splitting out material on encouraging through words, touch, and prayer. I could also simplify all this for a children's magazine.

Then my fiction-writer side kicked in. I was already naming the protagonist and antagonist for a story about the encouragement of hospitality.

I've learned that when I overresearch, I can birth more articles or stories out of my notes. As I redeem illustrations and insights, I'm reminded that even scraps can be used for effective ministry. Though they may need a little trimming and rearranging, with God's help I can always take the scraps and create something whole.

Lord, help me work with my writer's scraps to help others.

Gather the pieces that are left over. Let nothing be wasted. John 6:12 NIV

—Jeanne Zornes

April 20

In school, math was my forte; English, a subject in passing. Not that I didn't enjoy reading and studying Brontë's *Jane Eyre* and Shakespeare's *Hamlet.* I did. But when it came to grammar and spelling, as my cousin taught me to say, "my mother borned me wrong." As a result, my energies went into the areas in which I naturally excelled; writing never entered my mind.

As a teenager I poured my dreams onto a steno pad, using Pitman Shorthand to hide my poor English. With age, time became a precious commodity, restricting my stories to memory alone. All the while, I wondered what drove me to dream so much.

It wasn't until a math career, husband, and three children later that my desire to learn the craft of writing emerged. No longer squelched by the dreaded grading system, I was able to pour my thoughts freely onto my keyboard, syntax errors abounding. Where modern software fell short, critique partners appeared to guide and direct my words.

After years of questioning why I was such a daydreamer, when numbers seemed to be my calling, I finally understood that if I learned the proper writing tools, my dreams could be shared with the world, one story at a time.

Dear Lord, thank you for preparing the way for me to fulfill your will.

For my thoughts are not your thoughts, neither are your ways my ways. Isaiah 55:8 NIV

—Eileen Astels

April 21

It calls me before I fall asleep. It calls me in the car. It calls me at the job that pays. It calls me when I hear sad stories. The need to write calls me often.

But my kids cry. Sometimes their cries make me run to rescue them, scoop them up, hug them, kiss them, and say, "it's OK." Sometimes their cries also make me want to run the other direction.

For three years, their little cries silenced me. I couldn't write.

At the end of the silence was a deep, dark place. There was nothing left in me. I cried out to God, "Have mercy on me. Show me a way out of this pit."

Within twenty-four hours, my prayers were answered. Home-schooled girls came to my house in the mornings so I could write. After their commitment, I was blessed to find a job that paid real money. Even though it was a back-breaking, knee-swelling, aggravating-at-times waitress job, it allowed me to pay those God-given girls to watch my precious little ones.

Every morning I live my passion and hear laughter in the background. Knowing my little ones are well taken care of, I write.

Father, thank you for providing for my needs today. Please increase my faith and help me use the gift of writing accordingly.

Ask and it will be given to you; seek and you will find; knock and the door will be opened to you. Luke 11:9 NIV

—Nancy Lucas

April 22

As a young girl, I wanted the years to pass quickly so I could be on my own. I wanted freedom and new adventures. Fargo, North Dakota, seemed pretty dull.

At seventeen, traveling by train to work in different cities for Western Union, I found the freedom I longed for. Two years later, World War II was over and there was no special need for telegraphers in large cities. My last assignment was Cleveland.

One evening at a dance, I met my husband to be. That wonderful day changed my life and in four months we married. I prayed, "God, please let us have ten years together." Ten years became sixty.

With the children grown, writing gave me purpose and pleasure. After twenty-five years, I still enjoy my efforts. Sometimes I'm successful, sometimes not. I've published for teens, seniors, and children. I've written Christian songs.

But I wonder. How have I used my writing to further God's message? Should I have spent more time writing about his glory and blessings?

It won't be long before I meet my Savior face to face. I pray for his guidance to use this time wisely. Perhaps I'll work on a children's book, finish the article on the Biloxi mission trip, and write another song.

Help me with your wisdom, dear Lord, so that my writing will please you.

Teach us to number our days and recognize how few they are; help us to spend them as we should. Psalms 90:12 TLB

—Gloria Tietgens Sladek

April 23

After contributing stories to over thirty Chicken Soup for the Soul books, I was given the opportunity to coauthor one. Naturally, I was thrilled. Then I learned it was a companion book for *Chicken Soup for the Dieter's Soul* and I would have to collect 365 one-hundred-twenty-word inspirational nuggets about fitness from hundreds of writers who would each be paid twenty-five dollars.

The task seemed monumental. I didn't know enough writers who knew that much about health and fitness and I doubted that I could begin the task, let alone finish it.

Then I thought, Why don't you write the whole book yourself? You need to lose weight. Take the readers on a yearlong journey as you get healthier by eating less, eating better, and exercising more.

Even though every other Chicken Soup book is a compilation from many authors, I convinced the powers-that-be to give me a shot at writing the entire book myself.

Seventy-one days later, the book was written. I'd even lost ten pounds following my own advice! Trouble is, they asked me to coauthor *Chicken Soup for the Chocolate Lover's Soul* next and well, that book required research also, the eating kind.

But I learned an important lesson. We writers can always ask editors to do things our way, and quite often the answer is yes.

Lord, give me the courage to suggest new ways of doing things in this wild, wonderful world of writing.

You can't wait for inspiration. You have to go after it with a club. Jack London

—Patricia Lorenz

April 24

The angry caller probably thought she was dealing with one of those godless journalists: "You people can't stand God's word. That's why you won't run my letter to the editor."

I tried to explain: "In a general circulation newspaper such as this one, letter writers must present their own ideas. A few biblical passages are OK as long as they relate to the issues of the day. But your letter is 80 percent scripture."

"Well," she shot back, "I think your opinion page should be 100 percent scripture!"

Good-bye and click.

Given another minute with her, I also would have underscored the importance of discipline in writing. Beginning writers so often feel that as long as God guides their fingers on the keyboard, they need not follow the principles of composition. *The Elements of Style* by Strunk and White? Never heard of it.

But it was the scriptural overload that worried me most. I was left wondering: Why are fledgling writers often so enamored of borrowed material? Originality is the heart of effective writing. Copious quotes—no matter how inspired—cheapen a product, chasing away readers.

Lord, may all of us would-be messengers learn to think for ourselves.

The merit of originality is not novelty. It is sincerity. Thomas Carlyle

—Jerry Elsea

April 25

My love of flowers and plants has taken me on quite a life journey. My husband and I built a small green house. Then I read all the flower and garden books I could find. Finally, I dove into the task of starting, transplanting, growing, and selling beautiful bedding plants to friends and neighbors. This escalated into trees, shrubs, nursery stock, flower arranging, and, finally, a complete garden center and floral shop. It was so exciting to have my hobby also be my work.

I decided to share my life experience by writing a weekly newspaper column on gardening. At first I was afraid that no one would be interested, but I approached the editor of my local newspaper anyway. He gave me a chance to try my hand at writing.

The column, Ruth's Gardens, has been a hit. I receive many compliments on my writing. People even tell me they look forward to my weekly columns. I'm happy to have found a way to give back to others.

Thank you, dear God, for letting me work with your beauty and for the opportunity to share my experiences with others.

Begin where you are. Bloom where you are planted.
Robert H. Schuller

—Ruth Schlesser

April 26

Rulers! Rulers!
Who wants to buy
Five rulers
For five little school children?
Here! Here!
I want to buy
Five rulers
For five little school children.

Honestly, is there any hint of a budding writer in that scrawl of a second grader? This eighty-four-year-old reciting my childhood ditty to my three senior-citizen sisters caused them to double over in laughter.

But that ditty was only the first, followed by many more as well as articles, skits, and devotions and stories of the elderly, the teenager, and the Asian refugee. Deadlines met. A few dollars earned. I finally had the nerve to call myself a writer.

Recently, the words of another writer caused me to dust off a work started three decades ago. Rereading it was exciting, reminding me of the spiritual walk I'd been on. I had been mentoring myself.

Does it matter whether the retrieved writing becomes the book intended? I don't think so. Let the words fall where they will.

Lord, are you the one who has nagged and pestered me? Thank you for bringing me back to the closer walk.

Our job is to tap the revelation of the Lord in our own area of talent so that we can reflect the king and his kingdom. Bill Johnson

—Tamar Braden

April 27

My professor, a well-known radio personality, handed my recording back: "You sound like a housewife."
I didn't know what that meant, but it didn't feel like a compliment. Majoring in psychology and broadcasting, I was hoping to emerge as someone with something to say. That small comment planted seeds of doubt in my mind.
My life took a difficult course. Years later, I felt the urge to speak and write about my experiences. The professor's words, now shadowed with cobwebs, still carried great impact. Maybe I didn't have a message worth sharing.
On a whim and prayer, I attended a writers' conference. I sat with a radio personality at a roundtable discussion. She looked at me square in the eye and said, "If you have a message to speak, then speak it. Don't let anyone keep you from sharing the message God's given you."
Suddenly, I realized that I would have to let go of those words from my professor. God had allowed me to hear encouragement so I could press on and share my message. How appropriate that many of the people I share with now are housewives.

Lord, you've given me a message and a voice. Help me use them well.

Do your best to present yourself to God as one approved, a workman who does not need to be ashamed and who correctly handles the word of truth. 2 Timothy 2:15 NIV

—Jami Kirkbride

April 28

A year ago, I took a beginners quilting class. The instructor told us we would each make a wall hanging the size of a crib quilt. She told us how much fabric to buy in six different prints. We were all assigned the same quilt pattern, but we could choose our own prints and colors.

I purchased my fabric and was eager to get started. During the next class I sewed strips of material together and cut the strips to make blocks. Soon I realized the other students' blocks looked different from mine. It wasn't the different material and prints; it was how they were put together. Before I could rip out the threads and start over, the instructor approached and said, "Don't rip it out, you made your own pattern and it looks great." I finished my quilt and proudly displayed it on the bedroom wall.

As a writer, I cannot go to a pattern book for detailed instructions. Even though I am writing devotions with the same guidelines as others, mine are different because they are from my own heart. Writing would be pretty boring if I had to follow a pattern and was not allowed to be creative.

Thank you, Lord, for making us all different and allowing us to be creative in our thinking.

There is then creative reading as well as creative writing. Ralph Waldo Emerson

—Sally Devine

April 29

I walked into the conference meeting room wondering once again—what I was doing there?

I loved the idea of a week of writing workshops, guest speakers and a chance to meet with an editor. But all these other people must be REAL writers, with bylines and publishing credits and payment. I only had a couple articles in two community papers. Did that make me a writer?

During the week, I discovered that we were all writers. Some had brilliant creative ideas; some had the drive to self-publish and then tirelessly sell their books. Others had wild imaginative characters that graced the pages of comic books or horror stories. Some had sweet and funny short stories of their own history. Each had a unique form of writing talent.

I am a slow learner. Now that I've attended three conferences, I've begun to believe that I am a writer. People have affirmed my skills and talents. I am investing time in writing. I submit pieces to editors with the confidence that they are good enough to be published. I know I have been given a talent and that one day I will find its home.

Lord, help me to recognize and affirm myself as a writer. Help me to use my talent as you intended.

What you are is God's gift to you. What you make of yourself is your gift to God. Danish proverb

—Beth Granger

April 30

Reading some of my journal entries, I was surprised to notice the great difference in feeling and energy between sentences written in second person and those written in first person.

"You should write every day" has a finger-wagging quality about it. My friend June used to say, "Don't 'should' on me." You feel like the naughty child caught in the cookie jar. Hang your head.

On the other hand, "I will write every day" has a can-do quality about it. The coercion slinks away. My head comes up. Yes, I CAN write every day.

June bought a new computer when she was eighty-six years old. Her mentor attached a sign of encouragement to it: Yes I can. She reports that this sign has a better effect than her previous sign: You can do it.

I wonder if this is the heart of my problem with to-do lists. Whenever I write a list of things I have to do, my inner child rebels and says, "I don't have to, and you can't make me." Then my stern inner adult shakes her finger, "You have to...." To-do lists feel coercive to me.

I'm giving this a try. Instead of making to-do lists, I will make can-do lists.

God, help me remember I can do all things through Christ who strengthens me.

Yes, I said, yes I will, yes. James Joyce
—Connie Scharlau

May 1

"Do you have the poem for Mother's Day yet?" she asked on the phone. "I want to put a copy in the gifts for church. Also, maybe someone could read it with soft background music during the service."

"I don't have it yet," I answered. "I'm sorry. With the kids' schedule right now, I just haven't had time. "

I put the phone down slowly. A cold feeling settled around my heart. Would my poem be good enough to be read aloud in church?

"Lord, I have so many responsibilities," I prayed. "I know you want me to be faithful with my writing, but please help me find time to be quiet and hear what you want me to write."

"Mom, I gotta go to basketball," my son called.

In the parking lot at school, a cool breeze was swaying the trees. My window was down as I relaxed, enjoying the view. I decided to stay there and wait.

My thoughts drifted to my married daughter with her two young children. I thought about what a good mother she is and the gift and pain of a mother's love. Slowly, thoughts teased my mind until they came into focus. Grabbing a pen and paper, the words poured out until the poem was finished.

As my son came walking out, I wondered if the Lord was smiling as much as I.

Lord, thank you for making a way, when I see none.

All I have seen teaches me to trust the creator for all I have not seen. Ralph Waldo Emerson

—Elizabeth Sebek

May 2

I woke up laughing. As a GED teacher, I teach writing skills. Students who take the test must write a 250-word essay on a topic they are given that day. To many, that seems like an immense amount of words. I had to laugh, because when I am limited to 250 words I have to cut words all the time.

I have my students practice expanded writing. One year, at the jail, I gave the students a simple sentence: bears eat. Then we started expanding it. I asked, "Do you visualize the bears as brown or black? What and where do they eat?"

One student wrote, "The bare bears eat anything the foolish tourists throw out from their cars." Another wrote, "Big black bears don't eat anything in the winter because they are hibernating."

My favorite writing that day came from a muscular, tall guy who wrote, "My bear don't eat nothing 'cause he's stuffed." I know the grammar isn't correct, but the play on words is great.

Lord, thanks for giving us so many ways to describe just about everything in your world and for the gift of laughter to enjoy it all.

He will fill your mouth with laughter. Shouts of joy will come from your lips. Job 8:21 NIRV

—Margaret Steinacker

May 3

"Write what you know," I'd always heard. But what do I know?

Several decades of raising three active children left me feeling intellectually scattered and shallow. Sure, I could discuss laundry detergent and quote *Goodnight Moon*, but craft a writing career from this commonplace foundation? It didn't seem likely.

I'd always been fascinated by an old inn standing in a state of neglect by the side of a busy local road. Peeling paint and overgrown gardens informed the public it was closed for business. As the years passed, my curiosity about the old place never abated. What was its history? How had it fallen into such disrepair?

One day I noticed a swarm of workers carrying ladders, paint cans and toolboxes in and out of the inn. I pulled into the parking lot and asked the nearest workman what was happening.

"The new owner's right over there," he said, pointing. "Why don't you ask him?"

So I did. And what I heard was a story too interesting to keep to myself. I queried a local paper with enthusiastic results, and the relationship turned into a lively two-year stint as a reporter.

Write what you know? I didn't know a thing about that old inn. But with curiosity and an opportunity to learn, I discovered I could know, and write, about anything.

Lord, may your spirit continually ignite in me a curiosity about this wonderful world you created.

It's all a matter of keeping my eyes open. Annie Dillard

—Sally Murtagh

May 4

It's been two years since I first sensed God nudging me to quit my day job to write full time. For a year I wrestled. How did I know it was God's voice? How would we make ends meet?

I believed God would provide—it says so right in the Bible: "And my God will supply every need of yours according to his riches in glory in Christ Jesus" (Philippians 4:19 RSV). But it's easier to believe a verse like that after the fact.

This is where the rubber met the road.

After much prayer, I submitted my letter of resignation—and immediately the tension ceased. Editing jobs came in just when the taxes were due or the heating oil was low. We got a bigger refund because our tax preparer just happened to notice something she forgot the year before and filed an amended return. More grant money for our son's college expenses sprung up. And there was the change in our health insurance policy that provided the eyeglasses we both needed—at no cost to us.

Now when I sense God's nudging, I'm not afraid to step out in faith. I've learned that where the rubber meets the road is where God will be.

Dear God, you are just awesome!

For we walk by faith, not by sight. 2 Corinthians 5:7 RSV

—Michele T. Huey

May 5

My first published work sparked my desire to pursue my goal of being a writer. It didn't matter that the material published was a letter to the public forum of my local newspaper. It also didn't matter to me that I had no experience in the literary world. I foolishly felt that writing was enough. I was in for a big surprise.

I wrote a story and submitted it to *Ladies' Home Journal*. I typed it single spaced, and crammed it into a regular-sized envelope, addressing it to no one in particular. Writers' guidelines and query letters were not yet part of my vocabulary. I had no clue how to approach an editor. I sent in my submission, then spent the next two months checking the newsstand to see if my story made it in the magazine. It didn't.

I've learned a few things from those blissfully naive years. I now accept rejections as part of the writing process that makes me more determined to get it right. Still, I wouldn't change a thing. I've learned that writers become writers by writing and submitting, over and over. Real writers don't quit. With that as my motto I shall continue on.

Thank you, Lord, for planting the seeds of passion to write. Help me perfect your gift.

If you wish to be a writer, write. Epictetus
—Kathy Whirity

May 6

In the sixties, we teachers were trained to lead values clarification exercises. I invited my students to write in response to the prompt "What are you worth?"

That evening as I sat down with a cup of tea to read my sophomores' responses, I was shocked by the paper that began, "I am worth a used pickup truck—no more, no less. And my uncle reminds me of that almost every day."

As I read on, I learned that her father had traded her to his brother for a '58 Ford truck. The brother's wife had needed someone to help with the kids and the work around the house.

That evening, I didn't use my red pen. I didn't circle words and mark "Sp" for spelling or insert commas and periods.

Instead, I wrote a note in blue ink: "You are worth more than ten pickup trucks. I am so glad to have you in my class this year. I have noticed how kind you are to Mary, standing up for her when the other children pick on her. You are a special human being. When we write in our journals each day, try to say something positive about yourself. You might begin with how you picked Mary first when we chose sides for teams at lunch."

Lord, encourage us to write affirming notes to ourselves and to others each day.

Fear not therefore: ye are of more value than many sparrows. Luke 12:7 KJV

—Shirley S. Stevens

May 7

Preparing to leave for a speaking circuit, I boldly called a cousin whom I had not seen for years and invited myself to be her overnight guest. Just before closing my suitcase, I thought of the unfinished manuscript for my first book and tossed it in.

That evening as Roxie and I relaxed in her home, catching up with the events of the years that had slipped by, I casually mentioned that I was writing a book. She eagerly asked if she could read it. Remembering that she had been an English teacher, I thought this might be helpful, so I excused myself and prepared for bed, entrusting my manuscript to her care.

The next morning she said, "I read your book. I like it." Of course I was thrilled, but shared that I was at a standstill because I didn't know how it should end.

"I do," she said enthusiastically. "When you go back to your family home...."

I didn't hear anything else she said, for the jumble in my mind was becoming clear. It seemed like someone was adjusting my focus button. My fingers longed to sit down at the computer and allow those words that now made sense to appear in print.

Lord, thank you for the joy of following the lead of people you put in my path.

How unsearchable are his judgments, and his ways past finding out. Romans 11:33b KJV

—Ethel Jensen Stenzel

May 8

In second grade, I had a difficult time learning to read, so much so that my mom was worried. As it turned out, the problem had more to do with my second-grade teacher than my abilities. Seems she didn't take to children, at least, not to me.

In third grade, wonderful Miss Avery made every student feel important, including me. My grades surged. Soon I became attracted to the library table in our classroom and began reading every book I could find. I don't remember reading any poetry, but one day I was playing on the sidewalk at home when a complete verse came into my head:

> A couple of little fairies were dancing in the night.
> A couple of little fairies were dancing with delight.
> A couple of little fairies took each other's hand.
> Just a couple of little fairies going to Fairyland.

I carefully wrote out that verse and sent it to the children's column in our local newspaper, *The New London Day*, where, to my delight, it was published. Thus began many satisfying years of sharing my writing efforts with others. I've published articles, poems, and a book of poetry, and participate in poetry groups and readings in Pittsburgh.

Lord, thank you for dedicated teachers, like Miss Avery, who inspire students to learn and to share their writing.

Hold fast the form of sound words. 2 Timothy 1:13 KJV

—Marilyn Marsh Noll

May 9

By my fourth year teaching in a parochial school in New Jersey, I had become less nervous about classroom management. I loved contests and was moved to challenge my class with one I'd read of in the diocesan newspaper. When a team of them won an award with their art project, my confidence grew. I sent a fine poem by Jeffrey to the local paper—then forgot about it.

On the following Monday morning, Jeffrey dashed across the parking lot flagging the newspaper: "Look, Sister! It's my poem!"

Jeffrey's joy at seeing his work in print helped me continue finding and encouraging ways for my students to share their best written work beyond the classroom. In Taiwan, I assembled *A Message to You, America, from Chinese Students* in the bi-centennial year, 1976.

In the United States and in the Far East, I had my students in high schools and colleges submit their work to the institutions' literary magazines. One summer, I overpumped an old ditto machine, soaking all eight masters, so I spent an entire day retyping the students' pieces for the final assembly. But I found that all problems of seeking publication were rewarded by my students' delight at winning awards or just beholding their works in print.

Lord, thank you for granting success to my efforts so my students and I would continue to share our creative works with others.

All hard work brings a profit. Proverbs 14:23 NIV
　　　　　　　　　　　　　　　—Sister Jane M. Abeln

May 10

I was a late bloomer. Any writing talent I enjoy came in my fifties out of the blue. My folksy fodder spurs pure bliss from living on the edge and perceiving life through bold and often quirky views. I suppose living in big sky Montana doesn't hurt either.

I've become a nonfiction/short story writing fool and I like being a rebel. Nonetheless, when I'm moved, I can rope in enough pity and passion to leave you agonizing, but always ending with a smile. These trademarks just happen while I journal phenomenal life memories.

It's a feast or famine hobby, for I refuse to pay anyone to publish me and gratefully accept any pittance while contemplating the next yarn. I have a good memory, amazing energy, and grit at seventy-five, and when they stop publishing me, I'll hang up my story spurs and play Scrabble.

It pleasures me to sit in my den overlooking my little donkey herd, belting out my life with one old crippled arthritic left hand, for I'm now minus a right arm.

This essay stuff is like a burr 'neath my saddle, for wondrous words, and the good Lord, keep me alive and kicking.

Lord, whatever my hand finds to do, help me to write with all thy might.

For your born writer, nothing is so healing as the realization that he has come upon the right word.
Catherine Drinker Bowen

—Kathe Campbell

May 11

My mother was a missionary, teacher, and wife. She became a widow when I was just twelve years of age. She never had a large income or surrounded herself with worldly possessions. At age ninety-three, she left us to go to her home in glory.

I thought it would be easy to clean out Mother's apartment. She for the most part only kept the things you would grab if your house was on fire. No clutter, no hoarding, just the important things.

As my sister and I packed memories into boxes, we reminisced about Mom and our early days without Dad. We talked about Mom's life, that she never remarried and was always available to talk or listen. We were thinking about how we would miss her daily words of encouragement and advice when we found a treasure in the bottom of her closet.

We couldn't believe it. It was exactly what we needed. Notebooks. Yellow spiral notebooks. We began to look through them. The pages were filled with her favorite Bible verses and quotes from a lifetime of learning. She had bridged the chasm of death with her small, familiar handwriting.

Today, I miss eating her favorite rice cakes and sipping weak tea. But our conversations continue as I quietly reflect on her writings.

Lord, thank you for a wise mother and for the writings she left behind.

The commandments are to be upon your hearts. Impress them on your children. Write them on the doorframes of your house. Deuteronomy 6:6 NIV

—Ruth J. Otto

May 12

I had spent weeks at the library gathering data for my graduate class research paper on Jonathan Swift. The time had finally come to do the writing. After pecking it out on my trusty Olympia portable, I skidded it into the prof's office just hours before the deadline with a hefty sigh of relief, confident I'd done as good a job of writing as I was capable of.

When the papers were returned a week later, I grimaced at the huge red B+ plastered on the title page. My writing wasn't worth an A? I grumped.

Skimming through the pages, I found red marks on almost every page—commas and punctuation marks in reversed position, use of forbidden contractions and adverbs such as "very," and errors in the bibliography style. I looked again at the title page and his comment, "Written with verve and humor." Frown turned to smile. So he liked the writing but not the technical errors. And they do deserve penalty.

That penalty changed my writing life. It certainly wasn't the end of all careless errors, but I began allowing more time for revision and editing. Later in my writing classes, students had a favorite question: How many times must I revise? My answer? Don't even try to count.

Lord, teach me patience as I strive to make my writing worthy of your heavenly blessing.

Better is the end of a thing than its beginning; and the patient in spirit is better than the proud in spirit. Ecclesiastes 7:8 RSV

—Olga M. Williams

May 13

I have always loved reading books and telling stories. So, writing a devotional guide for my church was a chance to realize a dream. My son, Robert, knew that I was writing and even though he was only in first grade, he would patiently listen to what I had written and offer encouragement or criticism as only a six-year-old can. After the devotional guide came out, I learned that my son was not participating in the accelerated reader program at school. Robert would sneak books back into the library without taking the reading comprehension test. This frustrated his teacher since Robert was one of her best readers.

Evidently, his entire class knew he was struggling with this. As we ate lunch one day, some girls teased him about it. Finally, he leaned across the table on his elbows and said, "Oh yeah, well, my mom makes books!"

I was suddenly validated as a writer. My son realized that he might not have the accelerated reader thing down, but he was reading all the time for enjoyment and understood that his mom made books.

Lord, thank you for letting me make books about you.

We are cups, constantly and quietly being filled. The trick is, knowing how to tip ourselves over and let the beautiful stuff out. Ray Bradbury

—Brook Dwyer

May 14

The day I received my own library card, I felt special, almost grown up. Going to the library, strolling through the bookshelves, deciding which book to choose were adventures for me. I went alone. No parental supervision, no time limit.

Some books I chose by the cover. I liked the ones with dark leather binding. Some I chose because the name seemed exciting or exotic. I exhausted books of interest in the older children's section and felt quite sophisticated when the librarian allowed me to take a book from the general collection.

At the time, I gave little thought to the writers of those books. Now I realize the effort it took to complete the hundreds of volumes on those library shelves.

My life has been blessed by hundreds of people I have known only through the written word. I am grateful for writers who are willing to spend their lives putting their thoughts, imaginings, and creativity on the page. I am most grateful for the courage it took to give those pages to all who read them.

Thank you, God, for the written word. Thank you for writers. Thank you for readers.

Employ your time in improving yourself by other men's writings so that you shall come easily by what others have labored hard for. Socrates
—Nancy Remmert

May 15

When I was eight years old, my mother gave me a small diary with a lock and key. It was bright yellow with dainty flowers, not your typical gift for an athletic girl like me. When I realized I could pour my heart into those golden-edged pages and keep it a secret, my diary became my treasure chest and my best friend.

Growing up in an alcoholic abusive home is never easy, especially for an only child. Late at night, I would hear my parents yelling and calling each other names. In the still darkness of my room, I would quietly open my bedside table drawer, pull out my diary, turn on the light in my closet, and lie on the floor. Writing brought me peace, hope, and perspective. God listened to me pray over and over again, "Tomorrow is the first day of the rest of my life."

Even now, solitude is a daily necessity to continue using my spiritual gift of writing. Whether I'm sitting on my porch in the early morning with coffee or at my desk in the middle of the night, my pen is waiting.

Lord, thank you for sharing with me that even in the midst of the storm, your light prevails.

God not only knows where he is taking you, but he also knows how to get you there. Roy Lessin
—Tracey Williams Garrell

May 16

Most writers have the urge to write or discover a love for literature at an early age. Not me. I spent my time reading music, not words. My vocation for most of my life was a professional violinist and music teacher. Writing just happened, almost a random event, like a sting from a wandering bee. I felt a strong desire to express my thoughts.

As I approach seventy, I see the world with fresh eyes and listen with attentive ears, especially to the very young and the very old. Writing motivates me to look closer at life, even at life as it interferes with my plans. It teaches me to focus on the spiritual instead of the secular and to let go of preconceived notions.

Several years ago, my daughter went into labor with my first grandchild. She lived in New York City, fifteen hundred miles away. It was during a holiday and the flights were full. My frantic attempt to reach the hospital was the subject of a short story that was published in a collection for mothers and grandmothers.

Sometimes, commonly shared experiences form the background for the most poignant tale.

Attune my words, Lord. May my writing resonate and fill the void in another's soul.

Age is a matter of feeling...not of years. George William Curtis

—Emily Tipton Williams

May 17

I stared at the creek. It looked like it was narrow enough to jump, but I was in my Sunday best. Crazy? Yes, but I hadn't planned on a field trip. The flat stones marching across it tempted me to cross. Slick, leather soles, a lack of balance, and destiny sent me splashing into the brink. I was wet, but I survived.

Rejection slips get my stare too. What brought that article back to my desk? I read it until I think I see the weakness the editor caught. If it is unmendable, I toss it and go on. If I see the chance to make it successful, I give it another try. Rejections are learning tools.

Most often I've been presumptuous in sending my article. I didn't do my homework. I sent it to the wrong publisher or didn't follow the editor's requirements. But there's a real downside to being rejected. As a writer, I have to realize it was the quality of my product that did not meet the need, not my person. The piece may be dear to my heart, but it wasn't judged on my personality. I am still the same person I was before submission. I am wet, but I will survive.

Lord, help me to see across the creek and jump it successfully.

The sufferings of this present time are not worthy to be compared with the glory that shall be revealed in us. Romans 8:18 KJV

—Rose Goble

May 18

While sifting through a stack of writing strewn across my desk, I opened a worn paper covered with my hurried scrawl. One side revealed the bones of a poem titled "Everyday Missionary"; on the other side, thoughts punctuated with multiple corrections filled the page. Ordinary details penned about everyday life had unfolded into a devotion.

A plant had grown in a small space between concrete and brick that edged the flowerbed. Perhaps transported on balmy winds off the bay, seeds had grown into a perfectly shaped butterfly bush. As I warmed myself in the morning sun, I watched two yellow butterflies flirt and flutter above the vibrant color. Slender green spires lined with tiny amethyst blossoms were now a focal point of beauty.

I wondered if my writing was like that—seeds fallen in the most unlikely of places, taking root and eventually blooming in the lives of others. I cannot know where the winds of time will carry my words or into whose hearts they will land, but God does. God gave me a message in that butterfly bush and supplied the spiritual nourishment for seeds to grow in my life at just the right time.

Lord, thank you for transforming my ordinary writing into extraordinary beauty.

The one who plants and the one who waters have the same purpose, and each will be rewarded for his own work. 1 Corinthians 3:8 NCV

—Barbara Parentini

May 19

In 1953, Dr. Abraham Nasatir lectured in my history class when my professor was ill. That evening, I told my husband, "I learned more in one session than in all the history classes I've ever attended."

Thirty years later, fire devastated the hillside community where Dr. Nasatir lived. Interviewed on TV, his hand swept over the rubble and he wept. "My life's work is gone."

I wrote to comfort him:

> As one to whom writing is as important as eating, I understand. I too would be devastated if I lost files and treasures collected over a lifetime. Let me remind you of all that has been saved. Over the years, you have ignited the positive flame of interest in thousands of students. You gave us insight, knowledge, and a hunger to learn. You built in us a respect for the past and for our heritage. You infected us with a lifelong desire to go on learning. Never forget that an imperishable work has been indelibly written in the hearts and minds of your students.

His wife spoke at his memorial years later, remembering the fire. "What saved my husband in those dark times were letters from students. I would like to share one with you today." A chill passed over me as she began to read: "As one to whom writing is as important as eating..."

Lord, thank you for teachers who ignite the flame of learning and for words that heal.

In my misfortune, I called. The Lord heard me and saved me from all distress. Psalms 34:7 NAB

Tommie Lenox

May 20

After my book *His Name Is Joel: Searching for God in a Son's Disability* was published, speaking invitations started arriving. My initial response was Moses-like: Not me. I shake. I shudder. I can't find the right words.

God answered with one word. Go.

I gathered a cadre of supporters: Jenny, who teaches communications, gave me a crash course in public speaking; Patty prayed with me; Tui offered her favorite adult education books.

I accepted the invitations, panicked during the preparations, felt self-conscious during the presentations, and slept for hours afterward.

One day, I hit a wall. As the keynote speaker at a disability conference, I ran into two angry women. One yelled disparaging comments in the middle of my talk. The other wanted to strangle me for the deep emotions she'd accessed during my theological reflection. I handled both women diplomatically, saving my tears for the drive home.

You've called the wrong person, I told God. I'm through.

I never call the wrong person, God answered.

Through my son's autism, God has given me an important message to share. Fixing my eyes on that message—God's faithfulness in the midst of adversity—I forge ahead.

Thank you, Lord, not for only calling me, but for accompanying me every step of the way.

Don't worry about what you'll say or how you'll say it...the Spirit of your Father will supply the words.
Matthew 10:19-20 MSG

—Kathleen Deyer Bolduc

May 21

I decided to become a writer soon after I learned to write. Or rather, my grandfather decided for me. An immigrant who had come to the United States at fifteen, it was important to him that I, his first grandchild, become a lettered lady. So we became pen pals.

Eventually, I learned to tell him things on paper so he could see them in his mind. An avid reader, my own life became a series of adventures like the ones I read about as I began embellishing my accounts to my grandfather. He was a wonderful literary critic, encouraging me with questions that served as jumping-off points for more adventures.

In time, I had to go beyond the narrow confines of letter writing to story writing. Some called me a day-dreamer, but I saw myself as a writer, dramatizing things in my head as they happened before putting pen to paper.

Today, when I find myself stuck and thoughts won't come, I think of what I would say if I were writing to my grandfather. There's nothing like a loving and receptive audience to inspire creativity.

Lord, help me see with the eyes of a child the adventures in my life and to share them with the freedom from self-consciousness that children are blessed with.

Train up a child in the way he should go. Proverbs 22:6 NASB

—Lonnie Lane

May 22

Early in my publishing career, I read stories of import. Deep, profound, searing. Tales of capsized boats, mountain rescues, and people who gnawed off limbs to save their own lives left me awed. My personal experiences seemed inadequate and mundane.

But by the very act of living, I garnered my fair share of writing fodder: I dealt with cancer and surgeries. I survived teenagers, college decisions, weddings, in-law children, and an empty nest. I endured the death of a parent and accepted the role of caregiver to an elderly mother-in-law. I weathered the agony of a child on life support. I parented through amputations, resuscitations, and rehabilitations.

Such ground-shaking events certainly shape my life, and I riffle through them on occasion for topics to fill an assignment or anecdotes to illustrate points.

Yet, I find myself drawn to the ordinary; I write most often about the trivial. The universal. The common, day-to-day minutiae that teach, amuse, or influence me. I pen vignettes about grandbabies, shopping sprees, even gardening. I look for humor and significance. What's more, I discovered vast publishing markets waiting with open arms for these stories.

I think I've matured as both reader and author to understand that—sometimes—the most inspiring moments in life arrive as whispers, not shouts.

Lord, thank you for eyes to hear, ears to listen, and hearts to understand the meaning—and value—in our everyday encounters.

Enough experience will make you wise. James R. Cook

—Carol McAdoo Rehme

May 23

Several years ago, I received a printed obituary in the mail. It described my aunt, who had lived several states away. As I read, I thought of all the good times we shared. When I was a child, my aunt, uncle, and cousins visited each summer. Other relatives joined us and we had picnics outside with watermelon and homemade ice cream. The adults played softball games while we kids sat and giggled over their clumsiness. I also remembered the times our family visited them and the three days of travel in a hot car that it took to get there.

I let my heart experience all the wonderful memories of my aunt, then wrote them in a letter to my uncle. He loved it. It meant so much to him to see how his beloved wife was remembered.

That letter began a ministry for me. I now write letters on a regular basis to family and friends who have lost a precious loved one, sharing my wonderful memories of that person. Invariably, I receive a letter or phone call telling me how my words touched their heart. The letters are my flowers to hurting souls, carrying a sweet fragrance of their loved one's life while sharing their deepest sorrow.

Father, I ask your blessings on those who write for hurting souls and those who read their words.

I always thank my God as I remember you. Philemon 1:4 NIV

—Louise Tucker Jones

May 24

The word "epiphany" is usually associated with religion. But how about writing? For me, excitement comes when a character in fiction takes over and I become merely a scribe. Thrills come when a poem writes itself. Those are moments that writers live for.

I have also experienced epiphanies when writing nonfiction, for instance, when I published a biography of Judge Ira Robinson, who died in 1951. Among other noteworthy accomplishments, he was the only member of the West Virginia Supreme Court to vote against martial law during the mine wars. Among his papers are letters from United States congressmen, from attorneys general of the United States, from five U.S. presidents, even from Mother Jones.

Ira Robinson, Sunday school teacher and church leader, was one of those countless servants of the Lord who see that derelicts get fed, the penniless get their rent paid, and prisoners are treated with dignity. Robinson never sought recognition. He accepted defeat graciously. He treated with respect every individual whom he met.

I'm thankful that I was asked to write Judge Robinson's story, for it has inspired me to see my neighbor not only as someone I might be able to help, but as a child of God who may be quietly helping others.

Father, I praise you for giving me the desire to write the stories about unexpected role models.

See that justice is done, let mercy be your first concern, and humbly obey your God. Micah 6:8 CEV
—Barbara Smith

May 25

I met Elaine at our writers' conference. She was a lovely person with beautiful stories. When I was asked to deliver a children's sermon, I talked about how Elaine's mother had read to her daughter. When they came upon a beautiful word, her mother would write it down on a slip of paper. Then they looked up the word's meaning in the dictionary, practiced saying the word, and used it in a sentence.

They kept the word slips atop the kitchen cabinet and took down a few each day to savor them—words like dandelion, daffodil, rainbow, and grace.

One day a breeze blew through the kitchen door and caught the slips of paper, sending them showering down upon the floor. Seven-year-old Elaine exclaimed, "Look, Mama, look! Word butterflies!"

Elaine taught me to appreciate the beauty of words when she selected and arranged them, crafting her own stories that won so many prizes that she was inducted into the St. Davids Hall of Fame.

Today in church as I give the sermon, I invite the children to take a slip of paper and write down special words. Then they blow on them so that the words take flight.

Lord, help me to remember that words can take wing.

A word is dead when it is said, some say. I say it just begins to live that day. Emily Dickinson

—Linda M. Hagenbuch

May 26

I was twenty years old, a college junior, and about to be married. With an advanced course of student teaching and preparations for my wedding ahead of me, I knew I didn't have time for a correspondence course in writing. But the temptation to take the written aptitude test was too great. It was something I'd wanted to do for years. I completed the test, sent it in, and buckled down to finish my college classes.

It was a bittersweet moment when I received an invitation to take the course. Just knowing someone had seen my potential was vastly encouraging. However, married life, a final year of college, and financial challenges seemed all I could handle at the moment. Regretfully, I declined.

Five years and two babies later, I shared my aspirations with my friend Lynn. Her staunch belief in my potential was the catalyst to finally enroll. Before long I'd submitted one of my better compositions to a children's magazine and achieved my first paid publication.

Dear Lord, keep reminding me to use my talents, plant my seeds, and wait for you to bring them to fruition.

He is like a tree planted by streams of water, which yields its fruit in season. Psalms 1:3 NIV

—Andee S. Davis

May 27

I'd sent in my first piece of writing for critiquing. Others were going to look at my work, pull it to pieces, and tell me what they thought. What was I thinking? I'd checked my e-mail inbox dozens of times over the last few days. Who knew waiting could be so hard? It was so bad the dogs hid, fearing yet another bath. I'd dusted, swept, and even cleaned the fridge. I was just wondering whether I should save that interesting piece of purple-green cheese for a science experiment when my husband announced I had e-mails.

How could he announce something like that, so off-handedly? Didn't he know this was the moment? The moment when the world announced once and for all I stunk as a writer?

I'd like to say I casually sauntered over to the computer, but I didn't. Instead, I bathed the dogs. Poor things, but it was either them or me.

It took me three hours to finally sit down and read those e-mails. One by one I opened them and read their notes. I sat back and stared at the wall, dazed.

They actually liked it! Snoopy had nothing on the dancing I did. Hubby grinned, I danced, and the dogs...well they just hid again.

Help me to have courage to share my writing with others, even if it means getting hurt.

Wait on the Lord; be of good courage; and he shall strengthen thy heart: wait, I say, on the Lord. Psalms 27:14 KJV

—Lee Franklin

May 28

In 1987 as an exhausted new mother in a baggy house-coat, I had a crazy notion: I would become a stay-at-home mom and write. Crazier still, I would get paid to write.

On a whim, I entered a writing contest and nearly fainted when I won first place and a check for a hundred dollars.

But what started with a bang soon fizzled. My early offerings yielded nothing but rejection letters. They poured in, threatening to drown me and my crazy notion. I had no idea I'd be swimming against the tide. But I come from a long line of stubborn women; I wasn't about to go under without fighting, and that's precisely what I did.

I remember the day when I sold my first article. And then another. And then another.

In 1993 I sold my first book manuscript. A second one soon followed. And then a third. By this time, it was clear: to stay afloat in the publishing world, I have to keep swimming.

And therein lies one of the greatest secrets of success—perseverance. Never give up.

Olympic swimmers don't start out with a gold medal around their necks. They endure grueling hours of practice and agonizing defeats, but the key is to keep swimming.

And so it is with writers. I don't start out being the best, but I'll never be the best if I stop writing.

Lord, with you all things are possible.

Successful writers are not the ones who write the best sentences. They are the ones who keep writing. Bonnie Friedman

—Dayle Allen Shockley

May 29

I was attending one of my first Christian writers' conferences. I entered several contests, including the one that interested me most: a special competition based on the conference theme, "Faith." We were told in the opening session that the entry had to be no more than 250 words.

I recounted how God had strengthened my faith and given me peace during my husband's eleven months of battle with two aggressive cancers. I labored over my entry for the first four days, carefully counting each word, writing and rewriting. On the last day to turn in the entry, I retyped it again and typed out the complete scripture text that I had previously abbreviated.

When the awards were presented, I waited anxiously. No, my name wasn't called. I felt disappointed that I didn't win. Imagine how I felt, however, when I picked up my entry with the judge's comments. "This would have been first place, but you were disqualified for too many words."

Lord, help me listen more carefully to instructions so that I might always be obedient to your leading.

As an earring of gold, and an ornament of fine gold, so is a wise reprover upon an obedient ear. Proverbs 25:12 KJV

—Jan Sady

May 30

I wonder when a writer should retire his pen, pad, and keyboard. Four years ago, carpal tunnel surgery returned feeling to my numb, eighty-three-year-old fingers that had written thousands of poems, stories, and songs.

Later, cataract removal restored my eyesight. Last month, a plastic surgeon rebuilt my nose. A lack of normal breathing had curtailed my teaching the creative writing class at our senior center.

My wife asked me how much more I was willing to invest to keep writing. Were hearing aids my next step?

"Well?" My wife asked later when I returned from the audiologist and flipped on my laptop.

"No need to raise your voice," I replied.

My printer grunted and moaned. "Is that the way it always sounds?" I asked. A grin crossed her face.

I sat down at my laptop and wrote.

My reactions to life's happenings paint a picture to those I hold dear. No negative space occupies the canvas.

Best of all, when I printed out this devotion and showed it to my wife, she said, "I'm glad you're back at it, Bill."

Lord, thanks for restoring so many of my parts and allowing me to experience the pleasure of writing again. I still have stories to share and know that when I write, I feel most alive.

Some of the joy of life had come back to me. Charles Kuralt

—William Elof Peterson

May 31

It's been more than sixty years since I sat at the kitchen table in my parent's house with a blank sheet of paper and a number two pencil. No words would come. I was to be one of the speakers at our eighth-grade graduation and did not have the slightest notion of where to start.

My English teacher had taught me well. I knew the parts of speech and could diagram sentences, but that was much different from actually writing my own sentences. The next day, with great assistance from my teacher, I was able to write the speech and deliver it. No one ever knew how much help I had had.

I learned that day that there are people who care enough to help budding writers get started. Today, as I write at least one sermon every week, I still need help from someone better versed than I. Today, my help comes from above, from one who cares enough to give me words to put on paper. Then he helps me preach those words in a way that conveys his message to others. I doubt if anyone still knows how much help I have had.

Lord, help me today and every day to write that which is true to your word.

I will put my words in the mouth of the prophet, who shall speak to them everything that I command. Deuteronomy 18:18 NRSV

—Rev. James A. Fegan

June 1

Nobody really wants to remember sixth grade. But when I think about writing, my mind jumps to Mrs. Hilmoe's English class. It was there that a shy, skinny girl with thick glasses was told she could write.

I honestly don't remember what Mrs. Hilmoe wrote on that lined, beige paper. But if I had it, I'd frame it.

Mrs. Hilmoe not only wrote on that paper that I have a gift for writing, she told me. I remember the eye contact and her hand on my shoulder. I was miserable in math, and no better in science. But writing was a different story.

So every now and then I think of Joan Hilmoe with a heart full of gratitude. She was a teacher who recognized a gift and called it forth. Today, I make my living as a writer and editor.

I've tried to inspire young people I've encountered through the years. As I write this, I'm taking a detour to Google. Sure enough, there's Mrs. Hilmoe's address and a South Dakota church newsletter item about her eightieth birthday. That does it. I'm writing to thank her. I hope my grammar and punctuation hold up. For some reason, I think they will. After all, I had a good teacher.

Gracious God, thank you for those who recognize gifts in others. Help me to do the same.

The job of an educator is to teach students to see the vitality in themselves. Joseph Campbell

—Julie B. Sevig

June 2

Years ago, my mother began to use her wall calendar as a daily log. She wrote down visits, phone calls, and appointments each day. By the end of the month, there was never an inch of unused space. This was her minidiary, and she enjoyed writing on it.

She now suffers from dementia. When my siblings and I call or visit, we gently remind her to write it on her calendar so she doesn't forget and feel forgotten and unloved. We tell her, "Mom, go check your calendar and see who came to visit or called this week."

After checking, she says, "Oh yes, I forgot. Thank you, it's on my calendar."

We continue to encourage her to write on her calendar as long as she is able. After all, she is a writer. She has been the author of many calendar pages. She writes every day, a goal all writers need to make.

Thank you, Lord, for giving me the ability to write even simple things.

Writers don't write from experience, although many are hesitant to admit that they don't. If you wrote from experience, you'd get maybe one book, maybe three poems. Writers write from empathy. Nikki Giovanni

—Sally Devine

June 3

The keynoter droned on. At the next table, a woman's expression made her boredom obvious. I felt sorry for the speaker—and flashed back to an assembly in seventh grade.

A boy sang and accompanied himself on the piano. Two girls sitting beside me snickered and whispered cutting remarks. I glared at them and turned my gaze back to the stage. The two critics apparently resented my goody-goody attitude because later as we collected our coats to go home, one girl wordlessly slapped my face.

Thirty years later I remembered and felt I had to write a poem about the experience. Then I decided to make up a character and tell my story as if it happened to her.

I went on to write many narrative poems about Ellen Davis. The first one—"In the Grade School Assembly"— was published as were a number of others. I sent the poems to a poet-teacher friend, who used some as models for children's writing. For example, a poem about Ellen overcoming her panic during first-grade fire drills prompted an assignment on "the big scare that went away."

The device of changing me to her helped me to write about the past—and inspired young writers as well.

Lord, help me find ways to help others and myself through writing.

The potential for personal insight through altered point of view is great. Tristine Rainer

—Nancy E. James

June 4

Many years ago, I prayerfully attempted my first book. It was for parents whose children were undergoing long-term medical care. God had nudged me through a nephew, Mark Heil, who fought leukemia for seven years. Mark lived a vital relationship with Christ. Shortly before he went to heaven at age thirteen, Mark told his parents, "Something good must come out of this."

Those words clung to my heart as I interviewed mothers and fathers whose children suffered from many conditions. Mark's parents shared powerful stories. But at times I wondered if my work would ever be published. I sent proposals to several publishers. No takers. I kept on praying, writing, and remembering Mark.

Finally, I met an interested editor at a conference. I finished the book, did revisions, and received a contract. When the print galleys came, I was elated.

Then the blow: the publisher went out of business. I cried. I got the rights back and tried more publishers. Two years went by. Again, I met an editor. His house accepted the book in a week. The staff created an appealing gift book with photography. It ministered to readers and jumped into a second printing.

My journey to publication took five years, but I see God's workings in it all.

Lord, thank you for your faithfulness in leading Christian writers to persevere.

In all these things we are more than conquerors through him who loved us. Romans 8:37 NIV
—Charlotte Adelsperger

June 5

I never think I'm good enough. This is my first time writing for publication. I have always been afraid to try. Even though I am an English major and have written several essays, short stories, and poems for classes, I didn't think my work was good enough for others to read. I'm afraid of being judged, scared of being critiqued.

Still, I have always been a writer. When I was a child, my mother would punish me by sending me to my room, where I would write out my emotions on paper. Through writing, I gained understand and clarity. I understood what I had done wrong and the letters ended up becoming an apology to her.

Writing is my outlet for my emotions, thoughts, and needs. I write for myself, but now I realize that my writing can also be beneficial for others who are feeing the same way I am.

I am a writer! I want my gift to shine for others to see. I want to write for the whole world, a voice that was previously unheard. I want to write for those who don't have a voice of their own.

Lord, give me the strength and courage to believe in myself.

Only when we are no longer afraid do we begin to live. Dorothy Thompson

—David Carter

June 6

"What does that smell like, the smell of fear?" our writing instructor asked my classmate Jean. A discussion ensued. "Why are you afraid? Give a hint to set the stage for fear," the instructor said.

I may be the next to read, I thought. No, no critique for me today. My piece isn't half as good as Jean's. I'm not sure about the smell of fear but I know the feel of it. All I want today is applause.

Applause...yes, I remembered applause...the polite applause I received after giving a reading the previous week. I hadn't bothered to present it to anyone else beforehand for comment, and no one commented after the program either. That kind of silence is not golden. Later, I asked a good friend to be honest. She peeled the cataracts from my writing eyes so I could clearly see the need for major revisions. I became embarrassed that I had read the article in public. Never again would I be my only critic, I promised myself.

"Carol, do you have anything for us today?" I began reading my essay. I had changed my mind. I will be grateful for words of advice. Hold the applause until I deserve it.

Lord, it's never easy to take criticism, even when it's lovingly given. Help me be receptive to suggestions to improve my work.

The flexible and open person keeps accepting new pieces, rearranging them to modify his tentative patterns.
John Powell, SJ

—Carol Nilles

June 7

After my husband died in a commuter plane crash, I felt paralyzed and unable to write. The crash seemed to have taken not only Jim but also the only gift I had to offer the world: my writing. This immobilization went way beyond writer's block; it was a pervasive shattering of my spirit.

Then, the social worker leading the grief support group I joined gave me a suggestion: write a letter to Jim. Tell him how I was feeling; pour it all out on paper. I was skeptical. Could I do it? Would this really help me get back to my writing career?

I sat with one of Jim's legal pads and a ballpoint pen he'd used. "Dearest Jim," I began. A tear rolled down my cheek and dropped on the lined yellow paper, then another. The tears unlocked my words. "You left me so suddenly that I never had a chance to ask you how—if something should happen—I would be able to go on without you. I never had a chance to hear you say in your deep voice: 'You can do it.'"

I continued the letter to Jim until I filled five yellow pages. Then I knew I could do it. I could continue to write, despite the devastating tragedy that had temporarily stolen my gift.

Lord, thank you for helping me overcome my tragedy and continue writing.

But I will hope continually, and will praise thee yet more and more. Psalms 71:14 RSV

—Peggy Eastman

June 8

I did it. I'd been working on the book for twenty years or more, and I, at long last, sent in a proposal. My critique group and I were tired of looking at it. We had tweaked, cut, and corrected until we were sick of it. It was as ready as it could be. I called my son to find out how to burn a CD, and he talked me through that. I ruined three before I got one finished. Before I packaged it, I opened the files to make sure everything was there. As I started reading the first page, I found two mistakes—two. I couldn't believe it. Of course, I didn't know you couldn't correct on a CD—so I had to use another one.

I put the final product in its case, added all the necessary info, and sealed the package. As I handed it to the postal worker, I knew he had no idea what was inside. He weighed it and gave me a price.

Nothing may happen from this event, but nothing happened with it in my computer for all these years. The proposal is on its way. I did it.

Lord, thank you for friends who encourage me to stop procrastinating.

Whatever you can do or dream you can do, begin it! Boldness has genius, magic, and power in it. Begin it now! Johann Wolfgang von Goethe

Mary "Mike" Mikell Calkin

June 9

"I'm not taking swimming lessons anymore," my five-year-old daughter, Carrie, announced firmly as she arrived home from her second lesson. With as pleasant but authoritative voice as I could muster, I said, "Oh, yes, you are. You are going to take lessons until you can be the teacher."

While Carrie was in high school, where she was a good student and on the swim team, I found her studying yet again way after midnight. I said, "Unless you get enough sleep, all those extra swim laps are in vain." She became a college national swim champion, swim teacher, and attorney.

If I could raise four daughters to be disciplined adults, why can't I discipline myself to write regularly? Accomplished writers advise: write every day at the same time, in the same place with the door shut, never stop reading, or...stop reading and start writing, rewrite, rewrite, rewrite, turn off the television, etc. Hundreds of helps, but none seemed to be right for me.

Then one day I really listened to one help: "Start each day with prayer." I can hardly believe it, but each day I remember to pray turns out to be more productive, giving give me time for writing.

Lord, help me learn discipline so I can write the story of your love for all.

Follow me and I will make you fishers of men. Matthew 4:19 RSV

—Christine Rotto Hefte

June 10

After twenty-seven years of selling antique quilts, I moved my shop to my home. Feeling disconnected, I prayed for a new purpose.

While studying Beth Moore's *Believing God*, God revealed his dream for me—to write a book of quilt stories. Using my own intellect and abilities, this dream was absurd; my teachers in the 1950s and '60s had catalogued me as a halfwit. I had struggled through high school and college, graduating only because of my bulldogged tenacity.

At age sixty, I enrolled in my first computer and writing classes. The computer classes contributed major adrenal stress and migraines. But then I found a compassionate writing teacher who patiently critiqued every word I submitted. Still, the writing came hard for me and I began doubting my dream.

As despair turned to near hopelessness, I received one more nudge, a circular quilt appliquéd with grapes titled "A Winter's Harvest"—a real mystery.

The next day I solved the puzzle while studying *Believing God to Get to your Gilgal*. Gilgal means circle and a new beginning and is the first place the children of Israel camped after crossing the River Jordan into the Promised Land, flowing with milk, honey, and grape clusters.

During bleak, barren writing days when I'm seeing slim breakthroughs, my Winter's Harvest quilt is my touchstone that reminds me that even I can write a book with God's help.

Father, teach me to persevere.

Whatever things you ask in prayer, believing, you will receive. Matthew 21:22 NKJV

—Judy Howard

June 11

At eight years old I wrote my first masterpiece, a ballad proclaiming my love for Donny Osmond.

> Donny, Donny sitting in the shade,
> under the tree house that we made,
> We'll be together,
> loving one another, forever.

Even as a child, I felt the Lord's pleasure as I wrote that silly song. My ability to take what I was feeling and write it down was a gift given by God, wrapped up in a bow especially designed for me. All writers have that same gift.

I didn't really use my gift, however, until much later in life when I started journaling. I began to understand that the emotions that swirled within me needed a place to land. The deep longing I felt for the Osmond boys had vanished, and in its place was the deep longing to write. When I write, the words take flight and fall upon the ears of my creator. I still feel his pleasure.

At eight years old, God sat with me as I took my pencil to scribbling. At twenty-five, he put his arms around me as I poured my heart out in a journal. Today, at forty-four, I sit with my laptop, coffee cup close at hand. God's pleasure still flows through each word.

Lord, thank you for the pleasures, the joy of writing, published or not.

In your presence is fullness of joy; in your right hand there are pleasures forever. Psalms 16:11 NASB

—Robbie Iobst

June 12

Back in the '80s, my husband and I attended a Marriage Encounter weekend titled "Forty Hours to Make Your Good Marriage Better." At the time, we lived on the family farm with my husband's parents living one thousand yards away.

The weekend went like this. The whole group of us met together and the leaders would share an issue from their marriage, i.e., "We have trouble with our in-laws and we solved it this way."

After this briefing, we were sent to our rooms and told to each write about the subject at hand for a half hour without talking. Afterward we were to read our writings to each other without comment. The writing allowed each of us to be clear about our thoughts before we discussed an issue.

Most details of that weekend are long lost to memory except for one moment: I sit on a wooden chair in the dorm room reading to my husband, who sits on the bed in slanting afternoon sunlight. As I read I suddenly understand a painful truth about my relationship with my father-in-law. That moment began a process of healing among the three of us.

More importantly I saw how that act of putting words on paper has the power to heal.

Thank you, God, for moments of clarity. Teach me to use my writing to bring more clarity into my life.

Now we see in a mirror dimly, but then we will see face to face. 1 Corinthians 13:12 NRSV

—Connie Scharlau

June 13

Life in a small Iowa town fifty-plus years ago could be confining, interesting, and challenging. The editor of our local newspaper had not had a vacation for several years and wanted to take his wife to Florida for a few weeks. He inquired if I would take his place in the front office.

Wow! I had no technical expertise with the noisy monsters in the back room—two presses and a Linotype—but was assured that the boys in the back room would handle that. I just had to feed them all the copy they needed: news, advertising, and editorials. After all, I was the new young pastor at the Lutheran church. I should have automatic access to all the information of importance in the area. With some fear, but much hope, I said, "Yes." I now had two jobs and awesome responsibilities seven days per week.

All went very well and in due time the Robinsons returned to Iowa, refreshed and thankful to be safely home and ready for work. My rewards were compliments, a typewriter, and requests for repeat performances. My writing career had begun.

I learned by launching out into unfamiliar situations and by working through them to appreciate the meaning of the term, mission accomplished.

Lord, help me to say yes more often and guide me toward the goal you have for me.

I can do all things through Christ, who strengthens me. Philippians 4:13 NKJV

—Rev. P. L. Kvitne

June 14

Today, June 14, is Flag Day. I've always had the utmost respect for the American flag. My parents flew one from our front porch every holiday. Dad put one on top of the pontoon he built in the early '80s. I had a nice big sturdy nylon flag waving from my home in Wisconsin where I lived for twenty-four years. When I moved to Florida, I donated it to my condo building, and now it waves in the breeze right in front of my front door.

I've learned that most often it's things like the flag that inspire me to write and submit my work to editors. I think about my grandma's cookie jar, the hammock my son and I installed between two trees in our backyard, the old hand pump in Grandpa's backyard, the turtle ranch my dad made for me out of an old tractor tire, the airboat Dad built when I was a kid, the adjustable wooden stilts he made, and my first bicycle.

It's these small things that can pack a wallop with their emotional intensity.

Father, on this Flag Day keep me proud and loyal to this country of ours where we writers are free to write about anything we choose.

The chief glory of every people arises from its authors. Samuel Johnson

—Patricia Lorenz

June 15

During the twenty-four hours after registration, I peered into the response stack every hour to determine if an evaluation had been rendered for my devotional, "Donuts," submitted for critique at my first writers' conference.

One time as I left the desk, a magazine editor approached me. Pointing at my name tag, she said, "You're Lisa Herrin. I critiqued your devotional and would like to use it in my class to teach my students."

Beaming, I replied, "Sure."

"Don't worry. I'll cover up your name so no one will know who wrote it. I returned it to the response file. See you later and thanks."

Slowly I walked to the stack, grabbed the envelope, and fled to my room. Sitting on the edge of the bed, I tore open the envelope and quickly scanned the flaming red comments bleeding over the manuscript. "'Donuts' doesn't say anything to the reader. Rethink your title. Learn to transition. Use stronger verbs. Too passive. Your theology needs work. The conclusion introduces another thought."

Silence. Uncontrollable tears. Silence. I can't do this! Silence. I'll go home. Silence. I'll stay to hear the other speakers. Silence. I'll talk to her in the morning.

The next morning during breakfast, she suggested helpful books. I purchased the books, devoured them and returned to the conference each year. On the fourth year, I presented a nonfiction book proposal. It was accepted and published in 2005.

Father, thank you for helping me to persevere in the face of adversity.

Persist without exception. Andy Andrews
—Lisa Q. Herrin

June 16

Mmmm, just one more cup of coffee. Hey, I'll watch *Good Morning America* while I plan my day. As a writer, I need to keep up with current events. Like Barry Manilow's reunion concert and—say, what's this?—a woman who sells hand-painted girdles on eBay? Amazing.

Whew! Got the groceries unloaded, and I need a short break. I'll check my e-mail and play a little solitaire. Dang, why can't you get a red ten when you need it? Just one more game—honest—and then I'll outline my novel, if I can still remember the names of the characters. But first, I should alphabetize the spice rack.

Wait, is that my stomach growling? How about Bob Evans for lunch? It will get me out of the house, and maybe I can work on my novel. Or, you know, I could just read a novel instead. Yes, that would be relaxing. Solitaire makes me kind of tense.

Home again. Got my toenails polished—fuchsia fluorescence. Time to fire up WordPerfect and start writing. Oh—hi, Sheryl. Glad you called. I was going to call you…No, I couldn't believe that dress she was wearing. And who ever told her she can sing?…Nah, nothing new here. Just can't seem to find any time for writing. Busy, busy, busy. Well, gotta go fix dinner…

Lord, help me to use the writing time you've given me.

Seize the day. Horace

—Patty Krylach

June 17

"Oh, it's no use. It's no use." My emotionally fragile father repeated these words over and over as I was growing up.

"What's the use?" haunted me all throughout childhood and into my adult years. I gave up on college after two years. What was the use?

One day when I was in my thirties, I noticed a want ad in the newspaper. The editors were searching for correspondents from surrounding towns to provide more balanced news coverage. A new thought came to me: Why not try? I submitted a sample of my writing and was hired. This was the beginning of many years of writing and publishing.

In my fifties, I had another new thought: Why not finish my college education? Three years later, I had a bachelor of arts degree.

"Sometimes success—or even survival—is a matter of endurance, of sticking it out," says Dr. Michael A. Halleen.

My writer friend Thom would agree. He sent his first book manuscript out sixty times before a major publishing house finally accepted it.

Why not try? I tell myself this as I finish typing a manuscript and then begin searching for a publisher.

Father, you did not create us to be quitters. You created us to add your strength to ours as we write and search for homes for our words.

Let us not become weary in doing good, for at the proper time we will reap a harvest if we do not give up. Galatians 5:9 NIV

—Anne Siegrist

June 18

I placed a lifelong dream to write and be published on hold through college years, a short teaching career, marriage, and raising children. In my midfifties, the dream became reality. I decided to enroll in a correspondence course that promised to make me a children's writer. I sailed through the course and set a goal of publication within a year.

I prayed about it often for I knew how very competitive the writing world is and I had already lost a lot of years. "Please open the door for me, Lord" became my much-repeated plea. But the doors all remained sealed tighter than a jar of pickles. My rejection folder ballooned, and the acceptance one remained flat.

More than a year later, I sold a story to a children's magazine after an editor requested a major rewrite. Happiness! I began to submit to Web sites for no pay, and I moved from children's stories into writing creative nonfiction for adults. After what seemed like an eternity, the doors began to open.

God did more than answer my frequent prayer. He also taught me about three necessary tools for a writer. One is patience, another is perseverance, but most important of all is trust.

Thank you, Lord, for opening doors for me in your time, not mine.

Trust in the Lord with all your heart and lean not on your own understanding. Proverbs 3:5 NIV

—Nancy Julien Kopp

June 19

After some initial successes, I hit a snag. Although I labored long and hard over each project, rejection slips seemed to be the only response to my many submissions.

Even though I followed the instructions gleaned from workshops and critique groups, everything I sent out met with rejection letters. Every contest I entered came back with not even an honorable mention.

I asked God why all my efforts were coming to nothing. My questions went unanswered.

I joined an online critique group for help. No change. Perhaps God hadn't called me to write after all. For weeks, I penned nothing.

Then one day I received an e-mail that read, "Your words touched my heart and made me realize once again how important it is to share with others our experience of God. I so appreciate the gift you are in my life and in the lives of countless others."

Tears filled my eyes and blurred the words on the screen as I printed it off.

I made a kudos file and popped in that e-mail. Now when I'm discouraged, I pull the file for a quick refresher.

Lord, help me to remember it's all for your glory.

For from him and through him and to him are all things. To him be the glory. Romans 11:36 NASB

—Sally Jadlow

June 20

I am a storyteller and photographer, and I like doing historical research. I attend my Aunt Clyde's family reunion every June in Alabama, and have become the family scribe. My newsletters started out as three pages of family news and have evolved into sixty page booklets of the family's contribution to our American history.

I wrote about my aunt's ancestor who was among the first to be killed at Bunker Hill. I explained how the family arrived in Alabama through land grants they received from President Andrew Jackson when they scouted with him in the Southern wilderness.

When I learned my aunt's Confederate great-great-grandfather had been mortally wounded at Gettysburg, I combined my photographer's eye for detail and historical research to poignantly describe Granddaddy David's last hours on a rainy July night in a wobbly wagon rolling down muddy dirt roads.

My months of reading, researching, and writing every year are worth it when my young cousins return to school in the fall with my booklets to proudly share the role their ancestors played in America's history.

Father, thank you for giving me the insight, the writing tools, and the need to share what I learn with others.

Storytelling is the skill of looking at everyday people and really seeing them, and really appreciating them. When you look at them closely, you can find something worth keeping and handing down for all time. Kathryn Tucker Windham

—Elizabeth Mary Van Hook

June 21

There it was: an error in a book I'd proofread. And on the very first page, in the chapter heading! I was sick. I e-mailed my apologies to the publisher.

"Mistakes happen," she answered. "You're a great editor."

I knew she was wrong. Was I losing my eye, my ability to spot errors?

"God, I know this is silly," I prayed. "It's one error. But I can't stop thinking that I'm a total incompetent. Please help me understand the magnitude of my mistake."

The next morning, I got onto my apartment building elevator. There was a man with a red-tipped white cane.

"I'm new here," he said. "Would you walk with me to the subway?"

"Of course," I said. "Just take my arm."

We had a nice chat, then two blocks later, we were there.

"Thanks," he said. "See you around the building."

I took his hand and shook it.

"My pleasure. I'm Melanie."

"Reinhart."

Then it hit me. When I had prayed for perspective about my error, God had sent a man who relied on his memory, his remaining senses, and people's kindness. I turned back.

"Reinhart?"

He turned his head. "Yes?"

"Thank you."

He smiled broadly. "You're welcome."

Lord, let me see myself as you do, imperfect but yearning for you.

Open my eyes, Lord. Help me to see your face. Open my eyes, Lord. Help me to see. Jesse Manibusan

—Melanie Rigney

June 22

With a big grin, my husband handed me a brochure. "How would you like to take a tour to Spain?"

Being a gypsy at heart, I was thrilled. Plus, the trip would celebrate our twenty-fifth anniversary.

When I packed, I included a purse-size notebook, something I had never done before. That began a practice I have continued on trips big and small. I have written on planes, ships, buses, in cars, hotel, motels— anywhere and anytime I could take a few minutes to record memorable sights and feelings.

On the plane coming home from Spain, our tour guide, explaining that she had noticed me writing asked, "Would you mind if I read your journal?"

Since Wendy King was a well-known radio talk show host, I felt very complimented. She graciously wrote on the back page, "Thank you for allowing me to share your personal thoughts." It was an inspiration for me to continue.

Just scribbling has given me freedom. I'm not under pressure to produce a polished piece. As a result, I've begun journaling anytime I felt the need to record anything. My spiral bound notebooks (which I label *Scribbles*) are filled with large and little life experiences that provide a mounting supply of reference for the prose and poetry of my writing life.

Lord, for the blessings of recording your awesome creations, I thank you.

The divine isn't only good, it is all things. D. H. Lawrence

—Mary A. Koepke

June 23

Since retiring, I've begun to write and to garden. When I worked in the city, I didn't have time. I was too busy rushing from one function to the other.

In the garden, I learned the value of pruning and how it relates to my life as a writer. I have to edit my manuscripts. Like pruning, editing produces a better product. Only the best are picked and brought to the table. A publisher's trained eye recognizes those manuscripts that have been pruned and are the best they can be.

When observing the seemingly overabundant seeds plants produce to ensure some will thrive, I couldn't help realizing how my words too are overabundant. Not every word is meant to live on the published page. But the best ones, the right ones for the right soil and environment, will be published.

Lord, let my words find the right soil. Plant them in their destined places to bring glory to you. Let my words become beautiful blooms that bring pleasure to others.

But others fell on good ground and yielded a crop, some a hundredfold, some sixty, some thirty. Matthew 13:9 NKJV

—Grace G. Booth

June 24

"Virginia, *Eigenlob stinkt!*" my German-American mother strongly advised. It means, "Self-praise stinks!" To say I was a humble kid is putting it mildly. However, through the years, with a combination of assertiveness training and prayer, I was able to get my self-esteem up a notch or two.

Every once in a while, my mother's training would come to the fore, such as when I decided to advertise my inspirational book on a secular Web site and needed a caption under the picture of my book cover. My mind went blank. I struggled. Finally, I realized that my inability to come up with an appropriate phrase was not academic but emotional. "Self-praise stinks!" got translated to "My praise about my book stinks!"

How do we as Christians, who have been taught to be humble and meek, promote our writing? Perhaps we should look at Moses, the meekest man on the face of the earth. God gave him a message. He aggressively demanded of Pharaoh, "Let my people go!"

There's no reason why we shouldn't be as bold. God has given us a message. Let us be both proud and grateful for the talent God has given us and share it by aggressively promoting our work. *Eigenlob stinkt* sometimes, but not always.

God, give me the courage to promote the message you have given me.

A book lying idle on a shelf is wasted ammunition. Henry Miller

—Ginnie Mesibov

June 25

My assignment was to interview women in Toastmasters, a nonprofit organization that helps develop public speaking and leadership skills. I'd pitched the idea to my editor with an ulterior motive. I wanted to learn for myself what Toastmasters was all about—with no commitment to stand up and speak.

While I talked with several ladies in the club, the president listened. Finally, he spoke. "Would you be interested in helping me start a commercial writer's program through the continuing education department at my college?"

I immediately lapsed into my I'm-not-smart-enough-I-know-nothing-you-can-find-someone-better-than-me mode. The expression that crossed his face sickened me. Because I had such little confidence in myself, his opinion of me changed in a split second.

While writing the story, I read and reread how Toastmasters helped each woman gain confidence, and how that confidence had spilled over into her personal and professional life. I visited another meeting to take copies of the published article. When the club president asked me again to help create a commercial writing program at his college, I accepted with confidence.

Dear Lord, thank you for being a God of second chances. Help me remember that you are my courage.

And there we saw the giants, the sons of Anak, which come of the giants: and we were in our own sight as grasshoppers, and so we were in their sight. Numbers 13:33 KJV

—Jessica Ferguson

June 26

Twenty-five years. That's how long it had been since I had written one word besides advertising copy. It paid the bills, helped raise my child, and provided an outlet for my creativity. I wrote for car dealers, hospitals, banks, furniture stores... everyone, but me. Then, suddenly, I couldn't devise one more catchy jingle or slogan. This was more than writer's block; it was a death sentence—the end of my life as a writer.

One day, I was sorting through memorabilia from my daughter's youth. Buried among the yellowing report cards and doily valentines were poems and stories I had written for her. As I laughed and cried at my own words, I remembered why I had once loved to write: to capture feelings, share them with others, and try to make the world better...one word at a time.

I joined a poetry club and a writers' club. I began that novel I always thought I would write someday. Today, I write articles about people I find fascinating. I even teach creative writing at a local school. Best of all, I now realize what I instinctively had known as a child: true inspiration is never really blocked or lost. It's always out there among life and the living...just waiting for me to find it.

Lord, thank you for the gift of writing and the wonder of life. Help me remember that the rest is up to me.

I shall not die, but live, and declare the works of the Lord. Psalms 118:17 KJV

—Denise May

June 27

I joined a local writers' club hoping to master the trade in a year or two and get published. The group accepted all comers, requiring only an interest in writing. Eleven years later, I have gleaned a few tips on effective writing from these biweekly meetings, but more importantly I've learned an awful lot about would-be writers.

Our group has included a poet in his sixties who recites his multiverse works from memory with excellent meter, rhyme, and story line. A young man with Asperger's syndrome (inherent inability to recognize social cues and body language) writes fascinating children's stories. A woman who had part of her brain surgically removed is realizing her dream of becoming an independent businesswoman, and writes about her journey to recovery. A retired logger is making progress with his assessment of the U.S. Forest Service. A minister's wife is turning her mother's early years on the Alberta frontier into a novel about choosing between a nursing career and caring for her orphaned younger siblings.

I've remained in the group all these years not only for what I get out of it, but for the encouragement I can give others now that I have gone through writing, rewriting, surviving many rejection slips, and finally getting published.

God, please help me remember that it is blessed to receive, but even more so to give.

Well done is better than well said. Benjamin Franklin
—Keith Dahlberg

June 28

The last clear memory I had was the insect bite. And then, much of my memory disappeared.

"I notice you like to write," Gail said. "Does that help you to remember?"

"If my thoughts don't come out right, I change words until they make sense."

"Strange. You remember something as complex as writing, but have forgotten so much."

I liked writing letters to God. He didn't make fun of me when I made mistakes. He never used my words against me.

I smiled and turned my attention to Gail's last question.

"How do you know when you've got words out of place? What makes you think you need to change them?"

"They don't sound right in my head. When my mind bounces like a car going over a bump, I know something's wrong and change them until they read smoothly."

My fears subsided. She knew my secret; she wouldn't twist my answers and accuse me of lying.

"It's going to be OK," she said. "I'll get you a dictionary so you can look up words you don't understand. Don't worry; you have a good heart. Write what you feel. Who knows, one day you might be a great author. You won't have to remember what was, you can write about what can be.

Lord, thank you for sending guiding lights that pierce the darkness of those in distress.

Education, clear and simple, is power. Hill Harper
—Julia F. Bell

June 29

"Mommy! I am so glad you planted these." I looked up at my little boy to see a huge smile spread across his chubby cheeks. His eyes danced with excitement. "These are what the cowboys chew on when they get bored!" And with that, he balanced the long scraggly weed on his lips and tried to smile. I couldn't hold back my laughter.

I was sitting on my front steps looking at the patch of seeded weeds that had once again taken over what was intended to be a flower bed. Discouragement dropped to the pit of my stomach as I reminded myself that this was supposed to be the year I would grow something other than weeds. I wanted to grow my writing career.

Since then I've learned that I just can't do it all. When I'm busy writing, everything else goes wild. And when I am keeping everything else under control, I'm not achieving my writing goals. I just can't juggle four kids and the house, and write too.

That morning on the steps laughter dispelled my discouragement as I decided that I liked my son's perspective on the weeds better. Even those silly weeds served a purpose. Maybe the key to balancing writing with all my other responsibilities would be perspective.

Lord, help me see my writing, my time, and my tasks with a perspective like yours—full of grace.

My grace is sufficient for you, for power is perfected in weakness. 2 Corinthians 12:9 NASB

—Jami Kirkbride

June 30

I needed to gather realistic information for the final chapter of my novel. The setting? The top of Multnomah Falls in the Columbia Gorge.

Despite Oregon's reputation for rain, the skies were clear as my family and I huffed our way 620 feet to the top. We stopped for occasional breaks so I could photograph a bench my protagonist might rest on, a rusted fern he might notice, or a crag he might lean against. I grilled my husband and kids as to what they smelled, felt, or heard.

On the way down, we took a breather on a wooden bench overlooking the falls. As we relaxed in the warm sunshine, I noticed the soles of my feet were tingling. "It's from slapping against the ground," my husband explained.

As we resumed walking, my eight-year-old daughter, who was in my death grip to keep her from slipping off the edge of the trail, tugged my hand. "Mom, whoever the guy is in your book, his feet need to tingle from slapping the ground because your reader wants to feel what happens so they can be in the book too."

She understands the power of show, don't tell. Don't we want our readers to experience our stories as if they themselves are living it?

Lord, help me to show your love, not just tell people about it.

And Jesus ordered him, "Don't tell anyone, but go, show yourself to the priest, as a testimony to them." Luke 5:14 NIV

—Christina Berry

July 1

I hunched over my computer, fingers drumming on my desk, and fussed about writing. Or not writing. My mind felt like a black hole. I hadn't had an idea worth turning into words in days.

I thought about my favorite writers and wished I could write like them. Who was I to think I could write—especially write to honor God. Did the articles and devotionals I'd had published ever touch a soul?

But then a question scrolled through my mind: "What is that in your hand?"

Startled, I stopped my pity party and sat up straight. Where had I heard that demand before? I reached for my Bible and started searching. In Exodus 4:2, I found what I was looking for. God had asked Moses that question when Moses made excuses about not wanting to lead the Israelites out of Egypt. Moses had a staff in his hand, years of experience, and God to lead him.

What was in my hand? A computer, a vast array of modern technology, writing resources, fellow writers for support, and God to lead me. Since that day, every time I've been tempted to make excuses for not writing, I've heard God whisper, "What is that in your hand?"

Lord, thank you for not giving up on me, for not listening to my excuses, and for keeping me writing for you.

The real voyage of discovery consists not in seeking new landscapes but in having new eyes. Marcel Proust
—Carolyn Meagher

July 2

The instructions said to write pretending I was the front seat of the bus in Montgomery, Alabama, where Rosa Parks sat the day she refused to go to the back. I love to pretend because then, anything I write is OK. As the front seat, I saw and heard it all. I was as sweat-stained as any other seat on our old rig. Every passenger stared at me and wondered how I was going to respond to this lady who had chosen me as her desired resting place. I saw her despair and felt her pain. She literally shook with fright and determination.

It only took a moment for me to decide to be kind. The first thing I did was to whisper to her, "Welcome, I'm glad you had enough strength and fortitude to stand up for the blacks." A small smile creased her lips. Then I plumped myself up as best as I could to give her a comfortable ride. It was one of the best days of my life.

As I wrote, I understood that every day someone comes into my life needing a comfortable place to rest. With God's help, I can be that place and serve in kindness.

Lord, when I write, you teach me so much about myself and about how I should react to others. Thank you for those lessons.

We must be as courteous to a man as we are to a picture, which we are willing to give the advantage of a good light. Ralph Waldo Emerson
—Margaret Steinacker

July 3

One hot sultry summer day away from my watchful eye, my four- and five-year-old sons stripped down to their BVDs in the garage. They found paintbrushes and an open bucket of used motor oil. The first object they encountered was my white 1960 Chevy Impala parked in the driveway. Fortunately, they painted only the rear fender before their daddy discovered them.

This event was recorded in my journal. Between laughter and tears, I took time to jot down many events of their growing up. Journaling became my way of coping with life and expressing myself.

Another time I wrote about the day the boys were digging up the front lawn with their Tonka trucks and trenchers. Fresh sod was overturned, and they invited their friends to share their fun. Even though their father was less than pleased when he came home from work, I reassured him with, "Honey, we are growing boys now. We'll grow grass later."

Father, bless my writings about my boys and help my words bring joy to their families. Thank you for the grandchildren I am writing about now.

I can't remember when I wasn't scribbling something. I jot things down when I can't sleep or I'm too tired or I need to reflect on friends, family, funny moments. Each notebook is a storehouse of memories. Ruth Bell Graham
—Sheryl Van Weelden

July 4

I sat in a session of my first writers' conference, feeling like a fish out of water. When I learned that was an overused cliché, I felt even more alone and fearful of ever learning all I needed to know about becoming a successful writer.

As a lover of historical fiction, I remembered the stories of the men and women who journeyed to this land and were willing to undergo adversity, battles, and even death to assure the blessings of liberty for themselves and their families. They were also willing to give of their time, one of our most precious gifts.

I decided to follow the example of our forefathers and undergo the strenuous time-consuming training I would need to better my writing skills. I would battle clichés and trite phrases, holding out for the best word or phrase. I would be willing to let some of my time-wasters die and fade away to make more time for reading and study of books on the craft of writing. Most of all, I would throw myself into the battle for the hearts and souls of my readers.

Lord, thank you for the privilege of writing for you. Be my guide on this trip and give me joy along the journey.

Dream lofty dreams, and as you dream, so shall you become. James Allen

—Rose McCauley

July 5

It was Friday morning again. I looked forward to the weekly meeting of our new writers' group except for one thing—the opening exercise. Our leader would introduce a word, bring an object, or give us a topic to write about. We would have thirty minutes to write something spontaneous.

I am not a spontaneous person, nor a very creative one. My dread, however, ended the morning the object was a jar of buttons. My first thought was of my grandmother, who was an incredible seamstress. She had a big jar of buttons we used to play games with over the years.

I began to write expecting to write about my grandmother and her buttons, but that is not the story that evolved. As my pen flowed, a very different story appeared. Out of my heart came a story filled with love and adventure about the exciting summers I spent with my grandparents.

My lesson was learned. I didn't need to always be so structured and predictable. There were all kinds of things to write about. I only needed to be spontaneous and open my heart and my eyes to all the possibilities around me.

Lord, help me be sensitive to opening my heart that I might share stories that will speak to the lives of others.

That marvelous instrument, the mind, has for all practical, useful purposes, two layers: the conscious and the unconscious. The writer learns to use both in the begetting of ideas. Marjorie Holmes

—Pam Wanzer

July 6

I slaved over my entry for the *Guideposts* writing contest until the vowels wore off my keyboard. Finally, I packed my perfectly formatted entry in a tasteful packet (with coordinating stamps) and drove to the post office at 10 p.m., one month before the deadline. A hurricane blew in while I was mailing the package and I was stranded in the parking lot until midnight. Naturally, I found things I should have tweaked, reading the copy during lightning flashes. When I got home, I threw a comforter over my computer, as a visual clue that I was DONE.

Soon thereafter, I received the coveted envelope from *Guideposts*, informing me I was one of the fortunate few. I could hardly wait to trade war stories with the other winners. Surely someone had obsessed over her entry longer than I had. I was prepared to feel like the junior senator, not having logged enough hours of anguish to enter the ranks of the pros.

Then I met a woman who waited until the day of the deadline to write her story. When she ran out of printer toner, she finished it longhand, raced to the post office and thrust her envelope through the chute, one minute before closing time.

That was the day I realized that it really is all about the story.

Help us to remember your story, Lord.

I am careful not to confuse excellence with perfection. Excellence, I can reach for; perfection is God's business. Michael J. Fox

—Betsy Dill

July 7

It was my first writers' conference. I'm not sure why I received the brochure in the mail. After much deliberation, I decided to attend. When I walked onto the campus, I wondered why I thought it was a good idea. I felt like a thirteen-year-old on my first day of junior high. Scared spitless.

I had somehow mustered enough courage to sign up for an editorial appointment. I waited for my turn, fiddling with my single-spaced manuscript. Then the editor beckoned for me. Time stood still while she read. My hands sweated, my heart pounded.

Breathe, I reminded myself.

The women's magazine editor looked over the top of her glasses. "Do you want the truth?"

I gulped and managed a barely audible, "Yes."

"Well, you need to show, not tell in your writing. Your verbs are passive. Active verbs move your article forward. Always double space. You've got lots of work to do before this article is ready for publication."

I scribbled some notes, trying to hide my discouragement behind a grateful smile.

As I got up to leave, she added, "Oh, you do know how to write. You have a natural gift. Now go use it."

That's the most important news I received at my first conference. Someone believed I could write.

Lord, thank you for the many editors, mentors, and teachers who have helped me become more skilled at the craft of writing.

Just do what you do best. Red Auerbach
—Deb Kalmbach

July 8

TWENTY-FIVE YEARS OF REJECTION SLIPS
and what does it matter? How many trees have been pulped
for this constant susurrus: sending, resending, shuffling,
sorting?
Even the name *submission* suggests a certain deference,
servility, prostration: lying down in front of the mailbox,
and letting the great steamroller of indifference flatten
me into the ground. You could read the morning newspaper
through my bones. Maybe here is the lesson: Look
at the wind, how it turns the pages of the leaves, riffles
through chapter after chapter, whispers countless stories
that no one bothers to write down. Look at the stanzas
of light in the locust leaves as they bob and weave
in the hot July wind, their effortless green repetition
and refrain. Why not give it up now? The phone isn't going
to ring; the mailbox is full of circulars and bills. So maybe
I'll read to the cardinals and wrens, sink back in the hammock,
listen to the hot buzz of the cicadas' applause.
Look, clouds are writing their manuscripts on the big blue
book
of the sky. They don't fear the wind's erasure, or night's
emphatic black rejection. Tomorrow, a clean sheet comes up
in the roller, and we'll start all over again.

Lord, help me to be patient, and believe in my work.

Let not your hearts be troubled. John 14:1 RSV
—Barbara Crooker

July 9

A man sunk his retirement funds into property sold for taxes. An ugly old barn sat right beside the house, but before he tore it down, he grinded off the heavy weld on the iron doors that kept out everyone for over fifteen years. After strenuous labor, he opened the rusty door and discovered rows of vintage and classical cars.

That reminded me of the verse in Matthew 13:44: "The kingdom of heaven is like treasure hidden in a field."

Many wannabe writers, myself included, quit before they begin. They see only the cost of the mountain. Many of us forget our pact to minister and stoop to publish the unseemly. I've learned that if I try to write to build character and motivate achievement, I won't fall into the trap of writing for a pay check.

Writing can sap my strength but increase my wisdom. Writing demands hours and days to meet a deadline but when I meet that deadline, I can bubble with the joy of accomplishment. Writing can turn me into a monklike creature while at the same time introducing me to the world.

I may never receive incredible earnings like the man who bought the old house and barn for pennies on the dollar. But the joys I find from my investment in writing can far outweigh the struggles.

Father, keep my investment pure. Help my writings mirror your character and bless my readership.

Delight yourself in the Lord and he will give you the desires of your heart. Psalms 37:4 NIV

—Rose Goble

July 10

I'd heard the adage that when the student is ready, the master appears. But I had no idea what it really meant until a couple of years ago.

When I finally stopped running away from the idea of being a writer, I was led to an online writers' group. At first it was daunting; after all, these people were professionals and here I was, a newbie asking newbie-type questions. They reminded that we're all still learning and honing our craft, and there is no such thing as a dumb question.

Last year I learned about a critique group, the Pearl Girls, a small group of women who love the Lord and write for him. They've shown me friendship, prayed with me, and, of course, critiqued my work.

I've learned that the Lord knows me better than I know myself. He knows what I need and when I need it, and has shown to be faithful more times than I can count. Now it's up to me to keep going and be faithful to him.

Thank you, Lord, for knowing the longings of my soul and supplying my needs when I don't even know what they are.

For he satisfieth the longing soul, and filleth the hungry soul with goodness. Psalms 107:9 KJV

—Lee Franklin

July 11

In school I earned good grades, a scholarship, and a diploma. The fame and fortune supposedly were to follow. I strived at athletics, but that was to earn the attention of young ladies. I learned to enjoy winning awards, honors, and attention.

Six years later, I contracted the call to write. The success and recognition that were so easily accumulated in school eluded me as an author. Instead, like most writers, I languished in disappointment and anonymity.

The frustrations led me to serious soul searching. Why am I writing? Is it for money? If so, I think I flunked! Is it for recognition? Is it to unburden my mind?

I've wanted to quit many times. But one day, after deep thought and prayer, I sat before an empty page and the following words poured out:

I may not know, nor ever see, the fruit I hope for in this endeavor. But to this one truth I shall commit my life: not that it was fortune, nor that it was fame, but that it was God who called me to write.

I swallowed. Hard. I asked myself if that was true. For me, it is; and clinging to the purpose of my writing has been the only motivation that has sustained me through the struggle. That, and having been blessed with eleven children to write about!

Lord, thank you for revealing the reason for my writing, that I might find the courage to fulfill it.

A good cause makes a stout heart. Thomas Fuller
—Drew Zahn

July 12

In 1999, a loved one was an inpatient at a psychiatric hospital and I attended group therapy sessions as part of the treatment. After years of living with someone with mental illness and addictions, I was desperate for answers.

At night, alone in my hotel room, I journaled. Journaling had been a reassuring ritual for years as I recorded my perceptions and attempts at survival in my troubled household. A published author, I was writing only in my journal. My confidence was so eroded that I stopped writing for publication and never expected to again. But I kept journaling, thinking that took no skill.

So thousands of miles from home, the familiar comfort of pen and paper helped fill the empty hours. I wrote about therapy, how the exposure of my carefully guarded secrets slowly drew me from victimhood back into taking responsibility for my life. I wrote about my hope for a restored marriage, a peaceful home, and a stable life for my two children.

I would realize how journaling had begun to restore my dignity and self-worth. When I read my entries, I noted how I had grown through struggle. I had walked through many dark days and made it. My hope was slowly restored. Maybe I could write for publication again. I had lots of material.

Lord, thank you for using writing to restore my hope.

Still let me guard the holy fire, and still stir up thy gift in me. Charles Wesley

—Lora Homan

July 13

"I called three times yesterday, and you never answered," my friend whined over lunch at our favorite diner. "I know you were home. Your car was in the drive."

"You did a drive-by to check up on me?" I furrowed my brow.

At her shamed nod, I heaved a huge sigh and dug into my salad.

Home. Where I hang my heart... and all my hopes of publication. Freelancing from the same place I eat, sleep, and entertain is no small feat. It's difficult to discipline myself surrounded by so many distractions. Plants to water and weeds to pull. Letters to answer and laundry to fold. Dinner to plan and...someone at the door. On the phone. Instant-messaging me with a vengeance.

Not to mention the guilt trips from nonwriting friends, impatient adult children, the usually-knows-better spouse. As if writer's block and procrastination aren't enough to deal with.

How's a writer supposed to write?

What works for me, I'm discovering, is to treat it like a job. Commit to the time and the task. Calendar appointments and deadlines—allowing breathing space for meals, breaks, and, perhaps, the occasional lunch with a friend.

Then, avoid distractions. Focus. Stay on task. Write until the allotted time is up.

And—park the car in the garage!

Father, help me honor my talents by carving out time to write and keeping my commitment to my craft.

Neglect not the gift that is in thee. 1 Timothy 4:14 KJV
—Carol McAdoo Rehme

July 14

Life can be a zoo, especially when you work at home. A week of summer zoo camp for my daughter Beth would be a time when I would write. Then illness struck our carpool, and I became a designated driver on a deadline.

I found myself at the zoo, laptop computer bag on shoulder and cell phone in hand. I searched for solitude beyond camper chatter and lions' roars. A zookeeper suggested a spot on the other side of the Pittsburgh Zoo and Aquarium.

Fatigued, I focused on my destination as I neared the new polar bear exhibit. I only glanced as the gigantic bear on the bank dived into the pool—remembering polar bears spend only 10 percent of their time in water—but rushed on. Until the polar bear dipped beneath the surface and reappeared directly in front of me.

The largest land predator looked up. I looked down. He placed an enormous paw on his side of the glass. I knelt, dropping my load, and put my hand up to his paw. A single toenail was the size of my index finger. As the bear swam away, I reminded myself to walk through life with a bit more serenity. As a writer, it's life's really cool encounters that provide material for writing. I just have to make sure I don't miss them.

Dear Lord, help me to focus first on your world, then to write with abandon.

The beginning of wisdom is the realization that what is of concern today won't seem important tomorrow. Old Chinese proverb

—Jane Miller

July 15

I waited a long time to hear back from the editor regarding a story I submitted for a popular anthology book. One day while checking my e-mails, I noticed on the subject line that there was a note regarding my submission.

With my heart beating a mile a minute, I carefully opened it to read that my story had been accepted into the finals for the book. I was so excited! The downside was that I still had to wait a few more months to know whether it would be in the book.

Not long after that, I received my contract with the edited version of my story. Signing and sending it back made me feel hopeful over the next few months. Then, the day came when I received the crushing blow that my story wasn't selected.

As I struggled to hold back the tears, I remembered some advice from a writer friend. Whenever she received a rejection letter, she immediately submitted her story somewhere else. I scoured my writers' guide to find another place to submit. Several months later, I received a letter of acceptance. That experience helped me understand that rejection can be divine redirection.

Heavenly Father, thank you that even in my rejections you have a plan.

This manuscript of yours that has just come back from another editor is a precious package. Don't consider it rejected. Consider that you've addressed it "to the editor who can appreciate my work" and it has simply come back stamped "not at this address." Just keep looking for the right address. Barbara Kingsolver

—Annettee Budzban

July 16

I ran today. It felt good to run again. It's been months since my last encounter with the road and several years since I jogged consistently. I started running after my sophomore year of high school when my basketball coach required it to join the team the following season. Since high school, I've run sporadically, but always associated good physical health with this activity. It's simple enough for me to grasp: put one foot in front of the other and don't forget to breathe. However, it requires discipline and persistence, which I lack at times. Yet I desire a healthy life and a fit body, and those don't come without sacrifice. The road to a smaller clothing size looms in front of me as I work toward my goal.

Writing necessitates discipline and persistence as well. I correlate writing with good emotional health. If I write, I feel good. I put one word after another formed into sentences and paragraphs that I hope make sense. I work on my craft with the objective of publication and success. Above all else, I long to write well. So I continue down the path toward this goal. Giving up is not an option.

Lord, help me be faithful with what you've given me.

I have fought the good fight, I have finished the race, I have kept the faith. 2 Timothy 4:7 NIV

—Shannon Wine

July 17

Long before I had access to the Internet, I prayed that God would connect me with a writer friend. Though I enjoyed creating my weekly columns, there was no one for me with whom to share my passion for writing.

Then the most unexpected divine connection took place. A total stranger called one day from Wyoming, explaining she was an advocate for a women's shelter there. She had helped my sister escape an abusive husband. This woman was calling me, in Chicago, to keep me updated on my sister's situation since I could not have direct contact with her.

During one of our conversations, we shared some personal information and learned we were both writers. With my sister safely on her way to a new life, Gracie and I established a close friendship.

Our friendship only lasted a season, but I'm grateful for the memories and the powerful reminder. God found a way to bring me a writer friend from across the country amid highly unusual circumstances.

Since then I have met many wonderful writers online—special souls who encourage me to reach my goals. And now, more than ever, I know that God does indeed work in mysterious ways.

Thank you, loving Father, for the friends you've placed in my path for I know their presence is not by chance.

Friendship is composed of a single soul inhabiting two bodies. Aristotle

—Kathy Whirity

July 18

Maybe it's because I was taught not to brag. It wasn't OK to feel good about six As in school if there was one B among them. No matter how hard I tried, I wondered if I would ever be good enough.

At one Writing Academy seminar, I struggled with the session opener. The instructor had said, "In five minutes, write down the talents and positive traits that make you the person you are."

Hmmm. Sounded like bragging to me. I couldn't write a word.

The second direction came. "Begin your notes with the words, 'Because I am a child of God...'"

Words flew from my pen. The woman next to me said, "You sure are writing a lot."

I laughed. "Once you remember the source, it is easier to accept the gifts."

One Sunday at church my priest, who was speaking on Luke 14, said, "Humility doesn't mean hypocrisy, pretending to be humble to earn praise. Humility is accepting your unique talents as gifts from God, and using them to serve him."

It doesn't matter how many talents I have. It matters how I use them. Whenever I'm faced with a new challenge, I remember, "Because I am a child of God's."

Lord, thank you for reminding me that everything I have is a gift, not an entitlement. Open my eyes to the needs of others that I might serve you with humility and gratitude.

For everyone who exalts himself will be humbled, but the one who humbles himself will be exalted. Luke 14:11 NAB

—Tommie Lenox

July 19

Christian writers speak about their calling to write. Since I came to writing later in life, I've wondered: am I called to write, or am I faking it?

I felt like a pretender when I compared myself with real writers at conferences. They were confident in their callings, in their writing. They had no doubts.

Then, I overheard someone encourage a new attendee: "After you've attended a few times, you'll stop feeling like an imposter. We all feel like fakes at first." She glanced at me. "Right?"

I nodded, too overwhelmed to find words to thank her for making my writer self-doubts sound so universal, so ordinary.

How can I know God called me to write? In the same way I know that I didn't choose God; he chose me. He promises to equip me with all that I ask in Christ's name—even writing skills—necessary to bear lasting fruit.

Father, thank you for reminding me that despite my doubts, you called me to write.

You did not choose me, but I chose you and appointed you to go and bear fruit—fruit that will last. Then the Father will give you whatever you ask in my name. John 15:16 NIV

—Vicki Talley McCollum

July 20

I am by nature a shy person. I don't find it easy to walk into a room full of strangers. Exposing myself to possible criticism is something I avoid. My writing is personal and private. That is why I refused to consider joining a writing group.

A friend was persistent. For fifteen years she insisted I apply for membership in The Writing Academy. Reluctantly, I submitted the sample writings and to my amazement was accepted.

They must be hard up for members, I thought as I prepared to attend my first seminar. It won't be long before they discover I am not a writer.

Again, to my amazement, I found the members to be warm, loving, and supportive. It was a safe environment. The members were genuine, struggling to become better writers themselves. They encouraged each other by listening, providing honest criticism, and being a cheering section.

Because of these colleagues, I was encouraged to develop my skills. I no longer fear criticism but welcome it openly. I learned that peer review stimulates growth and that rejection slips are not the enemy but a way of measuring progress. Love conquered my fears.

Lord God, thank you for the community of saints that builds up through love.

Beloved, if God so loved us, we also ought to love one another. 1 John 4:11 RSV

—Gerald Ebelt

July 21

Commitment. A hard word for me to swallow. I've always approached things in a neutral kind of way.

In October 2005, an idea for a story came to my mind. I wrote a synopsis. The idea was so strong that I spent the next five days thinking and obsessing about it. However, as I dreamed of the storyline, I also questioned my dedication. I had written before, some essays, poems, and short stories. But this wasn't short story material.

So, I hesitantly took up a pen and paper and started writing, not knowing where it would lead. I knew this required a commitment just as big as a marriage. I began...slowly at first, one word and one sentence at a time. Two years later, after countless revisions, I completed my manuscript.

I sit in awe of the perseverance within me to complete a tale that had to be written, with the hopes for it to be shared to the world.

Lord, I am no longer barren of defeat and confidence, but rather clothed in your strength.

A serious writer is not to be confounded with a solemn writer. A serious writer may be a hawk or a buzzard or even a popinjay, but a solemn writer is always a bloody owl. Ernest Hemingway

—Chiara Talluto

July 22

I've always heard successful writers proclaim the benefits of writing something every day. I learned the importance of being consistent in 2002.

Feeling the urge to write, I started putting thoughts on paper and e-mailed them to friends in my address book. I called my little writings E-mail Tidbits. That was not a very impressive title because it didn't seem as though anyone would take them seriously. No one responded, so I quit sending them.

One Sunday morning just before our church service, I was examining my conscience about those tidbits, wondering if had been a wise thing to stop. I asked myself if I was being consistent. Those thoughts were bewildering but the reason for them was revealed just a few minutes later. A visiting missionary, whose name was in my address book, asked if I was still writing my Tidbits, as they were a blessing to him.

That spurred my devotionals writing efforts. In 2003, I started archiving them under the title Words for Kingdom Living. Since that time, I've written a devotional every weekday. I am in the fourth year of writing and have never missed a single issue. That can only be by divine motivation, as it's the most consistent thing I've done in my life.

Father, I ask that you continue to build in me a steadfast spirit.

Create in me a pure heart, O God, and renew a steadfast spirit within me. Psalms 51:10 NIV

—Roy Proctor

July 23

Attending writers' conferences, hard work, and perseverance returned pages of published credits for me, but few dollars—until *Christian Reader* selected my article for its cover. Soon thereafter, I took a writing sabbatical. When I re-entered the writing arena, I expected to begin where I left off. But editors, styles, and requirements had changed.

When an opportunity to write book reviews arrived in my inbox, I accepted without even praying about it. Probably because I thought like James Lowell once wrote: "He who would write and can't write, can surely review."

With the first book review column, I learned reviews were not simple. They were difficult, and you had to actually read the book, not just skim it. A ream of discarded computer drafts sent me to my knees, where I should have gone first.

In addition to prayer, I reread notes from various conferences and decided to use journalism basics for reviews. While I read, I noted answers to the questions of who, what, when, why, where, and how before I determined the book's focus. Once I understood the author's intent, that became the review lead along with a brief summary and my critique.

Lord, thank you for steering me in new directions with my writing and for the enjoyment I get from reading and reviewing all these books.

Writing is the only profession where no one considers you ridiculous if you earn no money. Jules Renard

—Gail Welborn

July 24

One of an editor's pleasures is helping aspiring writers polish their craft. But one of my earliest attempts found me grossly mishandling an ardent young reporter's big feature story.

All Jim wanted to do was cover college sports. He had no classroom connection with the journalism school that produced the newspaper. All I, the sports editor, needed to do was give him leeway.

But no. I had to rewrite huge sections of his most prized piece of work. Well, I told myself, I can't reach Jim. And I do want to get that feature in tomorrow's paper.

Still, I should have postponed publication and let him handle the rewrite. His drooping shoulders the next morning signaled my mistake. Not angry, he seemed defeated.

"I'm just so disappointed," he said before disappearing for good.

I like to think Jim's self-confidence remained intact. If so, it was with no help from me.

Lord, remind me to grant others the same freedoms I cherish.

Life is not so short but that there is always time for courtesy. Ralph Waldo Emerson

—Jerry Elsea

July 25

Several years ago, after a particularly trying emotional upheaval in our family, I stopped writing. I didn't have any words of hope or joy to share. All I had was grief and disappointment, and I wasn't about to bring others down with my despair.

I prayed, every day—and I cried, every day. I knew God heard my prayers, but I couldn't grab hold of his comfort.

After several days of watching me wipe my tears, my husband said, "You need to write what you're feeling. You won't get better until you get it all out on paper."

So, I wrote...and wrote. Many pages later, I finally found the comfort I had been seeking.

Now, I finally understand. God gave me not only a desire to write, but also a need to express myself through writing. Writings, like thoughts, don't have to be shared to be valid. As a writer, my feelings stay bottled up inside until I put them outside myself and onto paper.

So, I write. Sometimes, I share my writings. Sometimes, I don't. Always, though, I am grateful that God created in each of us a way to express ourselves and find the comfort only he can give.

Father, thank you for creating within me exactly what I need to find comfort in you.

Know thyself means this, that you get acquainted with what you know, and what you can do. Menander
—Dorissa J. "Prissy" Vanover

July 26

I grew up reading Nancy Drew mysteries and Cherry Ames nursing adventures. Cherry Ames won out, and I began my career as a registered nurse. After a decade of writing nurses notes, creative writing seemed light years away.

Occasionally, I'd write a funny story or poem for a family member, but I never took my writing very seriously. I thought you had to write like Maya Angelou, or at least as well as my sister who wrote beautiful Christmas newsletters, to call yourself a writer.

At age thirty, I attended a small college deep in the Blue Ridge Mountains. After a scholarly English professor wrote on my paper, "Have you ever considered being a novelist?" and, my music professor noted, "You are very articulate. I hope you use your writing skills in your future career," seeds of hope were planted.

Over the years, I plugged away at English courses and a full-time nursing job, all the while feeling in my heart the longing to write. It wasn't until a near-fatal accident that my writing life truly began. During the months of solitude, words flowed for devotions, stories, and poems.

I never dreamed my story of tragedy and faith would appear in a book to inspire people. Writing is now my joy and testimony.

Thank you, Lord, for words that create hope in our lives and the lives of others.

Writing is making sense of life. Nadine Gordimer
—Barbara Parentini

July 27

I scanned the dining room at the retreat center for a place to sit. As author-turned-guest speaker that weekend, I'd already shared a meal with retreat planners. Now I was free to sit anywhere.

I felt drawn to an empty chair next to a quiet older woman. She seemed surprised when I asked if I could sit beside her.

"Dagmar," I said, reading her name tag. "Do you have a German heritage? My great-grandparents came from Germany."

"Yes," she replied in a lilting accent, "I came from Germany." Despite the distracting din of conversations around us, we managed to share about our families. I learned she was a single-again mother of a son and daughter who'd turned away from God.

After that weekend, she wrote to say how pleased she was that I sat by her. "Most of time," she said, "the speakers don't sit with us ordinary people." Her comment saddened me. Had other speakers really been so aloof? She also said she wanted to pray for me regularly.

More than a decade has passed since that retreat, but we still keep in touch. Every few months, I get an e-mail from Dagmar asking for prayer updates. And each week, I pray for her and the salvation of her two adult children.

Sometimes that's what God calls ordinary writers and speakers to do.

Father, keep me sensitive to your divine appointments.

My heart is not proud, O Lord, my eyes are not haughty. Psalms 131:1 NIV

—Jeanne Zornes

July 28

I worked for several years on my collection of short stories and looked forward to the day when my book would be published, but was having little success. For me, these stories have a life, and I wanted to share them with others.

One day, I thumbed through the compilation. Would my babies remain in my filing cabinet and never be read by anyone else? I picked up two folders and thought about the experience of an answered prayer in Italy and the healing story of a Texas French poodle named Bubba. Could one of these stories encourage another soul?

I decided to send some out there into the world of submissions. Now, several are published in magazines and book collections. By letting go of my writing, I am able to share some of my Christian experiences.

I wrote a story and poem primarily for my grandson. It is a tale of nature's progression of life, death, and rebirth. Although the story garnered first place in a writers' contest, it has yet to be published. I hope someday "Maisy the Daisy" will be an inspirational story for other children. Tomorrow, I'm mailing out another submission.

May my words nourish another on the path along the way that leads to our eternal home.

Humanity continues to tell man that life has a meaning. Our purpose in life is to discover this meaning and live according to it. Thomas Merton

—Emily Tipton Williams

210

July 29

My workday began when the yellow bus rolled away. The first month, I'd sit at my desk and stare at a blank computer screen while my coffee went cold. I read Natalie Goldberg's *Writing Down the Bones*. Every day after that, I sat down and wrote at least one page.

My writing day ended when my husband came home. I'd turn off the computer and make dinner and hang out with my family until the next weekday. Eight months later, my memoir was three-quarters finished. I'd written thousands of pages, almost a hundred essays. One day, I began a screenplay.

Characters I couldn't get out of my head consumed my every thought. Every spare minute I could find, I was on the computer jotting down thoughts. If errands or housework took up any part of my day, I tried to reclaim it by writing in the evening. The computer was never off, only idling.

My husband said, "That computer is my biggest enemy." Heartbroken, I went back to writing when he and my daughter were away. I tried to keep perspective on what was important. I cleaned house.

When I finally finished my first screenplay after nine revisions, I handed it to my husband. That weekend he bought us matching laptops and a new office program. A week later, he bought me my screenwriting software.

Lord, thank you for all those who support my writing passion.

Don't get it right; just get it written. James Thurber
—Julie Morrison

July 30

When my friend Elaine died of cancer, her daughter, Karen, was only eighteen years old. I filed the letters which Elaine, a prize-winning writer, had sent to me over the years. I enjoyed savoring her poetic prose as she described the "hish of the corn in autumn rows." She wrote of how her husband had baked two pies for a farmer so that he wouldn't cut down the row of corn Elaine enjoyed watching from her bedroom window.

When Karen had a family, I mailed some of Elaine's letters to her and her children. Karen told me that her eldest daughter, Emily Elaine, carried the letters to school in her backpack and tucked them under her pillow at night.

For birthdays and Christmas, I selected cards and letters Elaine had sent me, some of which were still in their original envelopes, and mailed them to Karen and her children.

One of Elaine's cards was in the shape of a butterfly. That seemed the perfect symbol for how writing goes through a metamorphosis. After words sleep for a while, they spread their wings and come back to life, adding color to our lives.

Dear Lord, help me take time to write full-length letters. And give me the wisdom to share some of the letters with the next generation.

And now in age I bud again. After so many deaths I live and write. George Herbert

—Shirley Stevens

July 31

I am a collector of ideas. I try to be original in what I write.

When I became a mother, my writing took a "shelf" (no pun intended). I tried for months to sit down and write a short story or poem—even the occasional thank you card—but my writing was adrift.

When I got a moment to write, I was discouraged because it was forced and unnatural. It felt like the laundry and the dirty dishes stole my muse. The most frustrating element of writing is writer's block followed by writer's boredom.

Then one day at the grocery store, I ambled through the school supply aisle, pushing my two lovely boys. I picked up a fifty-cent notepad and began writing down different names of things I saw: wacky product names, labels, my sons' favorite cereal. Before I knew it, a poem was in the works. I titled it "The Grocery Story With Two Boys."

That evening after the boys' bath and sleepy time rituals, I finished the poem and, being as clichéd as any mother, I took a magnet and hung my final product on the refrigerator. No one noticed the work except me. It made me realize that first and foremost, my writing is for me.

Thank you, God, for the unexpected and for the ability to seize the moment.

All life demands change, variety, contrast—else there is small zest to it. Mark Twain

—Kimberly Lytle

August 1

In fifteen years of freelancing I've encountered more obstacles than a protagonist confronts in a good novel. Amarillo, Texas, was an opportune locale to start writing professionally, but was not a career market for a fifty-plus year-old journalist and ex-flight attendant with a bad back and arthritis. But I persisted and, after publishing over two hundred articles, I spent two years writing a nonfiction book and a year pitching it.

Then I became a caregiver for a mother with Alzheimer's and a husband with cancer. I slid into a two-year slump until I pitched a Narnia-inspired novel idea to a receptive editor at a Christian conference, but then ran smack into a copyright infringement. I needed a new angle but was discouraged, distracted, and drifting—my motivation murdered.

In preparation for a C. S. Lewis Foundation conference, I read a book that related the influence and support Lewis and J. R. R. Tolkien shared within their writers' group, without whose encouragement—especially Lewis's—Tolkien said he would never have completed *The Lord of the Rings.*

Epiphany! In bowing out of my writers' group, I had lost support and encouragement—a writer's lifeblood. I needed a transfusion. Conferences aren't just for pitching. I learned I have to be a sponge and soak up inspiration and hope from other writers. Unsolicited encouragement is a gift that takes courting and investing my time and energy first.

Lord, help me to encourage and build up my fellow writers and to be open to their support.

What I owe to them all is incalculable. C. S. Lewis
—Nan Rinella

August 2

It took a while to learn to respond to the urge. If I didn't immediately grab something and scribble down words, a thought or story would often leave me. Now I succumb to the unpredictable, sometimes untimely voice inside my head that says, "Write this down!"

I try to keep a notebook handy. However, I've been known to write poems or stories on paper towels from a public restroom simply because I knew the string of words bouncing around inside my brain wouldn't be there for long. A napkin, the back of a check, a paper bag, whatever I could find to write on became an adequate tablet and companion for my pen. Once I begged some legal pad paper from a stranger at an airport. The urgency to write gave me the boldness to ask.

My sporadic notes were like the first light of sunrise. More words were gradually added and soon a full-blown story illuminated brightly. Then I was on to the next day, another literary piece of work, and another struggle from my innermost being to letters on a page.

Some say being able to write is a calling. Perhaps. But I believe it's my response to an inner voice that communes with me repeatedly. Each prompt is divine.

You are a God who desires to commune with your children. Help me be obedient to your voice and respond.

Speak, Lord, for your servant is listening. 1 Samuel 3:9 NIV

—Alesia Skaggs Campbell

August 3

Learning to sing the correct notes or memorizing dialogue always came easily for me. So when the opportunity arose to return to the classroom as a student after a thirty-year absence and years of performing, completing a degree in theatre seemed a natural. To fill a required full-time student status, I added classes in subjects I'd always wanted to try, including creative writing. Before graduation, I received an unexpected suggestion from the head of the creative studies department.

"I think you should enroll in the master's program for creative writing," my professor told me.

"Oh, I can't imagine anyone wanting to read what I write," I replied.

She told me I needed to get over that attitude, then offered to recommend me for the master's program. There was even a job opening for a graduate assistant in the department.

I soon found the act of placing correct punctuation in coherent sentences was as pleasing to me as sustaining a perfectly pitched high C. Creating my own dialogue became a passion. What a joy when I discovered I could sing my innermost songs in the stories I created on a written page for others to read.

Thank you, Father, for encouraging me to try new things and fulfill dreams I never knew I had.

Getting ahead in a difficult profession—singing, acting, writing, whatever—requires avid faith in yourself. You must be able to sustain yourself against staggering blows and unfair reversals. Sophia Loren

—Bonnie Lanthripe

August 4

Lighting a candle I sink into a wingback chair in my study to think, read, journal, and pray. Only the tapping of my Lab's claws on the kitchen floor punctuates the silence.

Pictures of the people I love most adorn the shelves above the desk. My husband, Wally, rakishly handsome in tux and bow tie. Our eldest, Matt, third grade, showing off his new Bible. Justin, eight, perched on his birthday bike, right arm in a cast. My favorite sits center stage: Matt, Justin, and Joel sitting side by side, the three of them leaning forward, arms on knees. Joel sits in the middle, knees crossed, hands folded, right arm resting on Justin's knee. Gazing at this picture I imagine Joel a typical boy, the birth not traumatic, his brain not damaged after all. I take a deep breath, thinking what might have been, and let it out, still thankful for what is.

Finally, I pick up my pen to write. How I love the forging of words that make sense out of hazy thoughts and connections out of chaos; the communication of ideas half hidden in my heart, taking shape and form as they race from mind to fingers. It's mysterious and marvelous and magical.

Lord, thank you for allowing me to be cocreator along with you; for helping me venture daily into the danger and mystery of who I might yet become.

Fill your paper with the breathings of your heart. William Wordsworth

—Kathleen Deyer Bolduc

August 5

My friend and former neighbor Bruce Swezey is a Bible scholar and a pilot. One time I asked him to tell me the most important words he ever read or learned. I expected something profound from the Bible.

But without blinking, Bruce said, "That's easy: the thirty-word emergency action for spin recovery." Then, in twelve seconds flat he rattled it off: "Throttles: idle. Rudder and ailerons: neutral. Stick: abruptly full aft and hold. Rudder: abruptly apply full rudder opposite spin direction (opposite turn needle) and hold. Stick: full forward one turn after applying rudder. Controls: neutral and recover from dive."

Try saying that in twelve seconds!

I learned that recovering from a dive in an airplane is as important as recovering from the dive into despair I've often felt when one publisher after another rejects my writing. The secret is maintaining control. I don't call them rejection letters. I call them returns and then I send my manuscripts out to another publisher the day they come back. I try to keep my stories, articles, essays and columns out there, circulating, waiting to be discovered. When I do that, I notice that I don't even have those feelings of rejection anymore. It's my fail-safe method for recovering from a dive.

Lord, keep me busy writing. And thanks for the computer and e-mail that makes submissions so easy these days.

The fear of rejection is worse than rejection itself.
Nora Profit

—Patricia Lorenz

August 6

One morning while sitting on the deck of our lake cabin, I said to my husband, "John, we both love it here. This would be a great place to retire."

John pondered the idea for a moment and said, "Yes, but we have a lot of work to do first."

Without saying another word, he went into the cabin and returned with pen and paper. John loves to make lists and will not start a project without one. He writes down work to be done and sets priorities. He then makes note of all the supplies needed and faithfully takes his list to the home improvement center. He is like Santa Clause, making his list, checking it twice...

His lists remind me of writing. I find it is very helpful to keep a pad and pencil handy. When I have an idea for a story or devotion, I write it on my pad. During the day I write down thoughts relating to my original idea. Like John's list, I prioritize these thoughts, deleting some, adding new ones.

This has taught me to be organized and not stray from my original idea. As a writer I find writing lists very helpful.

Thank you, Lord, for giving me the ability to prioritize my thoughts, throwing out the bad ones and keeping the good ones.

No one can write decently who is distrustful of the reader's intelligence, or whose attitude is patronizing. E. B. White

—Sally Devine

August 7

I sat staring at my computer, my mind and fingers paralyzed. Under normal conditions, the keys would be clicking away, with words flowing freely. But conditions had not been normal for a long time.

My husband had died recently after suffering the ravages of early-onset Alzheimer's disease. My mentally ill son had been unstable during that entire period. And I had faced potential financial disaster due to the deceit of a trusted friend.

Somehow, in spite of all the stress, I had completed the course requirements for my doctorate of ministry. Now it was time to write my dissertation, and I approached the task with a mind that was burned out. I struggled to compose sentences. Sometimes after hours of work, I had written very little that I felt was acceptable. Often, I wanted just to quit.

One day as I approached my work reluctantly, I turned the page of a perpetual calendar that sits on my desk. I read, "If you keep doing what you're doing now, you'll have more of what you've got later!" I chuckled. That, of course, was the answer—just keep putting words on paper.

Every day after that as I began work, I read the adage and smiled. I kept doing what I was doing. Now my challenge is to be able to reduce what I have!

Lord, thanks for your empowerment to "keep on keeping on" when it comes to writing.

The best way out is through. Robert Frost
—Gloria Jackson

August 8

This morning I woke at 5; slipped into my favorite housecoat, a bright blue yukata purchased on a long-ago trip to Japan; and slowly made my way along the darkened hall. I was up early to bake a pan of chocolate revel bars to serve after worship that day.

As I lumbered down the stairs, it occurred to me that this quiet morning time without the telephone and other interruptions would be better spent writing than baking.

But if I decide to write this morning, I feel like I will let someone down. Will she be angry? I try so hard to please that I tend to forget my needs are important too. I need to write. It is the very life and breath of my soul. If I decide to nourish my soul I am honoring the gift that God has given.

Oreos and pretzels would work as well as homemade bars and by serving them I might give another person permission to opt out of try-to-outdo-the-competition in bringing goodies to church.

Best of all, using store-bought cookies will give me time to write. Finding time to write is all about making decisions. I can, I will, I shall write this morning. And I did.

Decisions, decisions. Dear God, help me make decisions that will nourish the gift you have given.

Choose this day whom you will serve. Joshua 24:15 NRSV

—Connie Scharlau

August 9

I agonized over beginning my final degree. However, as the home economics program I developed blossomed and matured, I knew that I would hinder its credibility if I selfishly maintained my reluctance to embark on a doctoral program. My dean offered wise instruction: "You started the degree; be sure you finish it."

Today, some twenty-five years later, my writing ministry benefits from his counsel. The constant editing required from my dissertation committee prepared me for the fact that when I write books, my manuscript editor is going to suggest some revisions. Since the editor has more experience than I do, I should not be offended.

Pleasing an entire doctoral committee was a challenge. However, the experience poised me for the reality that once I sign a book contract, the focus moves from "my" book to "our" book. Dealing with individuals on my committee equipped me with tools to help me interface with publishers.

My Ph.D. experience taught me that the heat will come. Yes, sometimes deadlines seem impossible to achieve. The drought is certain. Writer's block will happen. However, there is a supernatural source of vitality when I trust the Lord to help me see the project through to completion.

Gracious heavenly Father, please help me finish the projects I believe you challenged me to begin.

Blessed is the man who trusts in the Lord, whose trust is the Lord. Jeremiah 17:7-8 ESV

—Pat Ennis

August 10

I had been struggling with stress and anxiety. At my doctor's suggestion, I made an appointment with a family counselor. She suggested I write down everything I felt responsible for in my life.

A week later I said, "I have my list. It's five pages in a steno pad."

The counselor said, "You think you are responsible for everybody's happiness. You are not and can't be expected to continue this way."

I began to journal my thoughts, feelings, and anxieties. Getting some of my frustrations onto paper seemed to release the stress within. Writing my true feelings was not easy.

At a writers' conference I attended, author Patricia Lorenz said, "When I write, I unzip my soul and expose my foibles." That helped me understand that if I expose an oozing wound to the sun, healing can happen. Similarly, opening my troubled soul and writing down my woes is often one of the best ways for healing to begin.

Recently, I ran across the faded pink steno pad journal and started to skim though some of the entries. At the time I wrote them, they were so healing, but now that I'm past that pain, reading them only seemed to restart a sinking feeling of depression. So instead of reading, I turned once again to writing and thanked God for giving me a love for penned words.

Lord, thank you for encouraging me to share my pain.

The role of a writer is not to say what we all can say, but what we are unable to say. Anaïs Nin
—Margaret Steinacker

August 11

We once took a family fishing trip to Canada. Terrified of deep water, I strapped on my life vest good and tight, and clung to the small boat as it roared across remote lakes. The tasty walleye we sought could only be found in waters deeper than I cared for.

While others reeled in fish after fish, my line kept coming back empty—minus the slimy minnows I'd squished on the hook. Eventually I caught a keeper, but only because I finally released my fear and focused on what I was there to do.

Letting go of fear applies to my writing as well. Rather than risk one more rejection, I often wade in the shallow waters close to shore, writing and not submitting. I know I'm supposed to venture into the deep, forget my fears, and let down my net for a catch. I have to learn that if I don't go in over my head, I might miss out on the blessing of having my writing published.

It didn't take a lot of faith for Peter to make the catch of a lifetime—just enough to turn the boat around. Neither do I need a lot of faith—just enough to venture out and let down my net one more time.

Dear God, shore up my faltering faith and give me courage to submit more of my work.

Put out into the deep and let down your nets for a catch. Luke 5:4 RSV

—Michele T. Huey

August 12

A number of people have said that I'm talented for having written and published so many books. Others ask how I come up with so many ideas. Usually, I reply that writing takes more work than talent. Then I tell them that my ideas come from life and people all around me.

My mind, however, goes back to the eighth grade and a mathematics teacher named Miss Metts. One day after a particularly unruly boy disrupted the class, she made this statement: "You are becoming today what you will be tomorrow."

Perhaps she was only saying that to the boy. I never heard her make the statement again. It could easily have been taken as a passing remark. But it stuck with me. Many times, that statement has been my encouragement even after thirty years of writing.

My books don't get written because I have talent or because I have so many ideas. They get written because I know if I am to be a writer tomorrow, I must write today.

I've reminded myself that the principle of that statement should be applied to every area of life, for my actions have earthly and eternal consequences. Today I am becoming what I will be tomorrow.

Lord, help me commit my ways to you each day so I might become the kind of person you created me to be.

Commit yourself to instruction; attune your ears to hear words of knowledge. Proverbs 23:12 NLT
—Yvonne Lehman

August 13

Dad's construction job took us around the country. When each job was completed, we moved, often two or three times a year.

I loved seeing new places, but I missed my extended family. By the time I could write, I was writing newsy notes that told of the places we lived and the exciting things we saw. Each new place was an experience to share.

During Vietnam, I wrote letters to anyone who asked, even those I never met. A friend would say that his buddy did not get mail and I would add him to my list. When my own brothers entered the service, I wrote to them. When we received an answer, I let my children hold my brother's picture as the letter was read.

As my children went off to college, I loaded them down with picture postcards. With only a small space to fill in, they did write. They continued the habit as they traveled the world.

Technology advanced, and I now send e-mails along with letters and postcards. Not wanting to just say, "Hi. How are you? I'm fine," I began to write stories about events that happened in my life. Writing lets me share my world with others.

Lord, thank you for the gift of communication so I can share my world with others.

Like cold water to a weary soul is good news from a distant land. Proverbs 25:25 NIV

—Doris Jean Shaw

August 14

Mama said I popped out of her womb with a pencil in my hand. Later, I wrote for newspapers, radio, and television. After winning awards and with encouragement from the judges, I considered writing a call and promised to retire and write full time. I didn't.

Later, I had brain surgery to remove a tumor. My brain got infected with deadly spinal meningitis. My church and friends prayed unceasingly; I was spared. However, Southeastern Louisiana University offered me a job teaching writing and I took it.

Shortly after, I experienced sudden death. Home alone, with terrible pain in my chest, and the hiss of my last breath as my heart stopped, I only had time to think: If you don't do something, God, I'm dead. I fell against the wall.

My heart started up. My breath returned. At last, I knew I would retire and write.

This is a hard story to believe—for me, as well as for others. It took three times in the valley of the shadow of death for me to realize that writing is a call. The call is rarely as dramatic as the one I had, for God speaks also in a still, small voice: Write.

Lord, from your heart, to my heart, from my heart to my head, and from my head to my fingers, I commit my writing to you.

Commit your work to the Lord, then it will succeed. Proverbs 16:3 TLB

—Jackie Strange

August 15

I began my career in higher education administration at the entry level. As director of public relations for a Florida university, I wrote news releases. I researched my facts, polished my drafts, and paid attention to details. In short time, I could speak with ease on virtually any subject related to the school.

A few years later, I became director of communications at a Carolina college. Here I oversaw a staff of fourteen; my salary doubled. Staff members now did the majority of research and writing. I received most of my information through conversations or documents.

In spite of my higher position, I found myself less informed—almost ill at ease—in discussing the school. The difference, I am convinced, lay within the writing process. When I had written the information, I owned it. My brain's wiring, like a computer, kept the written words in a type of suspended memory. But when I received information secondhand, I required an extra mental step to fully digest it.

This experience taught me a wonderful lesson: Writing massages our brains and delivers a huge payoff in the retention of details. From that point on, I wrote daily, creating powerful "scripting" minutes to enhance my busy schedule.

Thank you, Lord, for the amazing powers you grant me through the gift of writing. Help me use my talent wisely to your glory.

I, wisdom, live with prudence, and I attain knowledge and discretion. Proverbs 8:12 NRSV

—Margaret W. Garrison

August 16

"Why can't I have my own?' I would ask every Sunday.

I would always get the same reply: "Let's wait and make sure everyone gets one."

I would walk slowly up the center aisle, hoping to find my very own bulletin, perhaps one that was left from a previous service. I would eventually get Dad's or take a bathroom break and pick up another one on my way back.

To me, bulletins were more than directions for worship and announcements for the coming week. They were my canvas for doodles, tic-tac-toe, connect the dots and hangman. They were the perfect size to place on a hymnbook or Bible and write notes.

The trick was to sit in a row that still had a pencil next to the visitors' cards. Without that, I would have to ask Mom or Dad for something to write with, and, depending on how the ride to church went, the odds were usually stacked against me. If I was able to commandeer a pen or pencil, the first order of business was to fill in all the letters, like the Os and the Ps.

Today, I still like having my own bulletin to write on. The ones I like best have a blank page. I use them to write sermon notes and on occasion ask, "Where do you want to go for lunch?"

Lord, thank you for taking us from being scribblers to writers.

I love being a writer. What I can't stand is the paperwork. Peter De Vries

—Lonni L. Docter

August 17

It was an August day in 1987, and I had journeyed to Washington Island to join my brother and his family for a little respite. Their campsite was deserted when I arrived, so I reached for my legal pad and pen and settled into a comfortable chair. My mind was swirling with the events of the past couple weeks.

Surely there was a story here that needed to be recorded. I had owned a Christian bookstore since 1973 and had been praying for seven years that God would release me from that responsibility for several reasons. I was looking for a buyer, not a shocking end to my bookstore. But one night, a fire that started next door destroyed my store.

As I sat under the trees on Washington Island, I began to experience a peace that only comes from God. Words began to pour from my heart, coming faster and faster as though I was taking dictation, and perhaps I was. As I penned the final words, my family arrived back at the campsite.

Today, I can trace the steps from writing those words to the publishing of my first book. What an amazing journey.

Lord of the journey, thank you for making a straight path for me to follow.

Be still, and know that I am God. Psalms 46:10 NIV
—Ethel Jensen Stenzel

August 18

While mother lay asleep, dying of cancer, I crept into her fourth bedroom. I thought, "I've got to start cleaning out this house. With all the stuff she's accumulated over the years, it'll take me months to sort it all out."

An only child, I had been her caregiver for the past three months. Daily journaling was the only writing I had been able to accomplish during that time.

I opened an antique cabinet and the aroma of musty-smelling newspapers assaulted my nostrils. As I prepared to shove the contents into a trash bag, I noticed that the papers dated back to World War II.

Halfway down the stack, I found a brown speckled, dog-eared journal held together with duct tape. Each yellowed page contained diary entries in the scrolly penmanship of the 1800s. Every line was dated with a short entry such as: Saturday, Aug. 5, 1889. Staked my claim in the Oklahoma Territory today.

This was my great-grandfather's diary, which he kept all of his adult life. His entries wove a tale of the struggles he and his family endured 118 years earlier, a story worthy of publication.

After mother died and we disposed of her house, I researched extensively and wrote that story into a historical novel called *The Late Sooner*.

Father God, keep us ever alert to the writing opportunities you place all around us.

The history of every country begins in the heart of a man or a woman. Willa Cather

—Sally Jadlow

231

August 19

After a year's work, my first full-length play was finished. As I delivered the scripts to the cast, I felt as if a child I had birthed was leaving for college. During the weeks I was barred from rehearsals, my mind conjured up all sorts of horrific outcomes. Sure, I believed the play was great, but as a Moroccan proverb says, "In a mother's eyes every beetle is a gazelle."

Would anyone else like it, the cast, the audience? What if it flopped? I was making myself sick with anxiety and self-doubt.

On opening night, wearing a chic, new dress, I greeted a full house of patrons with a confident smile but quaking knees. Seated down front, as the lights dimmed, my husband squeezed my hand and whispered in my ear, "A guy named Chuck Jones wrote about some great advice his uncle gave him. Once when he was in despair over an injustice a bureaucrat had done him, his uncle told him, 'Chuck, they can kill you, but they aren't allowed to eat you.'"

As the curtain rose, I settled back with a smile, ready to enjoy my play.

Today when I need courage to put a manuscript in the mail, those words help me keep it all in perspective.

Lord, thank you for the gift of writing. Help me to have confidence in that gift and the courage to face criticism.

Use what talents you possess; the woods would be silent if no birds sang except those that sang best. Henry Van Dyke

—Cathy Conger

August 20

I kept my novel hidden in the clothes closet when I was in the fourth grade. I loved to write, but I had to keep my precious document hidden because my brother laughed when I told him about it.

That was the beginning of my light-under-a-bushel feelings about my writing. I stuck to topics others found acceptable, rather than write what was meaningful for me. That approach took me all the way to a Ph.D. in sociology. I wrote more for others than myself. The topic closest to my heart—my faith in God—never got on paper.

When I entered my fifties midlife crisis, I felt compelled to use the writing skills I had accumulated to write about my own life. I was quite nervous. I had to tell myself this was not my fourth-grade novel. I need not fear laughter.

As I wrote journal entries and worked on a book idea, I felt invigorated. This was fun! Finally, I was writing from my head and my heart. I scoured the Internet for Christian writing opportunities. Then, on my fifty-sixth birthday, I received an acceptance notice for a short article in a Christian magazine. After I thanked God, the first person I contacted was my brother. He was thrilled.

Thank you, Lord, for the courage to overcome fear of disapproval and write about my faith in you.

Let your light shine before men, that they may see your good deeds and praise your Father in heaven. Matthew 5:16 NIV

—Sharon V. King

August 21

As I hiked alone along the muddy river, my body relaxed and my mind wandered along many topics before landing on my dream of being a novelist. I'd been kicking around plans for a young adult novel for over a year, but seemed to have a lot more good ideas than time to write them down. I get frustrated with the difficulty I have finding time to write in my busy life—kind of like finding time to pray.

Who am I kidding? I thought. Maybe I should just come out and say it. I will never write a novel.

I didn't know I was praying until I noticed I was desperately listening for an answer. Just then an old turtle on a log below caught my attention. We stood and watched each other, and I realized that the turtle is always there at the river, if only I take the time to come and slow down enough to look. Likewise, God's presence and inspiration are always waiting for me, when I remember to look to God instead of spinning around in my own head. The conversation I imagined with the turtle later became a devotional poem; sometimes, writing and praying are the same thing.

Lord, thank you for reminding me of the rewards to be found from spending time in your presence, at the river or at the page.

Take time to be holy; the world rushes on. William D. Longstaff

—Joy Salyers

August 22

I almost gave up on writing in 2005. It had been four long years since I had started this career/hobby that offered more rejection than hope. Maybe this industry was meant only for the young. They had the stamina.

One day I told my husband, "I'm done with writing!"

"Done? Didn't you just start?" he asked.

"You aren't a writer. You don't understand," I wailed. "This is painful."

"Pain builds character. Give it one more shot," he said. "Write one more thing. If you can't stand it after that, then take up knitting."

I moped for a day or so, then sat down and scrolled through a contest listing a friend had sent me. An online magazine offered a competition with a short word count and quick deadline. Hesitantly, I started typing.

Three weeks later, I received an e-mail: "Congratulations, you have been awarded first prize in our contest."

I shrieked. I had done it. I had achieved recognition for my writing, albeit small. I won a T-shirt and twenty-five dollars, but I felt like an Oscar nominee.

"Still want to quit?" my husband asked.

"No," I said. "I want to try harder. I know I can do this."

And I am.

Thank you, Lord, for making the impossible more than possible.

Many of life's failures are people who did not realize how close they were to success when they gave up. Thomas Edison

—Lissa Merriman

August 23

Several years ago, I lost my voice for a time. It wasn't laryngitis that afflicted me; it was self-doubt. I'm referring to my writing voice, of course.

I noticed that certain Christian authors sold lots of books. They'd take wonderful truths and present them in such a way as to bless many readers. What was I doing wrong? Would I bring more glory to God if I sounded more like them?

So I read the popular books, studying them not for their content but for the secret of their success. Then I'd try to copy the style of this author or approach a subject like that author, all the while watching my words sputter onto the page in fits and starts as from a rusty spigot.

One day I came across a Hasidic tale about a certain Rabbi Zusya who said, "In the coming world they will not ask me 'Why were you not Moses?' They will ask me 'Why were you not Zusya?'"

Was God posing a similar question, urging me to write with the unique voice he created and trust him with the outcome? So I study mechanics and vocabulary, yes. I read and research, of course. But perhaps my true task is to weave it all together in the only voice he ever asks of me: my own.

Lord, thank you for creating me to bring you pleasure and glory, just as I am.

Ask me whether what I have done is my life. William Stafford

—Sally Murtagh

August 24

In 1975, I wrote a song called "Shannon" that went on to find a place in the hearts of listeners around the world. As surprising as it sounds, the music and lyrics were created simultaneously in a matter of minutes with no subsequent revisions.

If only I had been clever enough to have written down the formula, I would not have had to endure the torture of being denied entry to that magic kingdom where the answer to every creative puzzle is instantly revealed. If only I had known the formula, countless dry spells could have been avoided. Merely great songs would've been replaced by the transcendent. I could've gone to the beach while there was still daylight. I might have become the flavor of the millennium as opposed to the flavor of the moment.

While it's true that as writers we have little or perhaps no control as to when, where, how, and if we reach that higher ground, it's also true that we cannot win if we do not play. As writers, it is for us to wake up every day, pick up our pens and instruments, and write our hearts out to the best of our abilities. Only after exposing our souls and deepest thoughts will we perhaps, find ourselves once again in this literary promised land.

Father, thank you for the times when writing comes easy and give me the strength to endure the times it doesn't.

A professional writer is an amateur who didn't quit.
Richard Bach

—Henry Gross

August 25

I know God chuckled when he listened in on the interview.

I looked over my questions and dialed the number the music artist's publicist had given my editor. I had never heard of this mainstream artist, but had gone home the day before and listened to the guy's latest CD.

When the artist picked up, I said my name and the magazine title before saying, "I'm going to record this if it's OK with you." He announced that he was on a tour bus and that I would have to speak loudly.

I attempted to, but the highway hum seemed to drown us both out. I crossed out yet another useless sentence as he murmured, "Well, you know, it's like...you know."

I asked another question. "How has your faith affected your music?"

The highway hum stopped. "Hold on," he answered. "I'm at a Subway ordering lunch."

I waited. Then came the more "meaty" answers.

"Well, my faith is like..." he began a few second later. "I think God is like...tomatoes, and yeah, my faith is like...lettuce... no hold the mayo."

The scheduled one-hour interview went twenty-four minutes before I heard him say, "I'm going to have to hang up now, but thanks for taping this. I hate it when reporters twist my words."

Lord, when I'm writing, help me laugh when things don't go the way I plan.

The Lord is my strength and my shield; my heart trusts in him, and I am helped. Psalms 28:7a NIV

—Kate E. Schmelzer

August 26

I recently signed up for a short story course at the local state university. Our first assignment was to write a "moment in time" piece that could stand alone, but from which one could deduce what happened before and conclude the possibilities afterward.

Perhaps because my husband is a cancer survivor, I wrote a story about love, marriage, cancer, and possible death. I asked an older professor to read my story, knowing his wife had died of cancer.

As I worked at my desk in the outer office, I heard him chuckling periodically and saying, "I know this is supposed to be fiction, but this is so you!"

I returned the laugh and replied, "That's right, it is."

It got quiet and I walked into his room, thinking he was still laughing. I asked what he thought. To my surprise he was crying.

"I'm sorry, I didn't mean to make you cry!" I walked over to him, not knowing exactly what else to say.

He sat there a moment, unable to speak.

When he spoke, he gave me the most sincere compliment I've ever received. "This is a beautiful and well-written love story. If you can make this old man cry, you've got it in you to help others get through trying times."

God-given talents are often hard to define. I am thankful through written words, I can help others laugh, and sometimes cry.

Thank you, Lord, for the gift of words.

Life is short, art long, opportunity fleeting, experience treacherous, judgment difficult. Hippocrates
—Alisa Dollar

August 27

"Ashlee is leaving the 27th," my daughter-in-law said.
"Oh, no! So soon?" I could barely speak.

I would have only a few days more with my precious granddaughter, who would leave home a carefree girl and return a mature young woman. I had attended ROTC drill meets and award ceremonies for three years while she was in high school. That summer when she made her eight-year commitment to the Navy it had been no surprise.

I am so thankful her grandpa and I had crammed the first eighteen years full of memories and photos: camping, boys, dances, swimming, family, and ROTC. While she is in boot camp, I will be retelling her story in a scrapbook journaling page by page. Writing while she is gone will be my therapy until I can again talk to her face to face.

Words on a page will be my only link. I will send newsy letters about the family and letters of encouragement to ease the waves of exhaustion and loneliness. Later, when she is in law enforcement training, I can send e-mail messages and eagerly wait for her response.

Father, I pray my letters will encourage and warm her heart and other seamen's hearts.

The Lord bless all that you write with his Spirit, in the life lessons you teach, and the people you touch. Rev. Jane Brown

—Sheryl Van Weelden

August 28

It was the writing class from anywhere but heaven.

The instructor encouraged us to lie to editors about our credentials. He showed us samples of his writing. He was published—he had a column in a local newspaper—but his writing wasn't very good. He talked more about his ex-wife, his children, and his current girlfriend than he did about writing. He spent whole class periods talking with one student while the rest of us sat there and eavesdropped.

Why did I continue going? I guess it was a combination of things: optimism—maybe he'd say something useful; stinginess—I had, after all, paid for this class and I was determined to get something out of it; and loneliness—it was my only opportunity to be out with people during the week.

Halfway through the course, he challenged us. The local newspaper would be putting out several special sections. Our assignment: write an article for one of those sections and submit it.

Fear and trepidation of being embarrassed in class for not submitting anything overcame my fear and trepidation of interviewing and submitting.

The editor accepted my article on kitchen design. She printed it. She paid me for it. I went on to sell numerous articles to that newspaper.

The worst writing class I have ever taken opened the door to the best writing opportunity I've ever had.

Lord, please give me the courage to go through the doors you open for me.

Duty is ours; events are God's. Samuel Rutherford
—Jean Fritz Stewart

August 29

Flying to the 1997 Writing Academy seminar in Colorado, my mind was racing. I had to give a talk about the Internet on Monday night, and I wasn't ready. My friend Kathy and I still had to practice our act for the talent show, and Nancy was hinting that she'd like some help with her clown skit.

When would we stuff the information folders for the seminar attendees? What if nobody met us at the airport? And what about the box of programs my husband had mailed fourth class to the ranch? Fourth class—what was he thinking? With UPS on strike, the postal service was jammed.

Eeek!—was that turbulence? What if we went down in a plane crash before we even got there? Flames streaking, sirens screaming, peanut packets flying.

Who would raise my four children? Who would stuff the folders?

I looked out the window. There in the clouds was the shadow of the plane, encircled by a perfect rainbow, a small reminder that God had it all under control. No what-if too big for him. No direction I could go—including straight down—to get to someplace he was not.

Things can get hectic for the planners before a writing seminar, but now I know that God holds us all in the rainbow circle of his care.

God, I'm resigning as CEO of the solar system. Here...you take the wheel.

Cast all your anxiety on him because he cares for you.
1 Peter 5:7 NIV

—Patty Kyrlach

August 30

I have been writing for years. I have attended conferences, had articles published, been given wonderful tips by well-known authors, and received cordial rejection letters. Discouraged by the number of proposals publishers reject every year, I often feel like hanging up my writing hat and giving up on that big book contract.

In early 2007, something happened that changed my motivation in writing. I had an article published, and although I have always written quite candidly, this article was full of raw emotion that topped them all. Soon after publication, I received countless responses from women all over the country telling me how the article touched their lives. Suddenly, I knew what God wanted me to do...to use my writing to glorify him and to help others through difficult times in their lives. It is not about earning money or about gaining fame.

Not long after, I discovered the world of self-publishing and realized that I no longer needed to wait on a publisher to share the words God has given me. My goal now is to continue to stay in the Word and to ask God put the words on paper for me. He will provide the audience when I seek his face first.

Lord, direct my path as your writer, leading me toward the light, so I may light the way for others.

Therefore, since through God's mercy we have this ministry, we do not lose heart. 2 Corinthians 4:1 NIV
—Sherri Wilson Johnson

August 31

New faces, new teachers, and friendships yet to be made encompass the fear of the first day of school. As a preschool teacher, each year my classroom is filled with parents experiencing these emotions while their children are ready to explore the unknown. It's usually the parents who need the written word to ease their unsettled hearts as they drop their children off for possibly the first time.

I have found written communication with parents is the most important tool I can use to touch their hearts and ease their worry. On the first day I send a welcome packet home to parents that often includes personal notes about their children.

> Bella took a while to warm up today after you left, but soon enough she jumped right in with the class and had a great day.
>
> Dylan missed you this morning, but he told me all about your special weekend. The picture he drew of you two made him happy. He can't wait for you to see it.

I've learned that the smallest note of encouragement goes a long way. Especially when mom and dad can't be there to see their child encounter the ups and downs of their first school experience.

Lord, help me to use writing as a way to communicate your peace to unsettled hearts and minds.

Encourage one another as long as it is called today. Hebrews 3:13 NIV

—Kimmy Howard

September 1

I sat in the back of my seventh-grade English class. This was the last place in the world I wanted to be. Summer vacation had come to an abrupt halt and the hot, stuffy classroom in our old brick school felt more like a juvenile detention center than a place to nourish my brain. The only thing worse was mom taking us to Sears for new school clothes and buying those stiff, formalde-hyde-smelling blue jeans and shirts.

It was tough for this twelve-year-old boy to concentrate on the newly imposed writing assignment. The paper lay blank on my old wooden desk. My number two pencil made a handy drumstick that attracted attention from Mrs. Barett, my teacher. She could sneak up behind me without making a sound. She would whisper in my ear, "Starting is half done." Throughout the school year she would remind me, "Starting is half done."

Those words have been powerful. So many times in my life, those words have made the difference between success and failure. I learned that I could do just about anything if I could just get started.

Now, forty years later, I rarely struggle with writer's block, or other tasks, as I quietly hear her say, "Starting is half done."

Lord, thank you for writing teachers who know just the right words to say and take the time to teach us.

Procrastination is the thief of time. Edward Young
—Lonni L. Docter

September 2

When the last of my four children started school, I decided to find a job. I applied to be a school librarian in the grade schools of our local community and was accepted.

My purpose for working was to expand my horizons, add to our income, and show the world there was more to me than a housewife and mother. However, multiple sclerosis, an unexpected incurable disease, left me hospitalized and I had to leave my job. All my plans fell by the wayside. Years passed, my children grew up, and my focus remained on my disease and myself.

Much later, due to relocation and a new expanded view of the world and life, my focus changed. I was still dealing with health issues, but I found I could inspire people because of the illness I lived with.

I began to write. Never did I imagine when I was carding and placing books on shelves of the school library that someday people would be checking out my books at my community library.

Thank you, God, for changing my plans in midstream.

They say that time changes things, but you actually have to change them yourself. Andy Warhol

—Betty King

September 3

I had to go and open my big mouth. At the first faculty meeting of the school year, I enthusiastically commented on the latest, greatest method for teaching writing I'd gleaned from a summer workshop. I was beginning my third year teaching language arts to eighth graders.

Eyes gleaming, my principal gazed upon me like a spider knowing he had trapped a fly. I would teach the new writing process and grade close to a hundred essays—every week! It was hard work, and many weekends I thought I would drown in those five-paragraph essays.

Although it took me years to see it, my big mouth resulted in more than paper cuts and red ink stains. I taught my students that good writing comes down to two things: know what you want to say, then learn to write it well.

Those principles help me crystallize what I want to communicate in my own writing. Whether I am writing a Bible study or writing in preparation for a speaking engagement, I always begin the same way: What do I want to say? Now write it well.

Thank you, Father, that amid the hard work in life you teach the teacher and inspire the writer.

Ease brings very little out of people. John Maxwell
                                        —Melanie J. Dorsey

September 4

As a child, I devoured books. I never dreamed of writing them. In high school, I was introduced to creative writing. Maybe I could be a writer.

My guidance counselor quickly squashed that dream with, "You'll never make a living at writing." She didn't know if I had talent, but she knew success in the writing world was hard. She steered me toward a business career.

For forty years I worked in accounting, and I forgot about my dream. I did write a few stories for my family. I also wrote articles for the businesses where I worked and for volunteer organizations.

Five years ago, my husband, Frank, saw an ad for a writers' conference and suggested I attend. Frank wanted me to write the story of an elderly friend. He thought it could be a made-for-TV movie. I would become a millionaire, and he could retire. Ha!

The conference inspired me to begin writing and make up for lost years. The unedited novel sits in a briefcase, but I continue to have other work published and accepted by magazines, newsletters, anthologies, and newspapers. I have also authored two devotional books and one novella.

My forty-five-year-old dream has become a reality.

Lord, help me faithfully use the talent that you have given me to write.

Never, never, never give up! Winston Churchill

—Jan Sady

September 5

Day one of the school year always meant writing an essay about our summer vacation, an assignment I thoroughly enjoyed. I loved describing the mountains, the lake, and swimming to a float anchored a little offshore. I wrote with ease about toasting marshmallows in the evening, snuggled with my sisters around a crackling campfire.

It is not so curious then, that my first publishing success as an adult was a similar piece. After vacationing in the Baltic on the Swedish island of Gotland, I wrote up my travels. Then, without much forethought, I sent my piece off to *Nordstjernan-Svea*, a New York-based weekly written largely in Swedish.

To my delight, the editor published it, and requested two more articles. One subscriber commented, "I loved the piece on Gotland because I don't read Swedish. If you would publish more articles like this, I could read more of the paper." What fun is that!

Today, I check the markets carefully before I submit my work; I seldom act on impulse. Yet, that one time I did, and success took me by surprise.

Lord, enrich me with youthful verve.

It is only by following your deepest instinct that you can lead a rich life, and if you let your fear of consequence prevent you from following your deepest instinct, then your life will be safe, expedient and thin. Katharine Butler Hathaway

—Helene Clare Kuoni

September 6

Milton was the dad next door when I grew up, but he was also like a favorite uncle. He was always giving out advice and hugs. Milton had been through an awful lot in his life—a debilitating World War II combat injury and a near-fatal heart attack. Despite it all, he could always make me smile with his wacky sense of humor and his special brand of charm.

We kept in touch even after I grew up and had children of my own. On his sixty-fourth birthday, Milton suffered a severe stroke and lost the ability to speak whole sentences. But he still found ways to communicate, and he could still always make me smile.

I was just starting to spread my writing wings then. I was shy about showing my words to others, but I really wanted people to know about Milton's courage. So I wrote a story about him, and a local newspaper printed it. Within a week, the editor forwarded a letter he had received from a reader. "They say we should bloom where we are planted," it read. "Surely Milton has. I pray my own roots will extend as firmly and gently. Thanks for the inspiration!"

With the receipt of that simple letter, I knew I had found my life's purpose.

Lord, let my words always tell your story.

We are all pencils in the hand of God. Mother Teresa
—Dianna Graveman

September 7

Creative writing assignments were the highlight of seventh grade. When I started writing, I believed everyone thought as I did. My classmates read aloud, disproving me. Articulating my thoughts felt as easy as breathing.

At college my freshman year, I passed English with high praise from my professor. I wrote every day. Second semester, a new female prof ruthlessly disparaged everything I turned in. Crushed, I stopped sharing my words.

Still, like a smitten lover, I chased words all over paper. In thank-you notes, letters, and greeting cards my words reached into people. Over coffee, Vera, my adopted mother, said, "You have such a way with words."

I laughed. Five years later, the compliment took root. In a leap of faith, I sent out five poems. The publisher selected one for publication. Since then, several stories have been accepted and published. Vera's timely words changed my life.

Lord, thank you for the people you send who bless us and encourage us by speaking truth over our lives.

Twenty years from now you will be more disappointed by the things you didn't do than by the ones you did. So throw off the bowlines...Explore. Dream. Discover. Mark Twain

—Jet Moore

September 8

Hello. My name is Carol and I am a binge reader. I admit it: I read everything I can get my hands on. Cereal boxes and Ajax labels. Vanity plates and microwave manuals. Periodicals, books, junk mail. I read because I'm hungry for words. I read because...I'm an addict.

Reading feeds me. It infuses me with a portable, potable wisdom and invites me to laughter, to insight, to passion.

Words—and the ideas they convey—entrance me. They summon me into placid ponds and deep seas. A tingling turn of phrase tickles my senses; a penetrating, profound sentence stabs my conscience; a passage of powerful prose forces me to pause in appreciation.

I actually taste the words, roll them around my tongue, and savor their flavor.

And, when I've read until I'm satiated—brimming, even overflowing—I feel my fingers twitch, my brain race. I burn and itch with the desire to write and create. To create my own pearls of wisdom. To mold a stunning phrase. To build a striking metaphor.

I admit it. I get my inspiration from other writers' words: Playing hide-and-seek in the classifieds, buried in a vintage autograph album, or peeking from a wall plaque.

I'm shameless. I'm a binge reader—a direct cause of binge writing.

Father, help me hone my own skills by appreciating the skills of others.

Originality is simply a pair of fresh eyes. Thomas Wentworth Higginson

—Carol McAdoo Rehmc

September 9

As a freshman at Suomi College in Michigan's Upper Peninsula (now Finlandia University), I accepted the position of class secretary with trepidation. My dad had held that same position more than thirty years earlier, and there were now faculty there who had been students with Dad.

One day, one of them asked me, "Are you going to be the same kind of secretary your father was?" My worst fears were being realized.

"I don't think so." I mumbled, feeling like an utter failure even before I'd taken my first set of minutes.

"So you won't be writing your minutes in poetry?" he continued. I managed a puny smile.

How could I not be as creative as Dad had been? I had to try. Yet when my attempts failed to turn mundane proceedings into verse scintillating enough to be read in public, I had to conclude that I was not destined to be a poet-secretary. Nor was I destined to live up to my father's reputation. This truth would require relearning many times over in the coming years. I had to learn to be me and to write like me.

Thank you, God, for the diversity of our gifts and for the unique contribution each of us makes in the creation of your kingdom.

Look for your own...do not write what someone else... could write as well as you. Care for nothing in yourself but what you feel exists nowhere else—and create, impatiently or patiently...the most irreplaceable of beings. Andre Gide

—Olga M. Williams

September 10

When my brother was in college on the G. I. Bill, he talked about his many writing assignments. I said, "Then I'm never going to college."

I hated junior high English compositions with topics like "My Summer Vacation" or "An Embarrassing Moment." We had to write during class, and I could never think of anything interesting.

One day in eighth grade, I groaned when Miss Bedford said, "Now you're going to write." The topic she scrawled on the board was "My Favorite Relative."

I grinned as I pantomimed snapping my fingers. I had something to write about! I had become an aunt in seventh grade when my brother's son was born. Now Howard was fifteen months old, and I thought he was the most delightful creature alive. Whenever he and his parents came to visit, it was my job to entertain Howard. I wrote my paper eagerly and happily.

Later that year the class was assigned to choose morals from Aesop's fables and create original stories. Again, I was inspired by something I knew. Pigeons inhabited the eaves of our house. My fictional pigeons made a decoy—a softball covered with mud and feathers—to drive a snake away to better hunting. He who laughs last, laughs best.

I loved writing when I wrote out of experience and imagination. And I grew up to become a writing teacher.

Thank you, Lord, for a life of writing.

Your passion is your power as a writer. Penelope Stokes

—Nancy E. James

September 11

As a priest in Arlington, Virginia, I'm invited occasionally to give congressional invocations. I had written a prayer themed "Welcome the Stranger" for the U. S. House of Representatives on September 11, 2001.

I was at the Capitol when news of the events at the World Trade Center in New York came. Then, fifteen minutes before I was to give the prayer, we heard the Pentagon had been hit. The billowing smoke was visible through the windows. (The plane had not yet gone down in Pennsylvania.)

The House chaplain and I decided that I should adjust my prayer. "Just keep it short," the speaker pro tem said. I wrote hurriedly, and at 9:52 a.m., I gave this prayer. It was the only action Congress took that day:

God of peace and life, send your spirit to heal our country: bring consolation to all injured in today's tragedy in New York and Washington. Protect us and help our leaders to lead us out of this moment of crisis to a new day of peace. Amen.

I repeated it twice to congressmen and senators before going home late in the afternoon. As a priest and as a writer, I hope my words provided some comfort that day.

Lord, fill me with words that will help people find healing and hope.

Few will have the greatness to bend history; but each of us can work to change a small portion of the events, and in the total of all these acts will be written the history of this generation. Robert Kennedy

—Rev. Gerard Creedon

September 12

After overdosing on television news coverage of the 9/11 terrorist attacks, I felt weepy, outraged, and helpless. The shock of the attacks, the replayed pictures of the New York towers crumbling and people jumping to their deaths onto the pavement below, some holding hands, were like a vision of hell. As an American, I was filled with hatred against the attackers, the same kind of hatred that must have motivated the suicide bombers.

After attending a candlelight interfaith memorial service, I was determined to put my feelings down on paper. What I wrote in the heat of those attacks was an overblown, patriotic reflection filled with waving American flags, phrases such as "land of the free," and righteous anger.

I sent my essay to a wise relative in his nineties. "What about the men who piloted the planes?" he asked. "Do you have any compassion for them and their families?"

Ashamed, I went back to my 9/11 reflection and completely revised it to add what was missing: love. I sent the new version to my wise relative, with an effusive thank-you note.

Thank you, God, for mentors who help us see when our own words have led us astray.

Where there is hatred, let me sow love. St. Francis of Assisi

—Peggy Eastman

September 13

As managing editor for *The Lutheran* magazine, I've received letters about articles I've written. Several years ago, one took me off guard. The writer, a single clergyman preparing to retire soon, asked if I would meet him. I live in Chicago and he lived somewhere in Pennsylvania. Not a showstopper, I guess, but I was in my late forties and not thinking of retired men.

He had read "Parish: Taskmaster and Mistress," my article on clergy divorce. A sidebar introductory piece I wrote explained that I was divorced from a clergyman and knew something of the demands clergy families face. I wrote that sidebar so readers would know that the article, while as objective as I could make it, came from someone who had experienced the phenomenon as well. I hardly intended it as a personal ad.

This is one of the realities we writers need to keep in mind. I've learned that as I open my life to readers, I sometimes get unexpected consequences. I may receive attack mail (I've had that happen), or I may be thanked profusely because I've helped or inspired someone who is experiencing what I have. Of course, that always makes the work of writing worthwhile.

Thank you, God, that sometimes my experiences can be used to help others.

A writer needs three things, experience, observation, and imagination, any two of which, at times any one of which, can supply the lack of the others. William Faulkner

—Sonia C. Solomonson

September 14

I saw myself as a storyteller, never as a writer. Making family and friends laugh or cry at carefully selected words was a delight. I used gestures, sound effects, and timing to take my listener to the end of the tale, but never dreamed of putting these stories on paper.

I penned a few poems because my heart would burst if I bottled up the pain. Still, I didn't see myself as a writer, just a melancholy person with intense feelings.

At prayer and share time at church, a friend insisted I write down the revelations God spoke to me through his word. I resisted. I informed her I was a storyteller, not a writer, and found a verse in the Bible for justification. She insisted.

So, I reluctantly joined a writing team at church. Until then, I had no writer friends. I don't know what I would do without them now. They inspire me to write, edit my work, and encourage me to record stories from life experiences. I am glad my friend insisted, or I may have missed out on these wonderful, creative people.

Lord, thank you for writers.

Whether you think you can or think you can't, you're right. Henry Ford

—Pamela Humphreys

September 15

I spent most of my teen years with pen in hand filling spiral notebooks with puppy love poetry. As I'd pour my heart out on paper I'd tell myself, Maybe I can write.

In my senior year of high school, my English teacher congratulated me on an assignment well written and encouraged me to hone my creative writing skills. Maybe I can write, I told myself.

When I married my husband, Bill, all those notebooks chronicling my teen-age love and angst were stacked at the curb. Being older and more mature and with the love of my life by my side I no longer felt compelled to keep them.

I was surprised to find that after my daughters were born, my passion to write was reborn. To this day I regret throwing away that treasure trove of teen thoughts, but it has taught me to always save my work.

The love of words that God placed in my heart so many years ago resurfaced as I wrote about my husband and children. Little did I know when I started recording the stirrings of my soul that I'd share them in a public way.

Ten years and hundreds of published columns later, I'm sharing the memories of my middle-aged soul. I tell myself that thanks to God's leading, I now know I can write.

Thank you, Lord, for filling my soul with inspiration and for blessing me with a loving family that continually gives me reason to write.

You have to expect things of yourself before you can do them. Michael Jordan

—Kathy Whirity

September 16

My first-grade teacher, Miss Glass, is an amazing woman. She plays the piano without looking at her hands, and she knows all her numbers up to a hundred at least.

But this morning, she amazes me even more when she tells the class, "Today I want you to write a story." Write a story? I have barely learned to make my crooked little letters, and here is this madwoman telling me to write a story.

Still, I pick up my thick black pencil and begin writing on the lined paper. It's kind of scary, putting down words without knowing what happens next. It's like swinging upside down on the bicycle rack—you might get dizzy and forget how to breathe.

To my surprise, a story begins to form on the page, a heart-rending tale about a girl who comes down to breakfast and finds that her father is missing.

"Where is Father?" asks the girl.

"Father has gone far, far away," says Mother.

I pause to read what I have written. "Far, far away..." What drama! What melancholy!

Other children are sighing and fidgeting and making crumbs with their erasers, but I am having the time of my short life. I have just discovered creative writing.

Lord, we grown-ups overcomplicate the creative process. Let us rediscover the joy of smearing words like finger paints on paper, just for fun.

Only the most mature of us are able to be childlike.
Madeleine L'Engle

—Patty Kyrlach

September 17

After years of raising my grandchildren, the eldest was moving out on her own, leaving a vacant room.

"Maybe we should make it a guest room for friends and family visits," I suggested as the conversation swirled and eddied inside the family room.

"I think it should be a game room and, you know, with the X Box and Game Cube and stuff!"

"No, no, an exercise room and I can move my weight set in from the garage!"

"A guest room for..." My words evaporated into air instantly as our grandson yelled, "No, wait! It should be a special place for Sparky!" our beloved minidachshund.

As the laughter and joking abated, my usually quiet husband said, "I think we should dedicate the space for Grandma to begin writing again." Agreement was joyfully unanimous.

Before the grandkids came, I had regularly written and published and spoken at seminars and retreats. My priorities changed the day our three priceless grandchildren, then nine, seven, and four, arrived. Now, ten years later, I had been saying I'd like to get back to writing. Suddenly I had a place and a space and the commitment and affirmation from my family.

The walls are still neon pink and green, but I'm writing again and using the gifts of the room.

God, thank you for this room and for the family who gifted it to me.

Creativeness in the world is, as it were, the eighth day of creation. Nicolas Berdyaev

—Char Forslund

September 18

Journaling was a daily assignment for students in my fifth-grade class. One aspiring author, Debbie, decided to write a book in the ten minutes a day allowed for journaling. Impossible, I thought.

"September 18: 'Once upon a time, long ago in a place far from here where nothing ever lived was a boy and a girl. The boy's name was Tommy and the girl's name was Wendy.'"

"September 19: 'And of course there was nothing but plants, rocks and trees.'"

"September 20: 'You are probably wondering why they are living there and most of all how they could live in such hot dry weather. Well, one spring ...'"

"September 21: '... afternoon...'"

Month after month, Debbie wove a fascinating story. In December, she came to me in tears.

"What's wrong?" I asked.

"My journal is full and I haven't written the ending of my story!" We went to the supply room for another notebook.

On February 23, I greeted completion of Debbie's book with mixed emotions. No worries. On February 24, Debbie started a sequel. Both books incorporated all the elements of good writing: descriptive narrative, conflict, adventure, pathos, drama, comedy. In ten minutes a day.

Lord, thank you for children who teach us not only to dream but also to get to work.

Under his direction the whole body is fitted together perfectly and each part in its own special way helps the other parts so that the whole body is healthy and growing and full of love. Ephesians 4:15 TLB

—Tommie Lenox

September 19

I had hoped to get a jump on this day to get some writing accomplished, but the alarm hadn't gone off. In the kitchen, one full pitcher of orange juice covered the floor. The bus driver, eager to get the kids to school ten minutes early, was outside honking. And we were only thirty minutes into our day!

"What's the matter, Sweetie?" my husband said with a quiet chuckle. He patted my backside as if to encourage. The pat felt more like the prod they give cattle going through the chute.

"If this is just the start of the day, can I please go back to bed? Better yet, can I just disappear and start writing?" I sighed.

With one child on the bus, I turned and faced three little ones.

"Read a story?" my younger son asked.

"Eat breakfast," stated my daughter.

My older son stared at me with a blank look. He felt like I did about mornings.

When things get tough, I find myself thinking that maybe my book won't get finished until they're all in school. But in the meantime, this morning will make a good story. It's a great way to refocus when things are falling apart.

Lord, help me take the moments I'd rather forget and turn them into stories worth writing.

I love those who can smile in trouble, who can gather strength from distress, and grow brave by reflection. Thomas Paine

—Jami Kirkbride

September 20

I recently visited Mrs. Holloman, my seventh- and ninth-grade English teacher. Grammar was not my strong point. As far as I was concerned, a final draft was the rough draft without the smudge marks. A dangling participle was something used to entice readers. She was surprised to find out that I am now a writer. My success is due to a new attitude toward writing.

I want to write. Writing is no longer an assignment; it's an opportunity to help, to educate, or to entertain others.

I've learned that I need to keep working on an article until I get it right. My final draft now is more than a neat rough draft. I've learned over the years that the secret to writing is rewriting. The constant rearranging of sentences and reworking paragraphs are all part of the process.

Still, there isn't any magical formula to writing. All I can do is my best, and let God take care of the rest.

Lord, give me the strength to work on my writing until I get it right.

Fall down seven times, get up eight. Japanese proverb

—Danny Woodall

September 21

As a busy nurse, wife, mother, and writer I have to work at making time for writing. When I procrastinated growing up, my mother would tell me, "Where there is a will, there is a way." I would will myself to least start a project, which made it easier to complete.

With snippets of time to write and facing a deadline, my idea notebook serves as inspiration to overcome writer's block. I never know where or when an inspiration will come, so I use a recorder while commuting. These ideas form the basis for characters, descriptive senses, or experiences that can be incorporated into my writing. Lunch breaks are spent writing, giving me time to rewrite the sticky notes and add creative thoughts.

Once as I strolled down St. George Street in Old St. Augustine, Florida, I stopped to watch two street musicians. One had his guitar case open for donations. Entertainers from establishments located on this strip frowned on this. Dressed in black from head to toe, a tall, lean, stern-faced man deliberately walked in front of the gathering close to the performers and kicked the guitar case lid closed; his menacing look told it was not an accident. I jotted these experiences on a note so that later I could form a character for a book.

Lord, help me to be determined to accomplish what is before me.

Never be lazy, but work hard and serve the Lord enthusiastically. Romans 12:11 NKJV

—Trudie Clem

September 22

"Speak? I have to speak?"

"Yes. Once your book is published, you have to market it," the workshop leader informed me.

"No," I argued. "The publisher will handle the publicity while I work on volume two."

"No, he won't," she insisted, "because you're not famous. Speaking to audiences to promote your book is a big part of the writing life."

My stomach went into knots. I had dropped my college course on public speaking because I was terrified of talking in front of people. What would I do? I quickly breathed that one-word prayer, "Help!"

A friend gave me a textbook on public speaking that introduced me to Toastmasters. "Become the speaker you want to be," the Web site read. I joined.

Initially, I spoke with fear and trepidation, with eyes glued to my notes. Gradually, I learned to speak with confidence and conviction. God gave me the poise I needed.

Now, I regularly speak at organizations, workshops, and women's groups and have been endorsed as an inspiring motivational speaker, combining enthusiasm with the ability to touch my audience with warmth and compassion.

Speak? I have to speak? Yes. And I do.

Thank you Lord, for giving me the strength to do what you called me to do.

Open your mouth wide, and I will fill it. Psalms 81:10 NKJV

—Ginnie Mesibov

September 23

"You're wanted in the superintendent's office." What a way to start the day. When I hurried through the door they greeted me—both the principal and the superintendent. I was a forty-seven-year-old secondary English teacher who was told she would be teaching physical education the following school year. How could I know the changes this would bring for me? However, I started walking for exercise.

I taught P.E. for four years. I walked for twenty. And when I returned from my morning walk, I wrote meditations. Sometimes I shared them with friends, but mostly they were my own devotion time.

In my retirement years, my daughter literally pushed me to a writers' conference in Florida, and God's plan came full circle. A wonderful editor read those simple morning writings and suggested I write a book proposal. Only God had known twenty years before that these experiences were preparation for the book of devotions that would be published when I was sixty-seven.

And now I am writing my second book, a newspaper column, and articles for Standard Publishing. If your dream is to write for God, never think that he can't use you. Perhaps it just isn't time yet.

Lord, help me to keep writing; keep waiting; keep trusting you.

Everything comes gradually and at its appointed hour. Ovid

—Clella Camp

September 24

Finally, the day came when my yearlong secret could be told. I made 9:00 a.m. reservations for a popular San Diego restaurant on a Saturday when the entire family could be present. After taking the hundred-mile drive, my wife and I arrived at the crowded establishment a few minutes early. I knew everything would be perfect.

I sported a huge grin. The curious owner asked, "May I ask why you are so happy?" When I told him of my special plans, he enthusiastically did everything he could to accommodate us.

Finally, everyone arrived. The owner seated us himself. After saying grace, we ordered from the enormous menu.

Before the food arrived, I addressed my mother: "I kept this a secret for a year. I have something to read to you."

I pulled out a book, *Letters to My Mother: Tributes to the Women Who Give Us Life—and Love*. I read her the title of my story, "Thank God for the Sandwiches."

With great emotion, I read my letter thanking my mother for struggling to raise young children alone, the example she set, and the sandwiches we lived on...and I'd complained about.

What a moment!

God, thank you for those sandwiches, the hardships you allowed me to endure, and allowing me the opportunity to pay tribute to my mother in print.

A mother is a person who, seeing there are only four pieces of pie for five people, promptly announces she never did care for pie. Tenneva Jordan

—Lawrence D. Elliott

September 25

A lion escaped from the Oklahoma City zoo one day. I wondered how that taste of freedom felt when she was caught and returned to captivity. I named her Leonessa.

That sparked a story I needed to write for a high school English class. The teacher gave me an A. A year later I needed a story for a college English class, so I submitted the same story.

"Did you really write this?" the professor asked. Got another A after I convinced him that I had. A flickering candle was lit in my mind that day.

I majored in elementary education, minored in journalism, and worked on the college newspaper. Taught kindergarten and believed strongly in teaching children to love books and libraries.

The candle flickered brighter when in retirement, at age sixty-eight, I returned to the university and took fifteen hours of writing classes.

Leonessa crept back into my imagination and I began writing children's stories as well as devotionals about people from whom I've learned spiritual lessons through the years.

Loving God, thank you for lighting the flame of the written word in my heart. I pray what I write will honor your name.

Imagination is more important than knowledge. For knowledge is limited, whereas imagination embraces the entire world, stimulating progress, giving birth to evolution. Albert Einstein

—Donna McCormick

September 26

While I was in the midst of a serious writer's block, I had a casual conversation with my friend Maurice. When Maurice was a child in a remote village in Rwanda, a missionary priest was handing out candy. Hearing about this, Maurice ran as fast as his five-year-old legs could take him, only to discover that he was too late. The priest offered him the empty box, saying, "You take this box and one day you will be rich!"

Over the years, Maurice saved money in his cardboard container to travel halfway around the world to attend college in Pennsylvania.

After telling his story, Maurice looked at me and, with a beaming smile, said, "Today I am rich!" With his permission, I wrote a story of hope titled, "The Empty Candy Box."

Writing that story taught me that being a good listener can be my most valuable writing tool. If I can hear with vision and creativity, stories will unfold, bringing to life an experience or string of events worthy of telling, retelling, and publication.

Lord, allow me to listen with an ear that will expose your magnificent hope, promises and grace to others.

The greatest compliment that was ever paid me was when one asked me what I thought, and attended to my answer. Henry David Thoreau

—Marcia A. Russotto

September 27

The Flathead Lutheran Bible Camp pastors are responsible for telling campfire stories. I dreaded that task. For years, I told a memorized story from a campfire book. It always fell flat. The campers talked while I spoke. A passing motorboat could distract them. A rock, thrown into the lake, produced giggles. I just couldn't hold their attention.

Then one summer, I discovered a solution. I wrote my own story. The setting was the little town where I had grown up. The central character was Uncle Emil, a man who couldn't hear or speak. The minor characters were two young boys. The story ended with Uncle Emil saving one of the boys from drowning at the cost of his own life.

There was silence around the campfire as the story unfolded. Even when a passing motorboat interrupted the story, they clamored for more. "What happened next?" a young camper asked. He and the others seemed spellbound.

Afterward, campers and counselors surrounded me to ask about Uncle Emil. They wanted to know if I was one of the boys in the story.

I learned that night the truth of the writing adage—write about what you know best.

Lord God, help us to tell the truth from our own experience.

If you don't have the power to change yourself, then nothing will change around you. Anwar Sadat

—Gerald Ebelt

September 28

"Sorry Betsy, but extreme circumstances call for extreme measures. You can't come back to critique group until you bring proof of submitting an article to a magazine." The group leader's smile was laced with steel. She said it was for my own good.

True, I had been writing for several years and hadn't submitted a single word, but so what? I had pored over how-to-write books and listened to how-to-write CDs until I was so overwhelmed by the don'ts, I couldn't remember the dos.

I spent hours polishing a funny turn of phrase. Any sentence that made me laugh was my signal that I could move on to the next one. Trouble was, I ended up reading and chortling at the same places, in the same stories, for months. Like the mother of a precocious child, my own creations never ceased to amuse and entertain me. Subject my darlings to rejection? I don't think so!

But I really wanted to stay in critique group, so I submitted five articles. And to my astonishment, three of them sold.

I still fight the fear that I'll always be a novice. But I'm learning to trust my peers. And when I'm feeling least talented, to send something out anyhow.

Because you never know.

Oh Lord, help me remember you don't require perfection, just reality.

Be who you are and say what you feel because those who mind don't matter and those who matter don't mind. Theodor Seuss Geisel

—Betsy Dill

September 29

I stepped into the publisher's office one morning to discuss an idea for a feature story. Ever since I'd been hired at the newspaper six months earlier, I'd been trying to convince him to let me write a devotional column for the religion page. I'd had a vision of such a column three years earlier when I was just getting back into writing after twenty years.

His answer was always an adamant "No! I want you to focus on feature stories."

But this day, he had the newspaper spread out on his desk and was complaining about wasted space. I saw my chance.

"Wasted spaced? I'll show you wasted space!" I flipped to the religion page and tapped the canned devotional they downloaded free from the Internet. "Let me write something fresh."

"I won't pay for it," he spat back.

"That's fine," I said.

That was ten years ago. The column has since birthed two books, a daily radio program, and three CDs. Today it appears in a newspaper, with three times the circulation, that pays well for what the managing editor said is one of the paper's most popular columns.

I learned that when I have a vision for my writing that it's up to me not to let it fade. Instead, I pray and then, with all the gusto born of purpose, I pursue it.

Give me the wisdom, Lord, to recognize your call and the courage to pursue it.

The one who calls you is faithful, and he will do it. Thessalonians 5:24 NIV

—Michele T. Huey

September 30

It was a bad day to be a writer. I had argued with an editor over rewrites. Her way felt awkward, stilted, and just plain wrong. But my original words were wrong too. Sitting in front of the computer I tried to pry loose the words that would convey my story and please my editor. I was not successful. Finally, in frustration, I quit.

My thoughts, however, would not quit. In desperation I grabbed my MP3 player, whistled for the dog, and set off for a brisk walk. When I returned home, ordinary tasks needed my attention; the writing would have to wait.

The next morning, I sat at the computer with new resolve. I took several steps back and began anew from a point in the story that worked well. The words were hard to choose. I did a lot of deleting and rewording, but this time, I knew it was right. My work rang true.

Some days writing is like that—chipping away at the raw rock trying to free the sculpture you envision inside. Progress is slow, painful, and frustrating. But the result, when it is complete, is a true vision of beauty.

Lord, help me to be tenacious and patient today. Help me find the right words to complete this work and be true to the vision.

I saw the angel in the marble and carved until I set him free. Michelangelo

—Beth Granger

October 1

A first book signing. It's a day an author dreams of, anticipates, and then one day savors with joy. Now, that day was approaching for me.

I would be one of the authors at a local book signing night. The manager was working on possible dates. June passed and July. Finally, the date was announced: October 1.

I joyously shared the information with everyone, including my older brother, who also was a writer. But his aspirations were slowing down. He had had a stroke and, now blind, his life changed dramatically. He and his sons had moved into my home.

Even with his disability, my brother cheered me on as the big day drew near. But during the last week of September, we found my brother lying on the floor. He never made it through the day.

October 1st was his funeral.

Up until 6 that evening, I wasn't sure about attending the book signing.

At 7:01, I was the last author to arrive.

How did I make it?

My brother would have wanted me to be there.

Father, my time is in your hands. I trust that my life is happening in a purposeful way for your will to be done—on earth as it is in heaven.

For this God is our God for ever and ever: he will be our guide even unto death. Psalms 48:14 KJV
—Audrey Marie Hessler

October 2

In the early '80s, after many, many rewrites, I wrote a story that was published in a literary journal. Using that and other publishing credits, I applied and received a much-needed respite from my husband and four children—a writer's retreat.

Unfortunately, the retreat—a cabin on a lonely dirt road, surrounded by pines and hardwoods—brought back unwelcome memories. That first night, my stomach lurched when the sun disappeared behind the horizon. Dusk turned to a night so black I couldn't even see my hands in front of my face.

The night dragged on, and I typed halfheartedly on a manuscript I'd brought. Soon, I put it aside. The long-ago fear gnawed at me.

The next day, I flung open the door, allowing the October sun to flood the cabin. After breakfast, I poured coffee and, warming my hands on the mug, meandered down a path to the woods. At the bottom of a hill, near a stream, I sat on a moss-covered rock and soaked in the peace that surrounded me. While the stream churned over rocks, my stomach no longer churned. I was in God's hands, and so was the work he'd prepared for me.

That morning, I pounded out my first personal experience story.

Lord, thank you for your perfect peace that heals all wounds.

A perfect faith would lift us absolutely above fear.
George MacDonald

—Nanette Thorsen-Snipes

October 3

Work. Kids. Home. Church. Husband.

Too busy. Too stressed. Drowning in responsibility.

I needed a break.

I packed quickly—efficiently, even—for the Green Lake Writers' Conference. Clothes. Shoes. Bible. Notebook. Hairbrush. Toothbrush. Even my cell phone charger.

I checked in and slid into a seat halfway through the introductions.

Breathe. Relax.

Yes, this would be a good week.

As I crawled into bed that first night, I remembered what I forgot to pack: Clean bras. They still were hanging up to dry in the laundry room.

Stress, overwork, and worry sweep over me. They swallow me in a flood that threatens to destroy me. They accuse me of failure to be all I think I should be.

The forgotten bras made me laugh at myself. They also made me realize I had waited too long to cry out to God, to quiet my soul long enough to see his hand reaching down to pull me from the flood.

I went to Green Lake not only for writing instruction, but also for spiritual renewal and time to reconnect with my husband who arrived two days later for a pastors' conference. I left Green Lake with a new sense of identity as a writer eager to apply journalism skills to inspirational writing.

There's always too much to do, Lord. Thank you for reminding me to de-stress.

Save me, O God, for the waters have come up to my neck. Psalms 69:1 NRSV

—Sandy Block

October 4

In the mid '80s, I developed an insatiable appetite to write. In 1994, my birthday gift came wrapped in a bittersweet package: an all-expense-paid trip to a writers' conference. Was I excited? Absolutely! But I was jittery too. Calling myself a writer was an aspiring dream, not reality.

The adrenaline rush and anxiety intertwined over the four days. Meal times were drudgery. "What do you write, Claudia?" The puzzled stares on the faces of those sitting around the table were evidence I was struggling. I thought fiction was true and nonfiction was false. Words like query, SASE, genre, niche, and marketing were foreign to me.

Still, that conference taught me much. One speaker's words pierced my heart: "If God has called you to write for him, he will see to it that you get published." Taking her advice, I wrote out of obedience and ceased my focus on publication. Thus began the cycle of writing, rewriting, revising, submitting, and resubmitting my work to publishers.

After countless rejections and two years, I received my first acceptance letter and a fifteen-dollar check for a devotional. Now I teach, encourage, and mentor writers at that same conference. I love it!

Father, thank you for giving me the gift of writing to glorify you and serve others.

You must do the thing you think you cannot do. Eleanor Roosevelt
—Claudia N. Tynes

October 5

A cartoon took on fresh meaning when a friend and I attended a writers' conference together. The drawing pictured two women, arms linked and each leaning on a cane. The cut line read, "You help me, and I'll help you."

At the time, I was recovering from eye surgery and couldn't read anything below 36-point bold type. My friend was getting over laryngitis and could barely speak above a whisper. None of this would have mattered, except we had appointments with a couple of editors to pitch a book idea.

So, we followed the lead of the two cartoon ladies. My friend printed our blurb in large bold type, guided us to our interviews, and sat where she could whisper corrections over my shoulder. I gave the pitch and answered questions. To our delight, both editors said to contact them when the book was ready.

Although we'd already worked together, we knew we hadn't gotten this far by ourselves. We'd undergirded our idea with prayer. We wrote and rewrote, and then trusted God to lead us to the right editors.

Depending on each other for physical assistance strengthened our trust in God and in each other as well as our commitment to an exciting journey that just might lead to a book contract.

Lord, thank you for writing colleagues who encourage and help us.

Commit your way to the Lord, trust also in him, and he shall bring it to pass. Psalms 37:5 NKJV

—Carolyn Meagher

October 6

When I was fourteen, I wrote a poem about asking God things happen that we can't comprehend. The verse that inspired me was Proverbs 20:24. I can still remember the day I wrote that poem. I finished it, put it away, and continued on with my life.

Two years later, my grandmother was diagnosed with breast cancer. I couldn't understand why something so horrible was happening. I took out my poem and read it. Then I wrote her a letter and included my poem. A year later, she passed away and my poem was read at her funeral. At the time, I didn't fully understand why I'd written that poem. Twenty years later, I know God had a plan and purpose for my words.

Although my poem remains unpublished, it touched my grandmother in a profound way. After she was gone, I found out she'd shared it with many friends and most of our family. That's when I knew God had blessed me with a gift for writing.

If nothing else I write touches another person, I am blessed to have touched one.

Thank you, Lord, for blessing me with the ability to touch lives with my words.

A man's steps are directed by the Lord. How then can anyone understand his own way? Proverbs 20:24 NIV
—Theresa Carouthers

October 7

"It's your move." My son grinned at me across the checkerboard.

I studied the board, certain his smile meant losing more checkers. What if I refused to take my turn? No, I couldn't let fear stop me. I made my move.

I had similar thoughts when invited to join a critique group—fear, risk, and hesitation. I found reasons not to participate: no time, a long drive, I had nothing to offer.

Finally, I bolstered my courage and attended one meeting. The session was long, the people were strangers, and I felt uncomfortable. Driving home, I told God I wasn't going back.

Just a minute, he seemed to caution. Don't be hasty. What if this is something good?

Once home, I e-mailed my niece, a writer, to express my apprehension.

Her reply was: "Aunt Lydia, if you cook something your family doesn't like, you don't quit cooking, do you? It's the same with critique groups. Don't give up. Try again."

I didn't like her advice. It would be easier to quit. Or would it? Reluctantly, I kept attending. The group offered help, strangers became friends, and my writing improved.

Ten years and hundreds of bylines later, I'm glad I stayed. I probably wouldn't have anything published without the help of fellow writers.

Thank you, Lord, for blessing me through other writers.

With courage you can stay with something long enough to succeed at it. Earl Nightingale

—Lydia E. Harris

October 8

On September 11, 1971, I gave birth to a beautiful baby girl. It was the first time I can recall bonding with someone. On October 8, 1971, she smiled at me and closed her eyes. She'd said, "Bye Mama, it's time for me to go to heaven."

Seventeen years later, I committed to telling the story of my memory loss. I didn't think her death was part of the story. I was wrong.

There were no words to describe the grief that consumed me whenever I thought about her. She insisted on being included in my story. Finally, I took a blank piece of paper and wrote her name on it. Joyce Lynn. From the last letter swirls, curls, and curves appeared. Sometimes an angle or line would form. Tears stained the paper as they mingled with ink. Months later, the words came.

I learned that characters, no matter what genre, demand to be heard. The people in my stories have a mind of their own. They entertain readers. I live through my characters' agony, and write about what can be. I experience ecstasy as I witness hurting readers step toward wholeness. Now, I can write to others who experience sorrow.

Lord, thank you for the healing power in writing.

It's about the audience and their energy and their story being told through you. Barack Obama

—Julia F. Bell

282

October 9

In 1968, my husband left our family to live with another woman. He never came back. We had three children, ages two, nine, and twelve, and we lived in a poor urban neighborhood where he'd been in charge of an inner-city ministry. We'd been deeply involved in the civil rights movement, an antipoverty program, and building bridges between people from all backgrounds.

When my husband left, our family was heartbroken. Our community was shocked. To add to our trauma, Martin Luther King was murdered a month later. Bewildered and frightened, I held on to my faith in prayer for dear life.

I scrambled to find substantial work to support the kids. Previously, I'd worked part time writing and editing articles for local newspapers. So, by turning to want ads and networking, I soon found opportunities for freelance jobs, one writing articles for a new Bible encyclopedia, another assisting a professional writer in compiling research. Although these jobs paid little, they tided me over until I was able to find an adequate full-time job near my home.

Over the next twenty-five years, my writing experience proved to be a valuable asset in whatever jobs I held, including twenty years working for the U.S. Congress. Now retired, I'm writing more than ever.

Lord, thank you for opening writing doors in times of trials and loss.

It is difficulties that show what men are. Epictetus
—Marilyn Marsh Noll

October 10

In my first year of teaching we had weekly spelling bees. I didn't think how students felt when they had to sit down quickly after misspelling a word. At that time, we had not learned about dyslexia, a condition in which students reverse and replace letters.

One of my junior high students wrote a two-line poem:

> Life is hard
> When you're tard.

I remember laughing and printing the poem in black marker on a piece of poster board. I shared it with department members who agreed that teaching is hard when you're tard. What I didn't realize was that misspelling words like tired as tard was embarrassing to students who sincerely tried to please the teacher.

On an in-service day, Ron, our special needs teacher, had each of us bring a mirror to the session. We had to look in the mirror and try to write. Our brain said to our hand, "Write normally," but the hand would not move in the right direction. Ron said, "In your frustration, you are experiencing what students with a learning disability have to deal with every day."

For the rest of the year, I reminded myself that school life is hard when students grow tired and frustrated as they try to learn to write and spell.

Dear Lord, help us to be patient with those to whom writing does not come so readily.

If you become a teacher, by your pupils you'll be taught. From *The King and I*

—Shirley Stevens

October 11

I was intimidated by my first writers' conferences. Everyone seemed so sure of themselves. The best thing that happened to me was taking a workshop in light verse from the well-known children's book poet Jean Conder Soule, whose titles included *Never Tease a Weasel*. We knew from the get-go it was going to be a fun time. And so it was.

After our first session, people remarked, "We heard you laughing all the way down the hall."

Jean taught us not only the form of light verse with its tight rhyme and meter, but to let to go and enjoy creating and sharing. I was very pleased with the response to my final class offering:

Our final verse class
I hoped to at last
come up with a poem quite witty.
To fill my blank sheet
with symbols concrete,
a metered and well rhyming ditty.
But my weary brain
from five days of strain
rebelled at mere thoughts
of more work.
I could only sit
with my burned out wit—
it sure made me feel like a jerk.

Thank you, Lord, for teaching us not to take ourselves or our writing so seriously.

To everything there is a season, a time to weep and a time to laugh. Ecclesiastes 3:4 RSV

—Mary A. Koepke

October 12

I loved to read mystery books in grade school. I read the Hardy Boys, The Happy Hollisters, and Nancy Drew. Still, the book reports my fifth-grade teacher, Mrs. Rutt, wanted were so hard for me to do. It wasn't that I didn't understand the assignment or know-how; rather, I just didn't want to stop reading long enough to write a report. Reading was fun. Writing was work.

Years later, writing was a tool I needed to gather information, write contracts, and survive in business. It became my best friend when my spouse filed for divorce. I had so many emotions inside me, with nowhere to put them. So, I started to write about the pain inside me. The more I wrote, the less anger I had. It was like the feelings would flow down my arm, through my fingers, then out my pen. As time passed, I would read what I had written. If I cried, I knew I was still working through that event. If not, I knew I had worked through it.

Now, I write because I have to. Writing is a tried and true friend.

Lord, thank you for so many different ways to express myself.

Keep writing. Keep doing it and doing it. Even in the moments when it's so hurtful to think about writing. Heather Armstrong

—Lonni L. Docter

October 13

"Only interrupt me if there's an emergency," I caution my five-year-old twins, Bryce and Andrew, "and keep an eye on the baby. I just need fifteen minutes."

I rush to my laptop, conveniently located in the kitchen, and open the article I'm working on.

"Mom!" Bryce calls from the family room.

"Are you bleeding?" I ask.

"No."

"Is there a fire?"

"No."

"Then give me fifteen minutes."

Now where was I? My article. "Balancing Motherhood and Writing." The words come quickly for the next two minutes. And then I hear the splashing water. Running to the bathroom, I find my one-year-old, Benjamin, playing in the toilet.

"I tried to tell you," Bryce says, shaking his head.

I wash the baby and give him a few toys, noticing the sticky floor as I walk across the kitchen. Where was I?

"Mom!" Andrew calls out. "I'm bleeding!"

Rushing to the next room I find him, in fact, bleeding. "Did you have to pick this scab off right now?" I ask. Sighing, I slap on a Band-Aid and get back to work, ignoring the breakfast dishes piled up in the kitchen sink. "It's a constant juggling act," I write, "but I wouldn't trade my roles as mom or writer for anything in the world."

Lord, help me find balance between my children and my writing. Thank you for both gifts.

A clean house is the sign of a misspent life. Author unknown

—Robyn Whitlock

October 14

After spending the hot, humid days of our Southern summer inside, I find that fall brings on my cleaning frenzies. One morning when there was a decisively autumn feel to the air, I began cleaning out an over-crowded closet I had not opened in a while. I found a large container filled with my journals at the bottom of a stack.

I've been a journal keeper for twenty-six years. My journals have been the friend to whom I would tell all, and hold between their pages both the happiest and saddest moments I have experienced.

I picked up a book and was magically transported back in time. Some entries brought laughter; others caused my eyes to mist with tears. There were things I had forgotten, and those I would never forget.

Reading some of what I had come through in life and seeing the lessons learned encouraged me to keep writing. Whether I'm writing for publication or in my journals, I just know that I must write. Period. Writers write.

Lord, thank you for the gift of being able to share myself through the written word.

I can tell you, honest friend, what to believe: believe life; it teaches better than book or orator. Johann Wolf-gang Goethe

—Linda Strong

October 15

One day, I was praying about feelings of painful inadequacy. Words poured out onto my paper from a deep place in my soul, vulnerable and honest.

Soon a cleansing filled my heart and I felt God's comfort surround my heart. This poem was just between the Lord and me, not to be shared with others. It was just too personal.

A few days later, I visited with a young woman going through a difficult time. I felt a powerful sense that I was to share with her my poem, the one that had been so personal to me. Still I resisted: Not that one, Lord. I'm too vulnerable. Please, no.

I felt the nudge again. Feeling foolish, I offered it to her.

"For me?" she said, surprised.

The young woman seemed touched as she read. Soon her teardrops fell on the paper. She looked up with softened eyes and shakily gave me a hug.

"Thanks," she said. "I needed that."

A lesson lodged in my heart that day. I was thankful I had gotten past myself and obeyed. Somehow the Lord used my vulnerable thoughts to speak to her hurt place.

Lord, help me to write as you lead, lay it down, and take the steps that you prompt.

So that we can comfort those in any trouble with the comfort we ourselves have received from God. 2 Corinthians 1:4 NIV

—Elizabeth Sebek

October 16

One of the hardest tasks in writing, especially poetry, is to learn how to say what we mean with the fewest words possible. Mies van der Rohe, the architect, preached that less is more, and I use that as a mantra when I'm teaching. The most cuttable words are often adjectives and adverbs; most of the strength in a poem comes from nouns and verbs.

When I was in graduate school, I had a professor who wanted the typical five-page critique paper done on one typed page. If you went over the limit, your grade went down. That was the best lesson in compression I've ever had. Because that was in the age of the typewriter, I came up with the method of penciling in tiny lines to show me where to begin to transition to the next paragraph. Using the word count function in Word is much more efficient.

Another way to do this is to make each word count. A couple of details like "palm tree" and "hibiscus," and we know we're in Florida. This is a corollary of that other mantra, show, don't tell. But not too much.

Lord, help me to see where enough is enough.

We shall be known by the delicacy of where we stop short. Robert Frost

—Barbara Crooker

October 17

I opened up the manuscript and sighed. "Boards" instead of "board's" and an exclamation point and a comma both outside the quotation marks, all in the first paragraph. A 163-word second paragraph. I quickly scrolled down: lots of "exclaimed," "declared," and "shouted" instead of good ol' "said."

I've reached the point in my freelance editing business that I work only with writers who I believe are interested in the craft and are aware of the market realities. John had seemed like a very nice guy via e-mail when he asked about an evaluation. At least I can let him know he needs a good copy editor, I thought.

But the further I read, the more I became part of this story of two seafaring men. The characters were compelling; the plot, taut, suspenseful, and believable. By about page 3, I was ignoring the grammatical errors. I was there, out in the Pacific.

As I started writing the glowing evaluation (which did include a suggestion John find a good copy editor), I couldn't help but smile and feel blessed he had contacted me. Yes, grammar and spelling and the rest are important. But they can be fixed. The ability to spin a good yarn...now that's a rare gift.

God, help me to see the big picture in your plan for us all. Keep me from getting stuck in the details.

Don't judge a book by its cover. Author unknown
—Melanie Rigney

October 18

The writing workshop started badly. My favorite writing instructor was unimpressed with the two things I written since my accident. She said the article about war didn't say anything new and that I used the word pain too much in trying to describe pain.

I asked myself what I should write about. The automobile trip had been unpleasant. The hearing aids my wife and I wore amplified the road noise to an unpleasant roar. When we turned down the volume, we couldn't hear each other. My efforts to write about war and pain weren't working, so why not write about the problems caused by lost hearing?

I entitled the article, "What Did You Say?" I included a description of the form at the veteran's hospital acknowledging that the hearing aids remained government property. I remembered thinking that as an infantryman I was expendable, but I was now wearing hearing aids that were not. Did I want to include that? Was it is poor taste? Was it a joke that only a combat infantryman would understand?

When I read it in class, the sentence was greeted with a roar of laughter. When the class adjourned, my classmates clustered around to tell me of their experiences with hearing problems and to urge that I share the story with others.

Perhaps God was telling me to spice my writings about war, pain, and the problems of aging with a little laughter.

Lord, grant me the gift of laughter when I write.

Laughter is the closest thing to the grace of God. Karl Barth

—Glenn W. Fisher

October 19

A few years ago I attended my first Christian writers' conference in the inspiring mountains of northern New Mexico. I didn't know anyone. After selecting my dinner from the cafeteria line, I wandered about, searching for a place to sit. At times like these, I often say a prayer for God to guide me.

I chose a table, sat down, and met a lovely lady named Charlotte Adelsperger, one of our workshop leaders. She took me under her wing, offering helpful suggestions on the best way to take advantage of the conference. She introduced me to other attendees and encouraged me in my writing endeavors. I was nourished by her insight into Christian writing.

Frequently at meetings we meet new people and promise to stay in touch, but never do. However, via the Internet, Charlotte has offered me continuing advice that has resulted in several published pieces.

Her poetry inspires me. I feel we share time together when I read Charlotte's words: "But God's love reigns best when he, in nearness, holds this very moment in his hands."

Yes, God brings others into our lives at unexpected and blessed moments.

Thank you, Lord, for Charlotte and the others who nourish me along the writing path.

And the Spirit of the Lord shall rest upon him, the spirit of wisdom and understanding, the spirit of counsel and might. Isaiah 11:2 RSV

—Emily Tipton Williams

October 20

New to the staff of a national Christian magazine, I had just turned in my first assignment. I was confident from my decade of publishing experience and my fresh master's degree and expected the editor, Jerry, to rave about my work.

Instead, after he called me to his desk, I wondered if he'd gotten a severe paper cut and bled all over my manuscript. My article bore copious editing marks from his red pen.

"We've got to cut this to the bones," Jerry said, asking me to retype it and see why he marked it the way he did.

As I struggled through the scarlet detours and deletions, I had to admit trimming away my excess words helped the piece.

Decades later, whenever I teach writing, I relate that experience. I want my student writers to realize that my editing—done in less-accusing green ink—has only their good in mind. They, too, need to learn to cut to the bone.

I'm still learning to omit needless words. Every time I have a piece published, I compare the edited version with my original. It's a free writing lesson, like I got from that busy red pen—before the mega-best-selling Left Behind series made author Jerry Jenkins famous.

Father, I ask for a teachable spirit, to learn from how others edit me.

The heart of the discerning acquires knowledge; the ears of the wise seek it out. Proverbs 18:15 NIV

—Jeanne Zornes

October 21

My entry in one of the first writing contests I entered came back with the words, "Find something else to do with your time," scribbled across the top. The judge's harsh comment could have broken my spirit and killed my dream. Instead, I decided to prove her wrong.

I didn't want to be just a writer. I wanted to be the best writer I could. I honed my skills with classes and conferences and joined a critique group. When fellow writers gathered, I listened and took extensive notes. I read writers' magazines and books. Was it sweet victory when my book took first place in the same contest where earlier I'd been snubbed by an insensitive judge? Definitely, but I didn't stop there.

Driven by that judge's devastating comment, I wanted to help promising writers whenever I could. I developed and taught Writing & Marketing the Short Story first at the local college, then online. My student roster spanned coast to coast with writers from ages thirteen to seventy.

When asked to judge contests, I try to offer something every writer needs to hear: encouragement and constructive criticism. We all touch other lives with our words. Why not make them count?

Lord, help me encourage others by considering the words carefully before I speak.

My method is to take the utmost trouble to find the right thing to say, and then to say it with the utmost levity. George Bernard Shaw

—Deborah Elliott-Upton

October 22

I had a session with my therapist today. We worked out why I was so angry and what I could do about it. My therapist lives nearby; she's always available; charges very little; and listens intently without judgment.

Yesterday, I went to a committee meeting at church. There was a remark at which I took umbrage and by this morning I was in a total kick-the-dog rage. By the time Paige and I sat down together, my emotions were ready to boil over.

She let me vent and then gently asked me to objectively describe what had happened. This took a little time, but she is a patient listener. At first I wasn't sure what had set me off. He said this, she said that. After some probing and thinking I settled on the heart of the matter.

Then she asked what I wanted to do about it. More thought. More patient listening. Finally, after a few more questions and answers, I was able to find a solution and go about the rest of my day in peace.

You may have guessed that Paige is my journal...a yellow pad available whenever I need her. She lets me vent and gives me time and space to shape the questions and the answers. We work well together.

Thank you, God, for providing the perfect therapist.

A true friend sticks closer than one's nearest kin. Proverbs 18:24b NRSV

—Connie Scharlau

October 23

It isn't like I always dreamed of writing. Writing simple poems and lyrics was second nature. But to be called a writer?

When I was accepted into The Writing Academy I was thrilled. Maybe I had a small, very small bit of talent.

My first article was published after much help from Writing Academy instructors. "King of the Dance" told about my father being crowned king of the yearly dance at his Lutheran nursing home.

It was exciting to get the check in the mail and share the story. Was I really a writer now? Enthusiastically I took the courses offered by the Academy, and started sending my work to magazines and music publishers.

I wrote three years for a local paper and had several articles and a Christmas anthem published. Then, I received rejection after rejection. This made me reexamine what I was doing. It was time to take the advice the Academy had given: write, write, and write some more.

Perseverance and hard work are my mottos now. And I'm turning on the computer more often.

Lord, thank you for the blessings, encouragement, and joy you have given me in writing.

Nine out of ten writers, I am sure, could write more. I think they should and, if they did, they would find their work improving even beyond their own, their agent's, and their editor's highest hopes. John Creasey

—Gloria Tietgens Sladek

October 24

Today, United Nations Day, reminds me of the time when I had to work for a manager who was my polar opposite. The experience was one of those mysterious little train wrecks that litter the railways of life, one that I'm sure is experienced often in the United Nations.

He and I were different nationalities; work styles; politics; religions; sexes; ages; biorhythms; and tastes in cars, pets, and lattes. He refused to try me out in the job the personnel department had hired me to do.

In what I suspect was an effort to get rid of me, he assigned me what was known around the office as the impossible writing job. I was too new to have heard about the difficulties, so I plowed ahead.

Because of a combination of good training in writing, beginner's luck, and the grace of God, I produced solid, cogent work. My manager, a knowledgeable writer, was won over. Oh, he still razzed me about my oddities, but I overheard him bragging about my work. "After I edited it," he said, "it read OK." When I moved on to another job, he actually gave me a hug.

Who would have thought that writing, not first aid, is the best train wreck survival technique?

Lord, thank you for the gift of communicating with those who are different from us.

The wolf will dwell with the lamb, the cow and the bear will graze, for the earth will be full of the knowledge of the Lord. Isaiah 11:6,7,9 NASB

—Rosa Lee Richards

October 25

The first time my work was critiqued, I felt like the arms had been sawed off my first-born baby. I grieved the changes and tried to accept this "improved" child. The feeling abated somewhat when the check arrived. Determined to improve even at personal expense, I chose the most brutal people I could find to edit my work, a sort of refiner's fire. I believed one of two things—or, possibly, both—would happen: I would get better or develop a thicker skin. I've never regretted my decision. It showed me where my blind spots were. It gave me new tools to shape my writing. Editors are the guardian angels of the written word.

I read a new author's self-published book recently. There's nothing quite like bad writing to remind one of the need for editing. If I could pass on one encouragement to serious writers, it would be this: find trustworthy people to edit your work. It will help you grow as a writer and groom you for success.

Lord, thank you for those who encouraged me through unswerving honesty.

That's what learning is, after all; not whether we lose the game, but how we lose and how we've changed because of it and what we take away from it that we never had before, to apply to other games. Losing, in a curious way, is winning. Richard Bach

—Julie Morrison

October 26

I've been writing for magazines, newspapers, and books since 1981. From 1976 to 1992, I worked for four different radio stations writing commercials. I wrote over forty thousand of those little buggers (thirty-nine thousand too many for one lifetime) and learned to say a lot in a few short words. When you only have thirty seconds to get an entire message across, you have to stick to the basics.

During that time I learned that the Lord's Prayer contains 56 words; the Twenty-third Psalm, 118 words; the Gettysburg Address, 226 words; the Ten Commandments, 297 words...and the U.S. Department of Agriculture directive on pricing cabbage, 15,629 words. Guess the government didn't get the message about less is more.

Even before my radio commercial days, I learned the lesson from my dad. When I was in college he wrote me long, encouraging letters. Once I wrote a complaining letter home about not having enough spending money. Dad answered quite succinctly: "Dear Pat: No mon? No fun? Too bad. So sad. Love, Dad."

Dad showed me you can pack quite a wallop with just a few words.

Lord, help me to write what I need to write and then stop.

Words are clothes that thoughts wear. Samuel Butler
—Patricia Lorenz

October 27

I knew about the Civil War as a child growing up in New England. But as an adult living in the South, I learned there was more to that story than freed slaves and a Northern win. What I didn't know would be obvious when I became a Yankee author writing a Southern tale.

I had worked for my local newspaper for more than ten years when someone suggested I write the history of our county. I enjoyed the project immensely until I reached the part about slavery, racial prejudice, and the Civil War.

I was outraged. How could anyone justify slavery, cling to the practice for generations, and even go to war to defend it? How could I write this chapter without venting my anger?

Before long, memories of my own childhood surfaced and I remembered I grew up with prejudice too. We may not have had slaves but, oh, what we said about our political leaders, folks from "that" part of town, and even those who attended a different church than we did.

It took time, but when I also remembered what I had been taught about judging others, I could finally sit down and write.

Lord, may the words I write always be as full of grace as they are of truth.

Do not judge, or you, too, will be judged. For in the same way you judge others, you will be judged. Matthew 7:1-2 NIV

—Barbara Seaborn

October 28

My honors English students asked: Is there is a simple word—a silver bullet, of sorts—to help jump-start our writing?

Like a concert pianist, I sat at my keyboard, hands poised. I mentally worked through the leads of various genres: memoir, political discourse, literary critique.

Eventually, the answer came: when.

When I husked corn on our family farm as a teenager, I learned some of life's greatest lessons in the cab of my grandfather's pickup truck.

When John F. Kennedy assumed the presidency in 1961, he became the first and only practicing Roman Catholic to serve as president.

When *Huckleberry Finn* was published in 1884, it immediately drew controversy.

My students embraced the concept so readily that I added ten more words: after, unless, although, while, until, because, as, before, if, and since. The first letter of each created a nonsense word—AWUAWUBABIS. Students memorized the list, chanting "awu-awu-BA-bis" like warriors preparing for battle.

Here's why this works: Each word introduces an adverb clause, so your brain focuses on an action and thus generates a ready flow of appropriate words. Try it. If you get stuck along the way, select another of the ten words to keep going.

When I am anxious about my writing, Lord, help me to listen to your still, small voice of calm.

I have stilled my soul, hushed it like a weaned child. Psalms 131:2 NAB

—Margaret W. Garrison

October 29

Begin a new career in the middle of my life? I always wondered about people who did that. Now, I was one of them. A career change wasn't something I ever thought about or anticipated, it just happened.

That very first day, I didn't know where to begin. I thought about a dozen different ways to arrange my time. However, being home for the first time in years presented many distractions for a multitasker neat freak. Sitting there on that very first morning, I picked up the book a dear friend had given me on writing by Anne Lamott.

It addressed my concerns. Lamott suggested you set aside a time and place each day to work. During that time you remained in your place. You were not allowed to answer the phone if it rang, put the laundry in the dryer, or do anything else. Some days you might write; some days you might not. That was OK. You could always spend the time thinking creatively.

How did I begin a new career? One day at a time. Writing is a process; the words will come. One day at a time.

Lord, help me daily find quiet times of solitude and use them wisely.

Bird by bird, buddy. Just take it bird by bird. Anne Lamott

—Pam Wanzer

October 30

Why am I doing this, I asked myself, slumping toward the door after presenting the pitch for my first book to an acquisitions editor.

I was attending my first writers' conference with high hopes and publishing dreams. Now my hopes and dreams had been shattered in less than two minutes.

"Your subject is flooding the market," the editor had told me. "I don't want to hurt your feelings, but why would anyone want to read a book by you? No one even knows who you are."

I nursed my pride and considered ending my writing career. No, I decided. There are four days left in the conference, and I'm going to make the most of it.

I made appointments with publishing house editors who might be interested in my subject and who worked with first-time authors. I revamped my pitch and the next day my idea was received with enthusiasm from two of them.

I listened intently during the workshops, took notes, and asked questions. I made lists of what I needed to do if I wanted to be published. I introduced myself to authors and speakers and paid attention to their advice.

During the next three years I honed my skills, expanded my speaking platform, and published two books.

I learned to turn rejection into direction.

Lord, help me remember to turn rejection by others into direction by you.

There's nothing like rejection to make you do an inventory of yourself. James Lee Burke

—Mary Englund Murphy

October 31

With my hair styled, makeup applied and wearing my best take-me-seriously-as-a-writer outfit, I arrived at the writers' conference anxiously seeking encouragement and inspiration.

"Where is the opening session?" I asked the desk clerk.

"This is the Holiday," the clerk said. "The writers' conference is at the Hilton across town."

A cold October rain fell as I walked down the circular drive.

By the time I arrived—late—at the right venue, my hair was matted, my mascara runny, my eyeglasses steamed, and my outfit soaked. Carefully reading the conference brochure would have saved time, frustration, and embarrassment.

To ensure my manuscripts don't suffer a similar fate of being misdirected and arriving bedraggled, I take every precaution during the submission process. In-depth marketing is time consuming, yet it's the only way to ensure that my manuscript arrives on the desk of the right editor at the right publishing house.

After reading a publication's description in a market guide, I send for current guidelines and theme lists; I secure a sample of the magazine if feasible. After checking for deadlines, I double-check the editor's name and address. Then I submit only polished work.

Lord, I am thankful that you accept me as I am, but love me enough to want me to improve—in all aspects of my life.

He who fails to please in his salutation and address is at once rejected and never obtains an opportunity of showing his latest excellences. Samuel Johnson
—Judyann Ackerman Grant

November 1

My assignment was a bit intimidating: do a telephone interview with an eminent university cancer doctor who was having his first collection of poems published. Then write an article about him.

As I talked to the doctor/poet, all his degrees, awards, titles, and training seemed to fade away. His compassion for his sick patients—which fueled his poetry—came to the fore. Here was another writer, struggling to convey his feelings about helping scared people confronting their own mortality. And he knew he could not save them all.

He talked about how maintaining a detached clinical manner was "probably the most difficult part of medicine." He described a young woman with two children who had an unusual tumor that stumped him and her other doctors. What kind was it? How should they treat it?

I was taking notes as the doctor's voice trailed off. Then, as he regained his composure, he began talking about how much the woman wanted to live, and how much he wanted to help her live. "She died before we figured it out," he said. There was a short silence between us, as if we were respecting her memory.

In that silence, all my concerns about this assignment evaporated like an autumn mist.

Thank you, Lord, for the unifying love that turns scientists into poets.

Whatever your task, work heartily. Colossians 3:23 RSV

—Peggy Eastman

November 2

The visit to my daughter's family in San Antonio would have an added treat. Two online writing critique partners I'd never met were joining me there.

Their honest feedback, tempered with gentle encouragement, had given me, a novice writer, the tools for needed improvement. But my plans changed drastically the night before their arrival.

"It's just indigestion," I said.

Then the pain increased like a vise squeezing my chest and a heart attack changed my life forever.

"You'll have to cancel your plans," my daughter told my writing partners. "There's no bedroom space at my house because Mother's in the hospital and extra family has arrived."

"We want to be with her," they said. "We'll stay in a hotel."

For two days they sat beside me, talking about their families, faith, and writing. In that hospital room God forged three cyberspace acquaintances into close friends.

When we each sold our first books months later, I knew God had blessed me again. On the road to publication he'd provided me with two friends who not only pushed me to be a better writer but also went with me into the valley of the shadow of death.

Thank you, God, for those whose commitment to writing goes beyond their own needs and reaches out to help others improve.

Keep away from people who try to belittle your ambitions. Small people always do that, but the really great make you feel that you, too, can become great. Mark Twain

—Sandra Robbins

November 3

Some years ago, I was part of a team who took care of an elderly couple in their home. Their appetites were no longer good, and Grandma in particular resisted nutrition.

One day, Grandpa picked up a large sugar cookie, held it in front of Grandma's face, and urged her to eat it.

"I can't eat that. It's too big," she protested.

"But it gets smaller as you eat," he answered.

Sometimes when I'm faced with a writing task, and feel I'm not capable, I remember Grandpa and the cookie. I can at least take a bite of the job, and immediately it seems to be smaller. If I have a thought, I can write it down. If I write the thought down, I can certainly transfer it to the computer. Once my thought is transferred to the computer, I find myself adding more sentences.

For several years I had an idea for a children's book, but it seemed like an impossible dream. One day I sat at the computer and wrote the first chapter. Ideas began coming faster and the task no longer seemed impossible. Several weeks later, the book was finished.

Even if that book never sells, I still have the satisfaction of having written a book for my grandchildren and great-grandchildren to enjoy.

Father, nudge me when I am slow to start writing, and remind me to take a bite of the cookie.

What is not started today is never finished tomorrow. Johann Wolfgang von Goethe

—Anne Siegrist

November 4

When I was a high school sophomore, I began my first journal in an *All Occasion Date Book for Engagements, 1949*. Each weekly page was a grid of seven dated rows and three small squares labeled Morning, Afternoon, and Evening.

My mother bought this book for her own diary, but only six spaces contained her fine penmanship. The last sentence written the evening of January 10.

Three weeks later, she admitted that her heart wasn't in the project and handed the book to me. "Maybe you'd like to use this."

My first entry, Friday evening, February 4, read, "Saw *Joan of Arc* wonderful movie."

As I worked my way through 1949, I made my handwriting smaller, but some entries still overflowed into the margins. For 1950, I bought my own four-by-six-inch black looseleaf binder and allotted half of each narrow-lined page to one day.

Over the years, my journals have come in many sizes and colors. I can't boast that I have written in them continuously from *Joan of Arc* until now. But journaling became a habit I couldn't and didn't want to break.

Among the many debts I owe my mother, this may be the most unusual. My lifelong interest in journaling as both writer and teacher began because she stopped keeping her diary and gave it to me.

Lord, I thank you for guiding my life's journey, sometimes in surprising ways.

Every good and perfect gift is from above. James 1:17 NIV

—Nancy E. James

November 5

Attending writers' conferences gave me the courage to keep writing in spite of rejections. I once received a rejection with ten pages of critique. I didn't learn until later that the publisher wanted me to make the changes and send it back. Instead, feeling humiliated, I didn't send out another manuscript for years.

I discovered that even great writers and best-selling authors have stacks of rejections. Not only were they rejected for years before publication, but some of them, well known today, are still being rejected.

I learned that writing is a business that requires financial investments. I need a strong editor to critique my work. At conferences, I talked with published writers and editors, asking one to look at a manuscript. She has been a godsend. When my book is finally edited and rewritten, she will recommend me to her agent. If he represents me and finds an interested publisher, I will hire a publicist, requiring another financial investment, who will promote me and arrange newspaper, radio, and television interviews.

In short, my manuscript must speak well of the master I represent. Not only do I need God's guidance, but I also need the help of experts to get his word out.

Lord, lead me to those who will help me write my best for you.

You have to put your heart in the business and the business in your heart. Thomas J. Watson Sr.
—Jackie Strange

November 6

I'm a fan of the *Dukes of Hazzard*. Bo and Luke's car, the General Lee, flies over barriers, road blocks, and rivers. Sheriff Roscoe P. Coltrane is hot on their tail with flashing lights and hound dog Flash. Boss J. D. Hogg plots to put the Dukes behind bars and steal Uncle Jesse's farm, but the Dukes always chase the bad guys. I often wish it was that easy to start a writing project as it is to watch that show.

There are one thousand four hundred and forty minutes a day. It takes ten minutes to turn the computer on and open up Microsoft Word. Adjusting my chair and cracking my neck steals another two or three minutes. Blankly staring ahead totals it to fifteen. I have already lost 1.04 percent of a day's time. One penny out of a dollar can be squandered or lost, and I won't feel the effect, but there are 365 days in the year. Fifteen minutes of every day equals 91¼ hours. I could put a lot of print on paper in 91¼ hours.

I know priorities rule, but if I just exchanged that hour of watching the *Dukes* for writing, I'd have a grand total of 260 more hours. Wow, enough time to author a book.

Jesus, please show me how to use my time wisely.

No one knows about that day or hour, not even the angels in heaven, nor the Son, but only the Father. Be on guard! Be alert! You do not know when that time will come. Mark 13:32-33 NIV

—Rose Goble

November 7

My adventure with Don Blanding, sometimes called the poet laureate of Hawaii, began in 1946 when I won his book *Drifter's Gold* in a poetry contest. In gratitude, I wrote, "The pen in his hand is guided by God..."

He responded: "Aloha friend. It is so wonderful to know that words from my own life can help and perhaps heal others. Your letter gives me additional courage to believe in my writings and myself. It means more to me than all the condescending pats on the head from highbrow literary journals. I seldom read the latter, but will read your letter frequently."

In 1947, after Daddy died, Don stepped in as a sort of father figure and sent me fifteen letters from Yap, Koror, Babelthaup, and other islands out of his Jabberwocky dictionary. In all, he sent me sixty letters over the next ten years.

With inimitable wit, he shared trials, triumphs, dreams. Don's last letter announced, "I think I'm with book again." He died in 1957, still working on *No Strings on Tomorrow*.

Don gave me encouragement, inspiration, hope, and a prayer, an acrostic carved into his mantle—LIDGTTFTATIM. Lord, I Do Give Thee Thanks for the Abundance That Is Mine.

Rereading his words, I knew someday I would feel tropic winds, savor the warmth of aloha, and become a writer.

Lord, I do give thee thanks for the abundance that is mine.

I came that so they might have life and have it more abundantly. John 10:10 NAB

—Tommie Lenox

November 8

I was standing in line to register when the lady next to me blurted out, "What are you doing here?" I was taken aback by her demeaning tone of voice and piercing brown eyes that examined me from head to foot.

I was already nervous about attending my first writers' conference, but now I felt as big as a mouse. "Well, uh…" I stammered, "I want to learn how to write."

"How old are you?" she persisted. A cold pallid breeze blew into the room as I explained that I was under thirty. The cool air numbed my hands as I listened to her judgment that I was too young and too spiritually immature to be there.

The next day, I anxiously awaited an appointment with a Bethany House editor. I enthusiastically prepared a formal pitch and presented my proposal for *The Abundant Life,* a devotional for college graduates. I was thrilled when the editor loved the idea and told me to mail in a hard copy of the book proposal. In that moment, it didn't matter what had happened to me in the registration line. I knew nothing could come between my writing goals and me.

Lord, when I feel doubtful about my journey as a writer, help me to remember that you are the author of success.

Always bear in mind that your own resolution to succeed is more important than any one thing. Abraham Lincoln

—Ann Michels

November 9

I squeezed my eyes shut. "I'm ready to give up, Lord! I don't think I'll ever finish this novel." Tears traced wet paths down my face. "If you have an idea...please, I could use it now."

"Commit your work to the Lord, and then your plans will succeed."

What? I'd dedicated my writing to the Lord long ago. Obviously, behind those twelve words, I was missing something important.

Several hours later, I stared at what I had distilled from my concordances, commentaries, and dictionary. So, that was my problem.

My saying a quick prayer before barreling into my writing simply didn't cut it. Committing my work was praying, "Lord, here am I. Use me. What do you want me to accomplish today?" It meant sharing my difficulties and delights, and inviting him into every aspect of my writing—manuscripts, plans, deadlines.

I learned a valuable lesson that day. Being a Christian writer wasn't simply a matter of my being a Christian and writing. It was laying my gift at the Lord's feet and obeying him. Looking back now, all of my published manuscripts were a result of God's plan. Painful as my years of struggle were, I am glad he has preserved that precious pattern.

Lord God, may I never forget that you are the giver of my writing gifts. May I faithfully offer my all to you each day and rise up to obey.

Obedience alone gives the right to command. Ralph Waldo Emerson.

—Beth Ann Ziarnik

November 10

After writing and teaching a Bible study for the women's retreat at my church, I was introduced to the idea of writing for publication by an author in the audience. I laughed at the idea at the time, but that published writer persisted. Eventually, I felt that perhaps God was opening a door, so I decided to give it a try.

Soon after my decision, medical problems surfaced. Symptoms appeared from a pinched nerve in my neck and back. A burning pain traveled through my right arm and hand, and right hip, leg, and foot. I suddenly needed a cane to walk and was unable to use my right hand.

Frustrated, I wondered if I misinterpreted God's direction and contemplated abandoning the writing career idea. But then I remembered that woman at the retreat and how much confidence she seemed to have in my ability to be a writer. So I decided to give it another try. I sat at the computer, prayed for pain relief and the Holy Spirit's help, and started working.

Hours later when I took a break, I was elated. I had been working unaware of any pain, enjoying the writing experience.

Lord, thank you for exercising your power over my opposition and enabling me to serve you through my writing.

Most people who succeed in the face of seemingly impossible conditions are people who simply don't know how to quit. Robert H. Schuller

—Cindy Rooy

November 11

On Veterans Day, I am reminded of my grandfather who arrived in America just before the outbreak of World War I. Hoping to have his wife and children join him the following year, he was greatly disappointed when travel between Europe and America was disrupted by the war. My grandfather clung to his dream of seeing his wife and children again. He was concerned about their safety, and wondered how long it would be before the war ended.

When the armistice was signed at the eleventh hour on the eleventh day of the eleventh month of 1918, travel between Europe and America resumed. My grandmother and her children finally arrived.

Waiting is difficult, especially when the outcome is unknown. As a writer, I have done a lot of waiting, wondering whether or not my hard work would be rewarded with publication. Like my grandfather, I held on to my dream and eventually realized it. Most important of all, I learned that waiting is an opportunity to grow in trusting God.

Lord, help me realize that waiting strengthens me as I learn to trust you more.

But those who wait on the Lord shall renew their strength; they shall mount up with wings like eagles, they shall run and not be weary, they shall walk and not faint. Isaiah 40:31 NKJV

—MaryAnn Diorio, Ph.D.

November 12

Lately, I find myself thinking about what technology has done to creative writing.

Often our e-mails carry an assortment of hieroglyphics understood only by those comfortable in cyberspace. Will this generation learn the art of the handwritten note and of its power to change a life?

Among my treasures nestled safely in an old shoebox, I find a handwritten letter from Mom, who died far too young. There is also the letter from our Marine son, struggling through boot camp, asking us to please send him his Bible. And of course I saved the love letters from my husband during the winter I was stranded on an island doing some substitute teaching.

As a writer, I sometimes struggle, trying to write chapters that I hope will become a best-selling novel or have a life-changing effect on the reader. But a few carefully chosen words penned in my handwriting can have an even greater effect on someone's life. If I remain open to opportunities, I can handwrite many notes. I often find this stirs my creative juices, allowing me to once again write those chapters. It's like priming the pump.

Dear Lord, thank you for those who encourage me. Help me to encourage someone who needs that written affirmation today.

Encouragement is the oxygen of the soul. George M. Adams

—Ethel Jensen Stenzel

November 13

I write because I must. I am a worder, watching for phrases as I go about my routines, grabbing at them and pinning them like fritillaries to paper. Phrases are stalked, eaten, paged.

I wrote ditties as a child, had a poem published as a young woman. I never took the art seriously until the day I read something in Exodus. It was no longer a dictum to Moses, but a stern command to me.

"Write these things down…"

"What things, Lord?"

Silence.

"But…I have nothing but shivering leaves and rattling bones to write about, nothing substantive like your friend Moses."

"Just write…"

I worked more regularly at my poems. I learned that when a phrase hit on the highway, I should try to pull over and write it down. If I waited, the words would be lost.

Journaling with the help of Julia Cameron's book *The Artist's Way* became a daily routine. I began to see myself as a writer.

Years later, I understood the Exodus reading: the stern command was God's way of saying that writing was to be more than a hobby for me. It was part of my calling.

And so I write. With the finishing of poem or story, a profound cleansing comes, lifting, joyful, the unsought blessing of much work. It is a deeply spiritual event.

Lord, forgive me for treating your gift lightly. Help me work with you in this call.

The Lord said: write these words. Exodus 34:27 NIV
—Ellen Strickland

November 14

Some time ago, I was active in Toastmasters International, a fellowship organization in which members improve their public speaking skills. Awards were given for the best performance at each meeting.

The president of our local club created a Round To It award. It was for those who didn't get around to doing assignments.

I often look back on that dubious award and laugh at myself. Whenever I sit down to write, that corny Round To It award stares me in the face. It's amazing the number of little distractions that arise: play spider solitaire, check for the mail, make a cup of coffee, play with the cat.

It comes down to self-discipline. Perhaps I could imagine a cage with a time lock on it. Once in, I'm there for at least one hour. Or, maybe I could simply observe ants at work. Perhaps their industriousness would rub off on me. It would have to be done in secret, or people would think I've lost my mind.

Better yet, I'll just pray for inspiration to write.

Father, give me the resolve to work diligently so that I might accomplish the task set before me.

Go to the ant, you sluggard; consider its ways and be wise! It has no commander, no overseer or ruler, yet it stores its provisions in summer and gathers its food at harvest. Proverbs 6:6-8 NIV

Roy Proctor

November 15

I think of myself as a writer with grandchildren. Actually, I'm a grandmother who writes. Between babies. Although with sixteen babies in seventeen years, there hasn't been much between.

Sometimes, I feel like a sparkler. I flame with an idea. But I have to change a diaper, search for a lost Hot Wheels, or empathize with teenage angst long distance. The idea sputters and dies.

Sometimes, I'm dry. The white page looms. Then, like now, a cuddly squirmer crawls on my lap. Three-year-old Justin says, "I hep you, Gramma."

I feel his blond hair against my cheek. His little fingers rest on mine as I type. There are too many spaces between words. Suddenly, he jumps over to the bulletin board. He finds "art" he made long ago and shows me. I'm glad I saved it. After mutual admiration, he remounts it.

"Good job," I say.

His smile nearly reaches his ears.

Back on my lap, his "hep" reminds me to "write what you know." What I know is connection with little souls.

"Can we send now?" Justin asks.

"As soon as I write words from Jesus' love letters," I tell him.

When I give him the signal, he'll "send" and say "Good job, Gramma."

Oh, gracious father, thank you for grandchildren who are Jesus with skin to me.

Suffer the little children to come unto me, for of such is the kingdom of Heaven. Luke 18:16

—Diane Perrone

November 16

I'm not a writer.

I kept hearing those words while traveling to my first writers' conference. All I ever did was jot down memories and stuff them in a drawer.

I thought about turning my minivan around and going home. But I'm so glad I didn't follow my fears, because the Florida Christian Writers' Conference was one of the greatest experiences of my life.

Here are a few of the reasons why:

First, I bonded with some of the most incredible people in the world, many of who are writing friends today.

Second, the teacher in my very first class challenged me to do something with my writing. He said, "My mom was a closet writer, and unfortunately no one ever had the privilege of reading what she wrote because she kept it all neatly tucked away in a drawer."

Third, I had an editor take the time to encourage me to try my hand at writing greeting cards, and that's what I've been doing ever since.

Lord, thank you for helping me to push past my fears to continue growing in the gift of writing you've given me.

Inaction breeds doubt and fear. Action breeds confidence and courage. If you want to conquer fear, do not sit home and think about it. Go out and get busy. Dale Carnegie

—Peggy Morris

November 17

Another rejection. I couldn't stop the tears as I cradled my gift book manuscript in my hands. The editor said, "Flesh this out, add some stories and send it to me."

I knew there was no guarantee, but I had hoped at last to have my name on the cover of a book. Now I just wanted to quit writing. What was the use of trying anymore? Other editors had rejected five other book proposals as well as various articles and stories. Could I truly not write anymore? Would I ever see my name on my very own book?

I'd been writing since childhood when I became family correspondent to aunts, uncles, and adult cousins living thousands of miles away. My grandparents, with whom I lived, didn't like to write. I discovered the fun of telling about Grandfather's teaching job, stories of his students' antics, music lessons, a book I was reading. My grandmother always read the letters before mailing them, rarely telling me to omit a story. Her smile and "Very good" are precious memories today.

And now I've taken that editor's advice and fleshed out my gift book manuscript and added some sparkling stories. I'm driving to the post office to set my dream in motion once more. Because that's what writers do. We never give up.

Lord, thank you for the love of writing you gave me and for helping me to persevere.

Keep all your senses acute and listening. Write all the time. Madeleine L'Engle

—June Varnum

November 18

I first began to think I had some talent for writing in college when my literature professor noted on my theme, "Oh Mr. Del Rosso, if you could only spell!"

I loved the fifteen-minute pop quizzes she assigned: write a story on any topic in the time allotted. No time for writer's block—I had to come up with something or fail the quiz. Hands sweaty, heart racing, I speedily scribbled something on the first topic that popped into my head. It was fun. It was exhilarating! I loved it.

Although I was a science major, I managed to sneak in an English minor by graduation—mainly because twelve credits of English were required and fifteen got you a minor, a mere matter of taking one extra course. I suffered through grammar and breezed through literature, graduating with a lasting taste for the written word.

A teaching career followed where my writing skills were put to use in formulating tests that were challenging but fair and unambiguous, and in writing reports and recommendations for graduating seniors. Many a time I thanked the Lord for that English minor.

Now, in retirement, I write for enjoyment—recounting the experiences of my youth to leave a life record for my grandkids. Writing is still fun.

Lord, thank you for the gift of understanding and the ability to write it down so that others may understand.

The pen is mightier than the sword. Author unknown
—Mario Del Rosso

November 19

My sixteen-year-old granddaughter Kalee went in for a routine checkup. After the examination, the grim-faced doctor said, "She's pregnant."

My daughter-in-law, who accompanied her, had also been a teenage mom. She knew with certainty she would not desert her daughter, deny her, or delegate her care to others.

I learned about it by phone. Even though I was stunned, I told my granddaughter, "God loves you, I love you, and I will walk beside you.

The letter I wrote to Kalee later that day, began, "I prayed for you and gave thanks for your life. Since you were an infant I have prayed Psalm 91:11 that God will command his angels concerning you to guard you in all your ways."

Praying the verses audibly and writing the scripture promises by filling in the names of my loved ones has carried me through many a family crisis. I write scripture verses of hope and strength in my leather journal each day, and pencil in comments in the margins of my Bible so I can return hours, days, or years later for comfort.

I've learned that not all writing results in credits in magazines and on books. Some writing is just meant for me or for a granddaughter in a crisis.

Father, pour out your love through my words, audible and written for my granddaughter.

Sharing our stories can be a means of healing. Susan Wittig Albert

—Sheryl Van Weelden

November 20

I am gradually accepting the dual roles of a writer—writing and marketing. For most of my life I have written primarily for my own benefit. The moment I published, however, my writing became public.

Before my book was published, I took my writing very seriously. Yet I did not think it was anybody's business. Once a friend phoned and asked what I was doing. I vaguely answered, "Working."

The day arrived when I needed my manuscript critiqued by strangers. This was a huge step for me. One Christian editor advised me to intersperse my testimony throughout the book. I felt even more vulnerable, but I did it.

What an exciting day when I held the finished product in my hands. My enthusiasm lasted about three months. Then the reality of what I had done engulfed me. There is much more to writing than putting words on paper and publishing them.

It has been an uphill battle to inform others that the book exists. A few months ago someone asked me, "Do you expect it to happen by osmosis?"

"Of course not," I thought. I've learned that it takes a great deal of time, organization, and energy to market a book. Most of all it takes determination not to quit.

Lord, keep me humble and energized as I try to market my book.

Nothing in life is to be feared, it is only to be understood. Marie Curie

—Heather A. Kendall

November 21

My confidence to write was increasing. This led me to take steps toward getting published. So I wrote and submitted to Christian magazines and Sunday school publications. I set my sights on one women's magazine in particular.

Each day I waited for responses. I received more rejection letters than acceptances, but didn't allow it to bother me since most were the standard form letters.

One day I received a personal response to my special submission. As I read through the letter my countenance began to drop. My treasured article had red marks on it, the kind I used to receive in English class. This editor took plenty of time to tell me what she thought of my submission. How dare she! I thought. The words stung my heart.

I slammed the letter down on the table. But after I cooled off, I took one more look. I read her words with an open mind; the remarks weren't so curt after all. Although I didn't agree with all of them, I took some to heart and decided to incorporate those suggestions in my writing.

It was a turning point for me. A few months later, I was writing a weekly newspaper column. I often wonder if my success was due to humbling myself and following the suggestions in that letter.

Lord, thank you for lessons in humility and for teaching me that humble actions bring greater rewards than prideful ones.

No one can make you feel inferior without your consent. Eleanor Roosevelt

—Annettee Budzban

November 22

I sat in my mother's basement, pecking out "I CAN'T FIX IT!" on a borrowed laptop. Newly separated and unemployed, with a teenage son who dressed all in black and carried a life-size rubber chicken everywhere he went, I was a bit overwhelmed.

A week later, I added a sentence, and then another, and couldn't stop until I had vented all my frustration. One day, my sister-in-law, a registered nurse, asked if she could read my journal entry.

"A Christian nursing magazine would publish this! You've described what nurses go through, perfectly. Just change the words 'wife' and 'mother' to 'nurse' and 'caretaker.'"

I told her she was nuts. I wasn't a writer or a nurse.

"They pay money."

My hands actually shook as I mailed the envelope. I knew it was a long shot, but the lure of the money was stronger than my common sense.

They accepted it! Apparently they agreed that I'm not powerful enough to fix the world's problems, even one by one...and I'm not responsible for anyone else's actions. Turns out, false responsibility never was God's plan for my life.

I wore the shine off that magazine page, handling it like a holy grail. Wow. My words of frustration had morphed into a magazine article.

And so I wrote another.

Lord, thank you, not just for the gift of healing words but also for new beginnings.

Troubles are often the tools by which God fashions us for better things. Henry Ward Beecher

—Betsy Dill

November 23

It's amazing to see your name in print. When my church printed my Advent devotional guide and I saw my name on my book, I was thrilled.

For two seasons, I was honored to write devotionals for different churches, each time with family and friends encouraging me to sell the books. I was reluctant to sell them and I finally figured out why. So far my work has been met with positive response. But I wonder, is it only good because it is free? Would a church want to use it if payment was required? Does that mean I'm not a real writer?

I started writing the Advent devotional guide as an opportunity to teach my son about Jesus. It worked. In my Bible right now is a drawing of a stick lady with the heading "People who teach me about Jesus" that he drew.

That drawing is priceless to me because it reminds me where my priorities are. To have a church buy my work would awesome, but this is for the Lord, not for me.

Father, remind me I have eternal rewards, even if I am never paid as a writer.

If you will think about what you ought to do for other people, your character will take care of itself. Woodrow Wilson

—Brook Dwyer

November 24

A critique group I attended refused to use the word "rejection," substituting other "R" words: response, return, and reply.

I've certainly received my fair share: The form letter, the terse insult scribbled by a harried editor, and, once, a critique of sorts that galloped on for a weighty, full page to shred my article and grind my concept to pulp.

In my early writing naiveté (or stupidity), I simply shrugged, noted the date in the appropriate column of my submission log, and tossed the slip into the trash. Then I popped the article off to the next possibility on my list.

After some trial and lots of error, I managed to sell a number of those early submissions. But now, as I look back on essays that never found a home, I blush in understanding—and almost wish I'd kept that weighty critique for a second read!

I'm grateful for my first "responses." They prodded me to persevere. They challenged me to believe in myself. They pushed me to research new markets.

And, to this day, I don't mind using the word. Rejection. It is, after all, what we make of it.

Father, thank you for road blocks and the challenge to find a way beyond them.

Worry often gives a small thing a big shadow. Swedish proverb

—Carol McAdoo Rehme

November 25

I knew it was bad news when my publishing house editor said he had to call me about my book, which was due to go on press shortly. My guess was that a last-minute rewrite of some content wasn't enough to allay some skittish executives' concerns.

I was right. The editor was totally professional, but his voice shook as he said the memoir about my return to Catholicism after thirty-five years was being canceled and went through the other things he had to say.

"How are you?" he asked, finally.

"I'm OK," I said. "How are you?"

"I think I'm more upset than you are," he said with a bit of a laugh.

Nine months later, I have an agent who's looking for a publisher for my book. The anger, disappointment, and sadness that once came with personal or professional rejection have never set in.

"Sorry about the book," friends and colleagues say. "I'm sure you'll find another publisher."

My answer is always the same—and always sincere. "Thanks. It's up to God, really. Either he'll find one…or the person who was supposed to benefit from reading it already has."

Lord, thank you for the patience and confidence needed to traverse the challenging road that is publishing today.

Be faithful to that which exists nowhere but in your-self—and thus make yourself indispensable. Andre Gide
Melanie Rigney

November 26

The nation was reeling from shock. President John Kennedy had been assassinated in Dallas. Camelot had come crashing down in a horrible scene played over and over again on national television. I was a young pastor, serving my first parish. Somehow I had to find words to write a sermon in that dark hour.

On Sunday morning, I struggled through a challenge to the congregation. If indeed Lee Harvey Oswald was the guilty party, our faith commanded that we were to hate the deed but not the doer. I told my little flock that they could not leave it to a jury in Texas but must decide in their own hearts to forgive their brother.

I felt pretty good about how I dealt with this event of such national prominence. I had written a sermon on forgiveness when so much was at stake. I went home that Sunday, turned on the television just in time to watch Jack Ruby take matters into his own hands and kill the accused. Everyone was off the hook. No one would struggle with the question of forgiveness.

I do not remember what I wrote for the following Sunday; nor, I suspect, does anyone else. The written word has power and life, but the trauma of history colors the best of manuscripts or erases them altogether.

Lord, give us words when none seem to suffice.

Whom the Gods love die young. Byron
—William Deans

November 27

Four major spinal surgeries in six years, then I lay encased in a body cast for six months. Frustration and anger filled me.

A wise friend said, "Char, journal! Write it down. Write it out." Even though I felt I'd been given a gift to teach, the only thing that comforted me was writing. I felt myself changing.

More and more of what I wrote became poetry. Astonished at what appeared on an empty page, I was too fearful of rejection to send it out to a publisher.

After reading some of the poetry my pastor said, "Embrace the new gift and use it." I vacillated, again and again.

Finally, he said, "Give me fifteen of the poems you love the most and trust me. I want to ask someone for his editorial opinion."

I took the risk and turned my work over to my pastor.

Weeks passed. Then one Monday my pastor rang the doorbell and handed me a Christian magazine. "Turn to page sixteen," he said.

Several of my poems covered page sixteen and were now in the hands of over forty thousand readers. I held it to my heart, embracing the new gift and vowing to continue taking risk after risk.

Lord, thank you for the courage to trust you implicitly and take risks with my writing.

Commitment at the point of my gifts means that I must give up being a straddler. Elizabeth O'Connor
—Char Forslund

November 28

Recycling—saving cans, papers, and bottles—is not my favorite thing to do, but I know it's for a good purpose.

Recycling reprints of my writing—well, that's a whole different thing. I love doing it. And I've had great results.

After my poems, articles, and short devotions have been published, I immediately look for new markets to send them. With *Writer's Market* in one hand and a pencil in the other, I scan through lists of possible publishers. I especially look for markets that accept simultaneous submissions. I also note which editors prefer an attachment and which prefer my manuscripts in the body of an e-mail.

While waiting for a response, I write something new or find other published pieces to submit. I keep track of my submissions and responses.

I get paid for the majority of my pieces, but I really write to touch lives. By recycling, I am able to reach hundreds and even thousands of people. What matters most to me is making a difference. If I can do that, so can you.

Lord, thank you for using me to touch others.

Success is getting what you want; happiness is wanting what you get. Anonymous

—Frances Gregory Pasch

November 29

For years I was reluctant to share the lessons God gave me, especially in written form. I did share occasionally with friends, who urged me to write the lessons down. They even gave me journals as gifts. But to offer them up for publication? No way.

When I started attending writers' conferences and workshops, I realized that if I wanted to inspire others, I needed to start recording and submitting. I chose the motto "If you don't submit, they can't print" for our local writers' group.

Now it's my desire to bring encouragement to others the same way that I'm motivated: by reading about the faith and success of others. As I share the way God has provided for me both spiritually and physically, I am greatly blessed.

It's an awesome responsibility and opportunity to be able to use the talent given to me at birth to write about all the things in this world that touch my heart. Then it's time for my motto "If you don't submit, they can't print" to come into focus. I consider it a privilege to pass my writings along.

Father, guide my pen as I write, so my words will bring honor and glory to your name.

For everything that was written in the past was written to teach us, so that through endurance and encouragement of the scriptures, we might have hope. Romans 15:4 NIV

—Jan Sady

November 30

I've loved writing for many years. So, why did I give up writing several years ago? I told people that my muse left me and I wanted to try my hand at visual arts. But I squirmed a bit inside when asked about my writing. I know writing is one of my God-given gifts. By turning my back on writing, did I turn away from a path he intended me to travel?

Perhaps I quit writing because it's such hard work: the writing, the rewriting, the submitting, the rejections.

I am not "work brittle," but I do fear working on a novel when success is uncertain. Basically, I am afraid of failure. My emotional mind still cringes at the thought. My logical mind knows that while failure (i.e., rejection) can happen, it doesn't define me or limit what I am capable of accomplishing. It's time that I let logic prevail.

This is my first baby step back into the realm of writing. For those who have encouraged me over the years, thank you for never letting me forget that God gave me this talent.

Lord, help me use the gifts you have given me. Thank you for writer friends who remind me I have a path to follow and for giving me a writer's heart.

Opportunity is missed by most people because it is dressed in overalls and looks like work. Thomas Edison

—Mary Benton

December 1

A dear Episcopal priest friend advised me to chew on the call to study for the priesthood. So I did. I prayed, wrote, and pondered. I argued with myself and conferred with others, finally deciding to enter the three-year process of vocational clarification.

My local parish voted to support me financially, and the psychiatrist confirmed my mental stability. In the third year, I traveled to a parish to teach adult classes and deliver the homily one Sunday each month. I submitted reports, lists of books read, and anecdotal accounts of my involvement in the parish. The parishioners sent me off with loving hugs, prayers, and good wishes.

I waited eagerly for the decision meeting with the diocesan bishop, totally unprepared for rejection. "Where would we place you as a woman?" he asked. After a few unsatisfying attempts at explanation, the final nail in my coffin: "You write very well." Was this a consolation?

In the following years, it didn't matter whether I wrote well or badly. It mattered only that I wrote—to learn to accept a blow delivered without an honest, clear explanation. I wrote to heal, to regain confidence in my worth, to forgive, and to learn to bathe myself in the oil of gladness instead of mourning.

Lord, teach us to search past our pain for the many reasons we have to be glad.

He has sent me to bind up the brokenhearted...to bestow on them a crown of beauty instead of ashes, the oil of gladness instead of mourning. Isaiah 61:1-3 NIV
—Olga M. Williams

December 2

"I never knew Dad, you know," my youngest brother said at a family gathering.

I couldn't forget his words. The youngest of nine children, my brother was only four years old when our father died of leukemia at age fifty-one. My youngest sister was only six.

Thinking I'd make a scrapbook for them, I sent a letter to the others asking for pictures, memories, stories, letters, anything that would reveal Dad's personality to the two who didn't know him.

One brother sent copies of twenty-three letters Dad wrote to him at college. Other letters of Dad's arrived from siblings who were in college, seminary, and military service in the early 1950s.

Those fifty-five letters from Dad and thirty from others put together chronologically, tell the story of his life.

After hours of typing and editing, I added original black-and-white pictures and newspaper articles. A project intended for my two youngest siblings became a book for my entire family, including extended relatives. Soon, people in our hometown and members of the church Dad served as a beloved pastor for seventeen years wanted a copy. Then orders came from their families all over the country.

So far I have given away or sold nearly five hundred copies.

Thank you, God, for speaking to me through the needs of others.

Listen, God is calling. Tanzanian hymn, translated by Howard Olson

—Christine Rotto Hefte

December 3

The most wonderful time of the year finds me penning our family's annual Christmas newsletter. It's a time of reflection and remembrance. Removing our marked-up calendar from the refrigerator, I thumb back through the year and recall the many events, celebrations, and even illnesses that have made up our lives for the past twelve months.

Memories of vacations, surgeries, and the birth of a new grandchild soon become our family's story, typed neatly onto festive holiday paper. Translating the joyful occasions into meaningful sentences causes me to smile. Reliving the difficult times proves painful. Yet in spite of hard circumstances, evidence of God's grace is sprinkled throughout the words.

As I write the newsletter, I am grateful for the gift of communication that enables me to stay in touch with family and friends. Our newsletters will eventually become history; the history of our family. Perhaps one day, my great-great-grandchildren will read the words penned by someone they never knew.

Thank you, Lord, for the gift of writing. Help me to write in a way that will touch people now and in future generations.

Be yourself. Above all, let who you are, what you are, what you believe, shine through every sentence you write, every piece you finish. John Jakes

—Julie Gillies

December 4

Ten years after I began writing, I wondered if I should be doing something else. The plentiful rejections and long stretches between successes left me doubting I was on the right path. I wanted my work to be used, my time to be well invested, and wanted to contribute more to our finances.

In the beginning, I had researched how to get started and then plunged in, hesitant and hopeful at the same time. I said my share of prayers and plowed ahead in the best way I knew how. But most of the time I felt like a lone ranger.

As time went on, I poured out my frustrations to God and shared them with my good friend Jeneal Rogers. Since she too had writing aspirations, we encouraged and acted as sounding boards for each other. Sensing my current struggle, she sent me a Bible study for writers. It left me reassured and refreshed.

Jeneal had joined the Fellowship of Christian Writers in Tulsa, Oklahoma, and could not stop singing the organization's praises. Even though the group was seventy-five miles away from me, I decided it would be worth the time and expense to attend. I was hooked after just one meeting. The support, camaraderie, and training have drawn me back again and again. No more lone ranger status for me!

Thank you, Lord, for the fellowship of other writers.

Think where man's glory most begins and ends, And say my glory was I had such friends. William Yeats
—Cheryl Barker

December 5

A poet is not truly free;
I am a slave unto my pen.
A writer has to write, you see.
I can't retire, cannot flee;
I am the most enslaved of men.
A poet is not truly free.
"Ah, what a life!" Most would agree,
"I am not ruled by laws." But then
A writer has to write, you see.
I leave my desk. "It can't hold me!"
But thoughts soon pull me back again.
A poet is not truly free.
My prison is hyperbole
Or image, plot, or stratagem.
A writer has to write, you see.
In this so-called democracy
Freedom's an illusion when
A poet is not truly free.
A writer has to write, you see.

Lord, may my writing be all for your glory.

I must be about my Father's business. Luke 2:49 KJV
—Bill Batcher

December 6

On a cold evening, I retreated to the sofa with hot chocolate and Grandmother's quilt. The warmth from the fireplace reached out to me, but the chill in my heart remained.

I'd not written a single word in months. After years of freelancing, I understood writer's block and rejection letters, but this felt different. I was tired of the struggle, the endless quest. Maybe I should quit.

So, for three months, I had. Some nights I tossed until dawn, wrestling with sentences, refusing to get up and write them down.

Watching the fire's flames consume the logs, I thought, What would happen if I lit a match to my desk? Computer, files, everything. Would anybody care?

Reaching for the phone, I knew if anybody could cheer me up, my friend Cindy could.

"I'm considering starting a bonfire with my desk," I told her.

"Dayle, don't think such things. You don't want to destroy the gift God's given you."

The flames burned low now, the room cold. I walked over and stoked the fire. Flames immediately shot up, flooding the room with hot colors—and an undeniable message: Fire left alone will burn out, but stir it up and it's a powerful source of light and warmth.

Cindy was right. God had given me a gift. It only needed rekindling. Armed with a fresh purpose, I marched into my office and wrote the story you just read.

Father, may I never allow my gifts to become ashes.

Stir up the gift of God, which is in thee. 2 Timothy 1:6 KJV

—Dayle Allen Shockley

December 7

Watching a television documentary series that covered World War II from Pearl Harbor in 1941 until August 1945 overwhelmed me with childhood memories. This was especially true of the movie newsreel footage.

Like many kids of that time, I often spent Saturday afternoons at the movies. After Bugs Bunny outsmarted Elmer Fudd and Roy Rogers chased the bad guys, the program switched to shocking reality. I can still remember hearing the reporter's serious voice describing beach landings and watching horrific scenes of our soldiers and marines pinned down by the enemy.

Sometimes when I'm trying to write, I feel like the soldiers and marines stuck on the beach. I'm not facing a hail of bullets, but a barrage of valid responsibilities claim me—family, a day job, phone calls, appointments, illness, emergencies, and even writer's block. Like the troops, I have to fight my way through whatever obstacles are in front of me. Often, I wonder if I'll ever make it. The troops had the beachmaster to direct and lead them. I have God, and he won't let me stay pinned down on the beach.

Lord, thank you for urging me on, for keeping my goal of writing for you ahead of me, and helping me to achieve it.

Do not pray for tasks equal to your powers; pray for powers equal to your tasks. Phillips Brooks

—Carolyn Meagher

December 8

"Why did you give up on writing books?" asks Bryce, my five-year-old.

"I haven't given up on writing books," I reply. "What makes you think I've given up?"

"Well, you used to spend more time writing."

"I still write. Just not quite as much as I did before Benjamin was born."

"Because babies are a lot of work." His twin brother, Andrew, joins the conversation.

"That's right." I said. "Babies take up a lot of time. And so does housework and cooking and everything else I do around here."

I try to stay positive, but the boys are right. When was the last time I sent out a query letter or wrote an essay? Maybe I have given up on my writing.

"What if we help you?" Bryce asks, cheerfully.

"Yeah! We could help with all that stuff!" Andrew agrees, walking over to the closet and dragging out the vacuum cleaner. Bryce races around, enthusiastically picking bits up off the floor while his brother maneuvers the plug. Soon, the roar of the vacuum drowns out any hope of further conversation. Andrew waves me off, mouthing, "You go write, Mom. We'll take care of everything."

I don't know whether to laugh or cry as they whisk me out of the room. So I open my computer and I write.

Lord, thank you for using my children to encourage me today.

Be strong, all of you who put your hope in the Lord. Never give up. Psalms 31:24 NIRV

—Robyn Whitlock

December 9

I used to think that only those who were published could be considered real writers. This idea was strengthened with each rejection letter I received. I considered giving up writing altogether.

Then I remembered the letters I'd written to comfort, encourage, and protect those I cared about over the years. Writing a note is the first thing I do when I learn someone is hurting or has a reason to celebrate.

Whether I become a published writer is no longer important. What is important is that I stay true to my calling.

Verse 45:1 in the Book of Psalms tells me to write from my heart, because God has put the desire to write in me. I may not be confident in myself, but this verse assures me that if I listen to the voice inside my heart I will be able to write just what I am supposed to for his purpose, not necessarily my success. He has equipped me and I stand ready.

With this in mind, today I'm going to finish editing the short story I've been working on.

Lord, when it comes to my writing, help me do my best for you.

My heart is stirred by a noble theme as I recite my verses for the king; my tongue is the pen of a skillful writer. Psalms 45:1 NIV

—Deanna L. Baird

December 10

As a teacher of writing in high school and college, I had my students repeat aloud and practice the mantra "Specific is terrific."

Instead of writing, "I rode different rides at the amusement park," I asked them to share the specifics. They learned to write, "I rode the Jack Rabbit and Thunderbolt roller coasters at Kennywood."

Instead of writing "I was scared on the amusement ride," they revised their writing to read, "When the car stopped at the top of the Ferris wheel, my stomach churned as we rocked."

Instead of putting up a sign that said "Beware of the dog," they learned to write, "A pit bull lives here."

One of my students wrote a corollary to my slogan: "Vague is not in vogue in Room 102."

When we looked at Frost's poem "Dust of Snow," I passed out the poem, inserting vague words like bird and tree. Students replaced the nouns with specifics and then compared their choices with Frost's crow and hemlock. Then they discussed the difference the specifics made.

When students edited their own writing, I asked them to take a piece of notebook paper and write the words "For example" in the margin on every third line. Seldom did I hear them complain, "But I already have specific examples on that line."

Lord, help us to see your world bird by bird, as Anne Lamott does, hawk by red-tailed hawk.

You can train yourself to see revealing specifics. Donald Murray

—Shirley Stevens

December 11

When my daughter was in grade school, she brought home a book she thought I would like to read, borrowed from her teacher. The title was *Chicken Soup for the Soul.* I read it from cover to cover and wondered what it would be like to have a story included in such a heartwarming anthology.

Around that time I started writing essays on family life. I also purchased quite a large collection of the Chicken Soup for the Soul series books. Each time I'd scan the author's bios in the back with an unexplained belief that one day my name would be among them.

Meanwhile, I found a home for my essays and stories in a local newspaper. Having my own weekly column was the first of many dreams to come true.

Many years and many submissions later, I added another Chicken Soup book to my collection. This time, my name is included in the back as a contributing author. When I handed my daughter a copy, her happiness said it all. I had made it!

I continue to submit my stories to Chicken Soup and other publications. I have proof that nothing is impossible if you believe.

Thank you, Lord, for placing a dream in my heart and for helping me see it through.

It's always too early to quit. Norman Vincent Peale
—Kathy Whirity

December 12

Staff and volunteers for Advancing the Developmentally Disabled streamed into the room. Leslie, a young disabled woman, gazed into the camera as if making direct eye contact with us. Her muffled words spoken in a whisper were hard to understand until she said, "I can make it."

She told of instances when people didn't let her attempt tasks or said she couldn't participate in activities. They meant well, but they deprived her of the opportunity to learn. Even if the quality of her work fell short of her peers' performance, she could do it.

Each time she gave an example, her words became clearer. Her voice strengthened as she described her determination to let everyone know she had the ability to achieve goals.

I wrote a letter to the host and included my impression of Leslie's story. The short piece captured the essence of succeeding in the world from a mentally disabled person's point of view. The host asked me to submit my letter to a newsletter for parents who had mentally and developmentally special needs children. People who didn't view the film were able to picture Leslie's story through my written words.

Dear Lord, thank you for the potential placed within each person.

Without faith, nothing is possible. With it, nothing is impossible. Mary McLeod Bethune

—Julia F. Bell

December 13

I was still learning to balance my time between my roles as wife, mom, volunteer, and freelance writer, and my calendar was jam-packed. As I penciled in my work for the week, I felt the familiar tug at my spirit.

When would I schedule time to write God's words?

These nudges happened more often than I wanted to admit. I overextended myself at home and at work and left little time for writing the words God pressed on my heart. I was frequently stirred to write a short piece or even a few phrases when a piece of scripture spoke to me. I knew it was the Spirit's silent persistence that wanted to guide me to a more personal essay or journal entry. But I frequently repressed the urge to write these nonpaying, unscheduled pieces until my calendar was clear. The result was missed opportunities and a growing sense of guilt.

Acknowledging that I needed to offer my first fruits instead of sloppy seconds, I marked off a section of my week for these divine assignments. The results might not be a paycheck or a published piece but I know I'll be rewarded in supernatural ways for putting God first on my writing calendar.

Dear Lord, help me put you first in my writing. Thank you for new opportunities.

I give you all the finest olive oil and all the finest new wine and grain they give the Lord as the first fruits of their harvest. Numbers 18:12 NIV

—Nicole Amsler

December 14

For my son's third-grade Christmas party, I wrote and read a short story that incorporated every child from the class. As research, I asked parents for a snippet of information about their child. The teacher was pregnant and due to deliver over the holiday, so I incorporated that as well.

"The Winter of the King" was about a magical old king who shows up, in a flurry of snow, right in the middle of the classroom. He is due to retire and is looking for the child destined to take his place. Each child states why he or she is perfect for the crown.

While I read the story, I watched faces light up across the room. The tale ended with the king announcing that the teacher's yet-to-be-born child would be the future winter monarch.

Several days later I received a note from the teacher. She had taken the story to share with her family, bringing all of them to tears. Her father had died weeks before, and the family had already discussed that phenomenon of losing one family member just as another was arriving. My writing brought her family comfort, she said.

I had no way of knowing the story would parallel her circumstances, but God blessed me by showing why he put it on my heart.

Lord, thank you for using our words to comfort others.

I wish thee as much pleasure in the reading, as I had in the writing. Francis Quarles

—Trish Perry

December 15

One of my writing instructors did all her work in children's spiral notebooks with silly covers. She said, "If I write pages of drivel it won't matter, because it's only a child's notebook."

I tried a spiral notebook, but it didn't fit my purse. Instead, I use an eight-and-a-half-by-eleven yellow pad folded in half with a rolling ball pen clipped to the side. It fits easily into my LeSportsac handbag and is always available. I love the sensuous quality of the ink gliding over the paper. It calls me to write flowing prose.

Fancy journals call for good grammar and real writing. In a yellow pad, I can do writing practice where I write without stopping for ten or twenty minutes; I can write a really bad first draft; or I can vent my feelings without dire consequences.

I may change my mind tomorrow; but for now I do much of my first-draft writing in a yellow pad and later transcribe it to computer for final edits.

This way, I am free to write mostly trash and mine the gems that occasionally appear. By giving myself the freedom to write badly, I am also free to write well. I have found that this strategy also keeps me from taking myself too seriously

Beloved God, grant me the grace not to take myself too seriously.

... not to think of yourself more highly than you ought to think. Romans 12:3a NRSV

—Connie Scharlau

December 16

After hours of delay, the Air Force transport lumbered into Glenview Naval Air Station north of Chicago. A woman and her two sons stood on the tarmac outside the small control center, unable to restrain their excitement. She cried. The boys jumped up and down.

The plane's door opened and Capt. Robert Naughton's frail form moved slowly down the stairs. He looked up as he stepped on the runway, and they ran toward him. The night air was thick with emotion. Even so-called hard-boiled newspaper reporters could not contain their tears. I know. I was one of them.

After more than five years of imprisonment at the infamous Hanoi Hilton in North Vietnam, Bob Naughton was home, reunited with his family. For seemingly endless months they had read and reread his infrequent letters, trying to put a face on the husband and father, inserting hope in between the lines.

Now, thanks be to God, they saw him in the flesh and they kissed him and hugged him. It took a while to make up for some five years of missed hugs.

It was one of the greatest stories I ever had the privilege to write.

Lord, thanks for precious life and the great opportunity to proclaim its wonder.

You changed my mourning into dancing, you took off my sackcloth and clothed me with gladness. Psalms 30:12 NAB

—Dale Kueter

December 17

The first assignment in creative writing class left me feeling inadequate. The sound of an egg frying? How could anyone capture that on paper? I cogitated for quite some time, then wrote and submitted my paper.

As we waited for the next class to begin, a few of us shared our angst about the assignment. When Professor Argent appeared, silence descended. In his distinctive British accent, he said one of the papers was particularly good and proceeded to read it. I made a soundless gasp. The piece was mine. "'Like the sound of a child popping bubble gum,'" he quoted. "That's an apt figure of speech." I tried not to seem too pleased.

When the professor returned my paper, he asked, "Why aren't you published?" I can't remember what else took place in the class that day because his words kept dancing like jewels before my eyes. Here were words affirming what I always wanted to do.

I left the classroom determined to be a writer. My inspiration resulted in two hurriedly written stories and two quickly received rejection letters. Yet I kept hearing those words and remembered them whenever I saw my byline or received a publisher's check. Those words spoken at the right time have been a lifelong inspiration to me.

Lord, let my words bear good fruit in a fellow traveler's life.

A word fitly spoken is like apples of gold in pictures of silver. Proverbs 25:11 KJV

—Judith P. Nembhard

December 18

I came out of church feeling angry with myself. A friend sensed my agitation right away.

"What's wrong?" she asked.

I told her that I gave in, once again, to a serious character flaw; I let myself be distracted by poor grammar. She didn't get it.

"Well, I'll tell you," I confided. "When Pastor made the statement, 'God gives good gifts to you and I,' I lost it. I tuned out the rest of his sermon. Why must I always be persnickety? I'm such a judgmental person."

"Not at all," she assured me as we walked along together. Even though Adele was a fashion designer, with talents very different from my own, she said she understood completely. "It's part of your job as a writer to be alert for such errors," she said. Then she added, "I stop listening to the sermon if the man seated in front of me is wearing a sports jacket and the plaid doesn't match at the back seam."

We laughed. Her sharing this about herself, helped put things in perspective for me. Now, whenever I hear "me" when it should be "I," or "I" when it should be "me,"— or even the word "myself" when a simple "I" or "me" would be correct—I tell myself, "Oops, another mismatched seam" and I continue listening.

Forgiving Father, help me to remember that I too make mistakes.

You and I do not see things as they are. We see things as we are. Henry Ward Beecher

—Helene Clare Kuoni

December 19

Seminar speakers stress the importance of writing each day. I don't question the wisdom of their advice. I just find it difficult to do. You see, I am plagued by a demon named Legion.

Legion convinces me that I am too tired. I need to shop for one more Christmas present. The walk needs shoveling. I have nothing to say. The third class catalogs demand my attention. The Christmas mailing list needs updating. Soon, the day has slipped away and I haven't written a word. Again, I have been seduced by Legion's siren song, "Trivia!"

All these reasons for not writing daily translate into a lack of discipline. I allow the less essential to replace the essential.

In my struggle to exorcise Legion, I adopted two strategies. Following my early morning walk, I reserve a minimum of two hours for writing. It's when I am the freshest and thoughts come easier. Second, I set a goal for the number of words to be written based on the task at hand. Only then do I read the newspaper or schedule the remainder of my day's activities.

This schedule is not for everyone. The important point is to set aside time each day exclusively for writing and a production goal set. Gradually, it will become habit and the demon exorcised.

Lord God, give me strength to become a disciplined writer.

Things which matter most must never be done at the mercy of things which matter least. Johann Wolfgang von Goethe

—Gerald Ebelt

December 20

My first book arrived by UPS. No one was home to see it except my four-year-old daughter. I wanted to show it to the world, but could only draw my little girl to me. "Do you know who this is?" I asked, pointing to my picture on the back of the book."

"Mommy," she said blandly. Well, at least she knew who I was.

"Do you know who wrote this book?" I asked.

She shook her head.

"Mommy did," I said. When she didn't show any reaction. I pointed to myself.

"Mommy wrote this book." Pause. "Isn't that wonderful?"

She sighed. "No."

Daunted, I asked, "Why not?"

She heaved a heavier sigh. "Because I can't read."

Although I was disappointed that no one was around to share my excitement over my first book being published, I learned a valuable lesson. There isn't always instant recognition or appreciation of a writer's long, lonely hours of work. However, when a note comes in the mail, an unexpected e-mail, or a friend or even someone you hadn't met before says, "I really like your work. It touches my heart." And even better when they say, "That strengthened my faith. Thank you for writing clean Christian books."

Lord, may my written words be an inspiration and encouragement to those who read what you have given me to write.

If my doctor told me I had only six minutes to live, I wouldn't brood. I'd type a little faster. Isaac Asimov

—Yvonne Lehman

December 21

A publisher approached the college where I work to write a book challenging believers to cultivate a Christian worldview. I was honored to be part of the team that would craft the volume, my first blush with writing for publication. At the first planning meeting, the administrator who would shepherd the project talked about the need for all of the authors to practice graciousness as we interfaced with the editor. "Some authors can be mean-spirited," he said. "Be sure you do not embarrass the college by falling into this category."

I prayed that God would grant me the ability to model his graciousness. He responded by challenging me to respond to the editor's suggestions with four categories of words—appreciative, quiet, affirming, and contented.

Now four books and numerous articles later, I continue to use these categories with each writing project.

Heavenly Father, as I write, please empower me to always model your graciousness.

Writers are not just people who sit down and write. They hazard themselves. Every time you compose a book your composition of yourself is at stake. E. L. Doctorow
—Pat Ennis

December 22

As I write my memoir, I notice it sounds like reporting. I try to find the shade of gray that describes personal despair or makes the everyday seem adventurous. Even though my story is true, it sounds too unbelievable. My story as fiction would likely never sell.

In many ways, I find writing fiction so easy that it seems unfair to write it. I create the universe, create the characters and create the problems. I can make sense of it because I see the end from the beginning. I know how each of the characters will grow through every tragic circumstance or wonderful event. Every action, thought, and character has a purpose from the outset.

In my life, things remain less clear, not so black and white. I wonder every day: am I a good enough writer? Who will read my stories? Will my words make a difference?

Pondering my life in an attempt to reconcile those things that do not make sense always delivers thought-provoking plot lines.

Lord, thank you for the trials you've carried me through. May their retelling in my stories touch others and illuminate their way out of a dark night.

The difference between fiction and reality? Fiction has to make sense. Tom Clancy

—Julie Morrison

December 23

"The poem's OK, but where's the Bolduc family letter?"

Ouch! My sixteen-year-old, Justin, cut, as usual, to the heart of the matter. For several years I'd found great joy in finding new words for the age-old Christmas story. Reclaiming the wonder of God-become-man. Excavating the awe that's hidden under mounds of wrapping paper.

Every December I sent out my musings in poem or story form, along with a family letter. This year, I'd decided to skip the much-maligned Christmas letter, which had become the butt of jokes on late night television.

"People want to know what's going on in our lives," Justin went on to say. "Letters are a way of staying in touch!"

I realized I'd bought into the cynicism and worldliness I'd been trying so hard to overcome in my Christmas writings. It's a lie that nobody cares—that we rip open holiday letters warm with news and throw them aside muttering "whatever."

Writing a Christmas poem or story to share remains my favorite holiday activity. Thanks to Justin, I make sure it's tucked inside the Bolduc family letter before I stick it into the envelope and mail it to far-away family and friends—people who love us; people who care about our ups and downs.

Lord, may the good news in our Christmas letters be reminiscent of your good news—a gift of connection, of caring, of love.

Behold, I bring you good news of a great joy. Luke 2:10b RSV

—Kathleen Deyer Bolduc

December 24

Family Christmases always meant a sparkling tree, laughter, my brother Eddie and me at the piano. But within a two-year period, everything changed. Mom died, Eddie died.

Where was God? Overwhelmed with loss, I couldn't write my annual Christmas poem. A long year of darkness followed. One sleepless night, I watched stars begin to appear in the night sky. I grabbed paper and pencil, and began to write.

How cold it must have been that night.
I can see the stars, if I close my eyes.
Listen! I hear the soft night air, rustling the leaves.
Or is it the rustle of angel's wings?
Suddenly, the skies fill with exultant song.
And so He came to the shepherds.
An obscure carpenter begs shelter for his wife,
heavy with child, and is led to a stable.
And so He came to the innkeeper.
When the tinsel and the tree are gone,
when all the carols have been sung, look for Him then.
He is not confined to a day, a season, or a place in time.
He comes to each of us in his own way.
He meets us in the oddest places.
In despair perhaps? He met me there.
And for me, for the first time, Christmas.

Lord, when it comes to helping me write, you meet my every need, turning darkness into light.

Even there your hand shall guide me, and your right hand hold me fast. Psalm 139:10 NAB

—Tommie Lenox

December 25

At age forty, I wanted more than just being mom, wife, and assistant in my husband's business. My old dream of writing and teaching resurfaced, but our home had no space just for me, no writing place.

I needed a desk, actually a rolltop desk, one I'd seen in a catalog. Throughout the fall, neither Jack nor the kids acknowledged my hints. That missing desk became a symbol of why I couldn't write.

On Christmas morning, I woke early to turn on the tree lights. There it was—my desk—warm oak, roll top invitingly open. Jack later explained how he'd hidden it in our neighbor's barn and then pushed it up our long driveway at 2 a.m. The kids cheered and praised each other for keeping the secret. I cried my way through Christmas morning.

I know material possessions are not what writing is all about, but that desk gave me space to become a writer. I went to graduate school, became a writing teacher, and published two poetry chapbooks.

Last year, I planned to redecorate my office with matching urban white office furniture. I couldn't do it. My desk means too much. What a blessing to be stuck forever with that symbol of my writing and the family who loved and believed in me enough to help make my dream come true.

Lord, thank you for your writing gifts and the people you use to show your love.

Where there is great love, there are always miracles.
Willa Cather

—Pam O'Brien

December 26

My friend Barbara sent me a rewritten manuscript that I'd helped her with. I saw how hard she'd worked on it and liked her final version. Knowing Barbara's eyesight was failing because of severe diabetes, I sent her piece to a newspaper editor. I didn't tell her because I didn't want her to be disappointed if the editor rejected it.

A month later I got a phone call from Barbara. Her voice was cracking.

"Barbara, what's wrong?"

"Well, my eyes began to hemorrhage and I'm nearly blind. But Pat, that's not why I'm calling. A friend came to read me my mail this afternoon. The last thing he came to was a big manila envelope. A newspaper was inside with a check and a note attached saying the editor loved my story and was publishing it.

"Pat, my story is in that very newspaper on the front page! I'm a published author! Imagine! Me, published!" she paused. "I know you sent it in. How can I thank you? I was so depressed with my eye problems and then this happened. What a wonderful Christmas gift! I was going to quit writing. Now I'm going to tape-record my stories and find someone to type them."

That day I learned that sometimes the littlest bit of encouragement makes all the difference for a writer.

Lord, help me keep the joy of writing alive in my friends as well as in myself.

What I like in a good author is not what he says, but what he whispers. Logan Pearsall Smith

—Patricia Lorenz

December 27

Most experienced writers caution again and again to let a goodly amount of time elapse before turning a painful recollection, experience, or feeling into an essay, story, or poem.

Keep it inside, they order. Don't rush it, they advise. Let it incubate, they say.

Rubbish, I say. I've learned the value in pouring out my heart while my emotional skin is scraped raw.

Write while the sensations sear, the goosebumps prickle, and the jagged holes of turmoil still gape wide. Bleed onto the page. Then set it aside. Let the writing incubate. Don't rush it.

After some time has passed (only the author can judge how long), take it out for a detailed, less biased review. Often, I discover a depth of strength in that initial draft that might be lacking had I waited until the wounds mended before I wrote. And I realize it's those first aching, wrenching words that might reach and connect with readers scarred from similar experiences. Moreover, I am often startled at the insights and lessons I discover from my primitive, penned reactions.

I've learned to risk exposing my innermost, private self—the good, the bad, and the unpleasant—while trusting my audience to empathize and sympathize.

And they do!

Lord, grant me insight into my own life, to understand the power of sharing my deepest emotions with others.

You're braver than you believe, and stronger than you seem, and smarter than you think. Christopher Robin
—Carol McAdoo Rehme

December 28

Her perfectly coiffed white hair and smooth, rosy complexion belied her eighty years. At a friend's urging, she joined my monthly journaling workshop at a retirement community, but protested that she was not a writer.

With the very first assignments, she revealed an ability to create prose as beautifully crafted as her paintings, and as lovely as her serene face. When the class decided to collect and publish a booklet of its best writings, half a dozen of this new writer's pieces appeared.

She was not the only late-blooming success in my workshop. A lady in her nineties struggled with the unfamiliar craft of putting thoughts and memories into written words—and earned her place in the booklet.

At each session, the students read their writings aloud. "What did you especially like in that story?" I asked after each reading, and the class learned to encourage the writer by singling out, for example, the image of love as a Ferris wheel, or the childhood memory of peanut butter and lettuce sandwiches cut into dainty triangles.

Without formal instruction in composition or close critique, these writers blossomed through listening to one another's work and responding positively. We were all proud of our book!

Lord, help us to support one another as writers, in your spirit of love.

When something can be read without effort, great effort has gone into its writing. Enrique Jardiel Poncela
—Nancy E. James

December 29

One of my greatest problems in writing is managing my day. Now that I am retired from a demanding office job, there should be plenty of time to write. Not so. I have children's and grandchildren's lives to relate to, household chores, church responsibilities, and the slowing down that comes with age, before even considering recreation, reading, or just plain relaxation. A "needs my attention" list is my constant companion.

Some discipline is needed, or the day gets quickly out of hand. Sleeping in until six or seven o'clock is only for weekends. Physical, mental, and spiritual exercise (in my case, about forty minutes each of bike riding, reading a technical journal, prayer, and a Bible chapter or two) plus breakfast with my wife and a quick read of the paper are all done by nine, leaving the rest of the morning for whatever I am writing, revising, or researching.

Distractions are inevitable: e-mail, phone, errands, the temptations of free-cell and solitaire, computer vagaries, guests, helping my wife, paying bills, attending meetings. Whenever possible, all this is done in the afternoon. I sometimes write in the afternoon or evening, but often yield to a good book or DVD after dinner.

The secret is balance, among God, loved ones, environment, and work.

God, please help me make time for my writing every day.

Keep your eye on the ball. Every baseball coach
— Keith Dahlberg

December 30

Christmas is past, but the last line of a carol replays in my mind. "The hopes and fears of all the years are met in thee tonight." I've sung those words since childhood. But what do they mean to me as a writer?

Sometimes I feel like a pendulum, swinging back and forth between hopes and fears. I hope editors will publish my work and my words will touch readers. But I fear rejection, isolation, and writing trials.

When I receive praise, I consider myself a good writer. But when rejection comes, I'm discouraged. Writing successes or failures influence my sense of worth.

As I ponder the end of the stanza, "are met in thee tonight," I realize those words hold the key. When my thoughts and emotions vacillate, I can turn to Jesus. God and his word will keep me centered. Verses such as Jeremiah 1:5 tell me how God views me: "Before I formed you in the womb I knew you, before you were born I set you apart."

Before I wrote or published a word, God sent Jesus as his word to be born and to die for my sins and to help me face my hopes and fears. I'm that worthwhile in God's eyes.

Amazing how wonderful it is to be a writer.

Thank you, Lord, that as I write, all my hopes and fears are centered in you.

Hope in God. Psalms 42:11 NIV

—Linda E. Harris

December 31

Autograph books were popular when I was in junior high school. My favorite way to write in them was to turn to the back page and write, "By hook or by crook, I'm the last to write in your autograph book."

Now, fifty years later, I find myself writing on the last page of this devotion book for writers. Members and friends of The Writing Academy and other writers from all over the country who wrote these devotions hope this book helps you gain confidence in your ability to write. We have poured out our writing joys, frustrations, pain, fear, struggles, and blessings in the hope that you know you are not alone and to give you courage to begin or keep writing.

If this were an autograph book, I would write on the last page...

This last page
Kept clean and new
Is waiting for a writer
Just like you!

Lord, may this New Year's Eve be the day that all the readers of this book will truly become inspired to write everything that's simmering in their souls for your glory.

Those who write clearly have readers, those who write obscurely have commentators. Albert Camus

—Sally Devine

ABOUT THE WRITERS

Sister Jane Abeln (5-9) is a professed Missionary Sister of the Immaculate Conception. She has taught English in the United States, Taiwan, and the Philippines, and worked in various spiritual ministries. She writes and ministers in the Paterson, New Jersey, area. sisterjane2004@yahoo.com.

Charlotte Adelsperger (1-29, 6-4) is a speaker and the author of three books, including *When Your Child Hurts: Hope for Parents of Children Undergoing Long Term Medical Care,* as well as hundreds of articles, poems, and stories. She lives in Overland Park, Kansas. author04@aol.com.

Sandra P. Aldrich (1-19), president-CEO of Bold Words, Inc., Colorado Springs, Colorado, is an international speaker who presents life's issues with insight and humor. She is the author/coauthor of seventeen books and contributor to two dozen more, including several Chicken Soup for the Soul books. BoldWords@aol.com; www.sandraaldrich.com.

Nicole Amsler (12-13) owns Keylocke Services, a freelance copywriting business in Springboro, Ohio. She wrote her first book at age five and charged ten cents a page for her middle-school novellas. After a career in marketing, she began her freelance writing business and is working on her next book. nicole@keylocke.com.

Eileen Astels (4-20) lives in southern Ontario, Canada, with her family. She is learning the craft of writing while dreaming up big plots and intriguing characters. She has written book reviews for the American Christian Fiction Writers' *Afictionado* e-zine. www.eileenastels.com.

Linda M. Au (1-27) has worked as a proofreader since the late 1980s. She is also a coach for an online writing course for homeschoolers and is an award-winning writer of humor essays and novels. She and her husband, Wayne, live in New Brighton, Pennsylvania.

linda@austruck.com; www.austruck.com.

Deanna L. Baird (12-9) lives in Armada, Michigan. She is the wife of David and mother of Devin and Kelsey. She works part time at the Armada library. Her work has appeared in *The Upper Room* and *Just Between Us*. d_baird1@yahoo.com.

Cheryl Barker (12-4), a freelance writer and home-maker, lives in Coffeyville, Kansas. Her work has been used in compilation books, greeting cards, magazines, and other publications. She is working on two book projects and is active in her church. ckbarker@gmail.com; cherylbarker.blogspot.com.

Bill Batcher (2-26, 12-5) considers himself a poet under construction. A retired teacher, he leads a writers' group in Riverhead, New York. His poetry has been published in magazines, anthologies, and online collections, and has won several awards. A book of Easter poems, *Footsteps to the Resurrection*, was published in 2005. bbatcher@optonline.net.

Julia F. Bell (1-21, 6-28, 10-8, 12-12) of Dayton, Ohio, is the mother of three children and grandmother of four. After losing her memory in 1970, she laid the foundation of her new life based on flashbacks of her grandfather's lessons about God. She discovered the healing power in writing as she recorded her story. jbell9347@aol.com.

Christina Berry (6-30), a stay-at-home mom from Gaston, Oregon, balances her compulsion to write with managing a young family and spending time with her husband. Though she's written on her own, most people are fascinated that she and her mother coauthor novels. www.ashberrylane.net.

Mary Benton (11-30) lives in Lubbock, Texas, with her husband, Jack, and Maggie the cat. She has two grown children and three grandchildren. She enjoys reading, writing, and various arts and crafts. She has been a member of writers' groups in West Texas and has published short stories and nonfiction. merribee02@yahoo.com.

Sandy Block (10-3) works twenty-five hours a week as the community page editor at the *Wausau* (Wis.) *Daily Herald*, although she would really rather be quilting. She lives in Rothschild, Wisconsin, where her husband is a Lutheran pastor. They have three daughters, one son-in-law, one grandson, and a dog. sblock927@hotmail.com.

Kathleen Deyer Bolduc (1-15, 5-20, 8-4, 12-23), from Cincinnati, Ohio, is the author of *His Name is Joel: Searching for God in a Son's Disability* and *A Place Called Acceptance: Ministry with Families of Children with Disabilities*. Kathleen speaks on disability and faith issues, and leads workshops on writing and contemplative prayer. www.kathleenbolduc.com.

Grace G. Booth (6-23) is a freelance writer, published in numerous periodicals including *Guideposts*. She codirects the Southern Christian Writers Guild in Mandeville, Louisiana, and teaches The Write Way, designed to help others polish their writing skills. She and her husband, Doug, live in Picayune, Mississippi. ruwriting2@datastar.net.

Ivie Bozeman (3-8) submits her work on a regular basis to *Eternal Ink* and *Presbyterian Daily* of Canada. She's an adult church school teacher in the United Methodist Church and lives in Thomasville, Georgia. ivie@rose.net.

Tamar Braden (4-26) lives in Sanford, Florida in her purple, second-childhood playhouse, sharing the porch with a once-vagrant cat. Her four adult children have provided her with twenty-six grandchildren and great-grandchildren.

Joy C. Bradford (4-17) graduated from the University of Texas in Dallas. Her writings have appeared in periodicals and anthologies. She and George, her husband of forty-six years, enjoy retirement and grandchildren.

Sharon Beth Brani (4-1) is an adoption consultant, speaker, counselor and writer living in Culpeper, Virginia. Her greatest joy is being the mother of two wonderful girls she adopted from Russia. She works to assist in the growth and nurture of adopted children. www.sharonbrani.com.

Annettee Budzban (2-3, 7-15, 11-21), Wildwood, Illinois, is a Christian author, speaker, and newspaper columnist. Her writings have appeared in *Guideposts Angels on Earth, Family Circle, A Cup of Comfort Devotionals,* and more. She is also a teleseminar speaker. www.AnnetteeBudzban.com.

Mary "Mike" Mikell Calkin (6-8) is a freelance writer and speaker from Clifton, Virginia. She is a cofounder of the Capital Christian Writers club and leads retreats to help women find their identity in Christ. She is a wife, mother of two, and granny of three. mike-calkin@cox.net.

Clella Camp (9-23) is the author of the devotion book *Just Walking* (AMG Publishers), published in 2005. She and her husband live in Paris, Illinois, in summer and Pinellas Park, Florida, in the winter. They have two children in Christian service and four grandchildren. www.clellascorner.blogspot.com.

Alesia Skaggs Campbell's (8-2) work has been published in various magazines and Christian books. She, her husband, and son reside in Edmond, Oklahoma. She is also a published author on speech-language pathology. mabcampbell@cox.net.

Kathe Campbell (5-10) lives on a mountain south of Butte, Montana, with her mammoth donkeys. She is a writer on the topic of Alzheimer's, a contributing writer to the Chicken Soup for the Soul series, numerous anthologies, *RX for Writers,* and medical journals. She is grandmother to eleven and great-granny to three. bigskyadj@in-tch.com.

Theresa Carouthers (10-6) is a second-grade teacher and the mother of two boys. They live in Hamshire, Texas. theresa.tlc1@yahoo.com.

David Carter (6-5) received his B.A. from Western Washington University and a master's from Seattle University. He lives in State College, Pennsylvania, works as an English as a Second Language (ESL) instructor at Pennsylvania State University, and is a private English tutor. dtrauts@yahoo.com.

Kay J. Clark (1-12) is a retired English teacher from Chesterfield, Indiana, and the widow of a Disciples of Christ minister. She spends her time writing, reading, quilting, and sharing lunch with friends. auden@sbcglobal.net.

Trudie Clem (9-21), a school health nursing supervisor, lives in Bunnell, Florida. She is the author of *Adoption Affair*, an inspirational romance. Life with her husband, family, and pets provides material for many stories. disgirlbejammin@aol.com.

Cathy Conger (8-19) lives with her husband in Wisconsin Rapids, Wisconsin. They have five grown children. Her work includes humorous essays, a book of poetry, a Christmas carol for choir and orchestra, and D-MAIL, her weekly online devotional column. She is writing a Christmas musical for 2008. conger@wctc.net.

Rev. Gerard Creedon (9-11), a Catholic priest, is pastor of St. Charles Borromeo parish in Arlington, Virginia, and chairman of the Peace and Justice Commission for the Diocese of Arlington. Educated in Ireland, Father Gerry has been published in the *Ireland Poetry Review* and the *National Catholic Reporter.* www.stcharleschurch.org.

Barbara Crooker (3-20, 7-8, 10-16) from Fogelsville, Pennsylvania, has two books of poetry, *Radiance* and *Line Dance*. (Word Press). Her work has appeared in *Christianity and Literature, The Christian Science Monitor, Perspectives, Literature and Belief,* and *America*. In 2003, she won the Thomas Merton Poetry of the Sacred Award. www.barbaracrooker.com.

Keith Dahlberg (6-27, 12-29) is a retired physician and medical missionary who has published a biography and a novel and is working on books three and four. He and his wife, Lois, live in Kellogg, Idaho. They have four adult children. keithdahlberg@hotmail.com.

Andee S. Davis (5-26) is a teacher, writer, wife, and mother. When she isn't plotting her next story, tutoring students in Latin, or reading her favorite historicals, she likes to sew for charity or take long drives from her home in Bismarck, North Dakota, into rural areas. www.andeesdavis.com.

Christy A. Davis (3-21) has a bachelor's degree in English/writing and lives in her hometown of Bismarck, North Dakota. She hopes to publish a series of chick lit novels starring full-figured women. cadavis01@ hotmail.com.

William Deans (11-26) of Fort Wayne, Indiana, is a retired American Baptist pastor. He served eight congregations in four states and taught in six colleges and seminary. He's an award-winning poet, playwright, and photographer. He now directs Clergy on Call, providing volunteer chaplaincy services to nursing homes and retirement centers.

Cheri L. Dedman (3-23) is a chaplain with Marketplace Chaplains USA. She earned a diploma for adult leadership, women's enrichment ministry through the Women in Seminary Doing Other Ministries (WISDOM) program at the Midwestern Theological Seminary in Kansas City, Missouri. She and her husband live in Plattsburg, Missouri. They have two grown sons. cheri@centurytel.net.

Mario Del Rosso (11-18), a retired teacher, lives in South Milwaukee, Wisconsin. He writes for the *Lake Geneva Regional News* and *The Wisconsin Regional Writer.* He has authored two books: *Geneva Days* and *Verse, or Worse.* Mdelrosso@wi.rr.com.

Sally Devine (1-4, 2-2, 3-3, 4-28, 6-2, 8-6, 12-31), a retired church secretary, lives at McGregor Lake in Montana. She is a member of The Writing Academy and coeditor of its newsletter. Sally is the mother of three children and grandmother of two. devine_59427@yahoo.com.

Betsy Dill (2-5, 7-6, 9-28, 11-22) of Centreville, Virginia, taught creative writing and journalism for five years in a private school. An award-winning humor and inspirational writer and director of Capital Christian Writers in Virginia, she has been published in newspapers, magazines, and anthologies such as Hallmark's *Laughing Out Loud.* www.betsydill.com.

Angie Kay Dilmore (3-6) lives in Lake Charles, Louisiana and is a member of St. Davids Christian Writers Association, Bayou Writers' Group, and the Society for

Children's Book Writers and Illustrators. She writes primarily for the children's magazine market. adilmore@bellsouth.net.

MaryAnn Diorio, Ph.D. (11-11), lives in Millville, New Jersey. Her writing has appeared in hundreds of publications including *The Saturday Evening Post* and *Human Events*. She's authored four books, contributed to six, and hosts Musings That Matter, a writers' blog. She's working on her first novel. www.maryanndiorio.com.

Lonni L. Docter (4-10, 8-16, 9-1, 10-12) is president of The Writing Academy. He enjoys writing poetry and short stories. A retired contractor, he uses his experience to write do-it-yourself articles for homeowners. Lonni lives in Tucson, Arizona. lonnidocter@hotmail.com.

Alisa Dollar (8-26) of Lubbock, Texas, works for Texas Tech University. Wife, mother of two, and Nana of two, she writes a weekly humor column for the *Frankston Citizen* newspaper and a monthly article for her church newsletter. She has received numerous awards for her fiction and nonfiction. texpeso@aol.com.

Melanie Dorsey (9-3) is passionate about languages, writing and teaching the Bible. She holds degrees in communications and foreign languages from Lee University. She lives in Clearwater, Florida, with her husband and children. mdorsey@tampabay.rr.com.

Brook Dwyer (2-17, 5-13, 11-23) of Dayton, Texas, a mother of two, began writing Bible study curriculum and Advent devotionals to teach her children about Christ. www.brookdwyer.blogspot.com.

Peggy Eastman (6-7, 9-12, 11-1) lives in Chevy Chase, Maryland, and is the author of *Godly Glimpses: Discoveries of the Love That Heals*. Her work has appeared in many publications including *Guideposts, The Living Church, Washingtonian, SELF, Ladies' Home Journal* and *Chicken Soup for the Caregiver's Soul*. peggyeastman@cs.com.

Gerald Ebelt (1-22, 7-20, 9-27, 12-19) is a retired pastor of the Evangelical Lutheran Church in America. He and his wife, Kathy, live in Cut Bank, Montana. They have four children and five grandchildren. Gerald enjoys writing, woodworking, camping, and gardening. ebelt!@ theglobal.net.

Annette M. Eckart (1-18) of Wading River, New York, founded Bridge for Peace (www.bridgefor-peace.org) in 1988 with her husband, Ed. Annette has ministered in Africa, Asia, Australia, Oceania, Europe, North America, Central America, and the West Indies.

Deborah Elliott-Upton (10-21) is published in *Writer's Digest*, Great Britain's *Fiction Feast* and *Mystery Reader's Journal* and two anthologies: *Carols and Crimes, Gifts, and Grifters,* and *Seven By Seven.* She writes a weekly article for www.criminalbrief.com. www.expressedimagination.com.

Lawrence D. Elliott (3-12, 9-24) is a published author and has been a Realtor in Southern California since 1989. Along with his wife, Lisa, and his dog, Lacie, he lives in Ontario, California. He also runs a network of real estate Web sites. www.LawrenceElliott.com.

Fran Elsea (1-25) is a former newspaper reporter and feature writer and a charter member of The Writing Academy. She now considers herself mostly a mom, grandma, and keeper of the dog and cats. She is married to Jerry Elsea and lives in Cedar Rapids, Iowa. jflz20@ mcleodusa.net.

Jerry Elsea (1-7, 2-21, 3-4, 4-24, 7-24) is a retired newspaper editor-writer and former Writing Academy president. He delights in writing on behalf of an inner-city mission established by United Methodist churches in Cedar Rapids, Iowa. jflz20@mcleodusa.net.

Pat Ennis (3-24, 8-9, 12-21) is the establishing chair and professor of the Department of Home Economics-Family and Consumer Sciences at The Master's College in Santa Clarita, California. She is author of *Precious in His Sight* and *the Fine Art of Becoming a Godly Woman,* and coauthor of three books. drennis@masters.edu.

James A. Fegan (5-31) was born and raised in Michigan's Upper Peninsula and educated at Michigan Technological University. After forty-one years in mining, he was called to Christian ministry in the late 1990s and now serves two United Methodist churches. He lives in Ishpeming. lorpman@aol.com.

Jessica Roach Ferguson (2-18, 6-25) is a novelist, a freelance writer, and coordinator for the Lamar University Write Site. Because of her husband's work, she bounces back and forth across the Texas/Louisiana line—with one fun jaunt to Scotland. She lives in Lake Charles, Louisiana. www.jessyferguson.blogspot.com.

Glenn W. Fisher (10-18), a retired Wichita State professor, has written his war memories, *Not to Reason Why: The Story of a One-Eyed Infantryman in World War II*. His journalistic journey through the Old Testament appears on the Residential Aliens Blog. He is married to Marvel. gfisher18@cox.net.

Char Forslund (9-17, 11-27) is a freelance writer from Bellevue, Washington. She has published numerous articles and over one hundred poems, and contributed to a devotional book. Char has led seminars on spiritual formation of children and has spoken at retreats. charforslund@comcast.net.

Paul Forsyth (3-1), originally from Arcadia, Wisconsin, graduated from Wartburg College in Waverly, Iowa. He now lives in Tokyo, Japan, where he teaches English to elementary school students, Ph.D. candidates, grandmothers, and everyone in between. tcsfj324@yahoo.co.jp.

Lee Franklin (3-18, 5-27, 7-10) lives in Australia with her husband and son. When not writing, reading, or home schooling her son, she loves going for long walks with her family and three dogs. www.LeeFranklin.com.

Eleanor Ramrath Garner (4-16) of San Diego, California, was an editor for Harcourt Brace Jovanovich Publishers for fourteen years. She's written fiction, articles, and the award-winning young adult memoir *Eleanor's Story: An American Girl in Hitler's Germany*. She lectures at educational institutions and is an exhibiting artist. ergarner@sbcglobal.net.

Tracey Williams Garrell (5-15) lives near Charlotte, North Carolina, with her husband, David, and two children, Jacob and Michael. She has worked for a variety of nonprofit agencies and ministries. Besides devoting time to her family, she is a freelance Christian writer and avid reader. traceygarrell@carolina.rr.com.

Margaret W. Garrison (3-26, 8-15, 10-28) has worked in higher education in Florida, South Carolina, and Indiana. Founding editor of *Kelley* magazine at Indiana University, she taught writing at Indiana-Purdue in Indianapolis and the University of Indianapolis. She teaches English at Lenoir-Rhyne College in Hickory, North Carolina. garrisonmw@lrc.edu.

Rebecca Willman Gernon (1-30) lives three-and-a-half feet under the sea in New Orleans, Louisiana, with her husband and cat. She writes plays, short stories, and essays. She attends a local Lutheran church. writer-rrg@cox.net.

Julie Gillies (12-3) has over thirty articles published in *The Bradenton* (Fla.) *Herald.* Julie serves in the women's ministry at her church. She lives in Bradenton with her husband, Keith, and two of their children. Their eldest son is in the U.S. Army. www.juliesjoyfuljourney.blogspot.com.

Louise Glimm (2-6), new to The Writing Academy, was the editor of two newsletters for several years. Louise lives in Conrad, Montana, and serves on the Montana Lutheran Women's Synodical Board. laglimm@hotmail.com.

Rose Goble (1-5, 4-6, 5-17, 7-9, 11-6) writes for *Vista* and *Standard* Sunday school papers. She published *A Horse Named Funny Bits* (D. C. Cook) in 1983. She hopes to sell historical Christian romance fiction. A Colorado gal, she now lives in Winamac, Indiana, and dispatches loads for her trucking hubby. mortrose@pwrtc.com.

Meredith Gould, Ph.D. (1-1, 3-9) of Princeton, New Jersey, is the author of six books, including *The Catholic Home* (Doubleday). She provides editorial and marketing communications services for individuals, organizations, and churches. Her adventures as an adult convert from Judaism to Christianity inform her work. www.meredithgould.com.

Beth Granger (4-29, 9-30) lives in Richfield, Minnesota. She and her husband, Gordy, have parented ten kids—foster, adoptive, and biological—leaving not much energy for writing. However, in 2007, she won second place in the Green Lake Writers' Conference contest for short fiction. Beth55423@yahoo.com.

Judyann Ackerman Grant (10-31) of Mannsville, New York, is a devotion writing instructor for The Writing Academy. She's had numerous devotions, inspirational articles, newspaper columns, and Bible curriculum published, including an essay in *Cup of Comfort for Weddings*. Her first children's book will be released in 2008. jagrant@tcenet.net.

Dianna Graveman's (9-6) work has appeared in several publications including *Chicken Soup for the Shopper's Soul* and *Cup of Comfort for Grandparents*. In 2007, she received a first- and second-place Missouri Writers Guild award and a first-place Catholic Press Association award. She lives in St. Charles, Missouri. www.diannagraveman.com.

William H. Griffith (1-9) is a chaplain for the Hospice of South Central Indiana. He lives in Columbus, Indiana, and is the author of *Confronting Death*, and *More Than a Parting Prayer: Lessons in Caregiving for the Dying* (Judson Press). wmgriffith@aol.com.

Henry Gross (8-24) of Nashville, Tennessee, is a singer, songwriter, recording artist, actor, and comedian. His 1976 hit, "Shannon," received a gold record. Co-founder of revival band Sha Na Na, he's working on a documentary about making "One-Hit Wanderer," a one-man show about his life and musical journey. henry@henrygross.com; www.henrygross.com.

Linda M. Hagenbuch (5-25) of Lewisburg, Pennsylvania, has published devotions and edited her company's newsletter. She has won prizes for fiction and poetry. lindaboo@jlink.net.

Amy J. Harrelson (3-17) has enjoyed writing stories since the second grade. She wrote "Bible Study Corner" for her church's newsletter for two years and is working on a children's story and a family history. Amy lives in

O'Fallon, Missouri, with her husband and three children. spamomma@centurytel.net.

Lydia E. Harris (10-7, 12-30) of Seattle, Washington, has contributed to twelve books including *The Write Start*. She's written stories, devotionals, articles, and book reviews. Her column, "A Cup of Tea with Lydia," is published across the United States and Canada. A former schoolteacher, she teaches at writers' conferences. LydiaHarris@Qwest.net.

Christine Hefte (6-9, 12-2) of Fergus Falls, Minnesota, was an English teacher, church youth director, student counselor, Bethel Bible Series teacher, Minnesota Public Radio board member, seminary student, and charter member of The Writing Academy. She self-published a book of her father's letters. crhefte@prtel.com.

Paulette B. Henderson (2-7) owns Page One in Anadarko, Oklahoma. She has written for clients in the corporate, nonprofit, and public sectors and has authored articles for *Christian Communicator, Northwest Christian Author,* and *Seattle Presbytery Spirit*. She is the host of *Community Forum* on KACO radio. paulette@hendersonhouse.net.

Dennis E. Hensley, Ph.D. (1-16), directs the professional writing major at Taylor University in Fort Wayne, Indiana, where he is a professor of English. He is the author of more than fifty books and is a columnist for *Advanced Christian Writer* and *Writer's Journal*.

Lisa Q. Herrin (6-15) of Plant City, Florida, is the author of *Life Interrupted* (AMG Publishers). She's had articles in *Proclaim, Inspire, The Evangel,* and various Church of God publications. Lisa is a women's conference speaker, pastor's wife, and local church mission director. www.lisaherrin.com.

Audrey Marie Hessler (2-19, 10-1) is a Christian author, speaker, and teacher. Her first book, *They Call Immanuel, God With Us*, is a Christian poetry and prose devotional. She is featured in *Refined by Fire*. Audrey teaches near Chicago, Illinois, where she lives with her family. www.AudreyMarie.com.

Dorothy Holley (4-3) combined gardening, poetry and photography in her book *The Garden Journals* (2006). FootHills Publishing also published her first book, *A Whole Quart Jar* (2005). She is a member of the Madwomen in the Attic Poetry Workshop at Carlow University and lives in Pittsburgh, Pennsylvania. dorothyh@verizon.net.

Charlotte Holt (3-19), author of *Praise the Lord for Roaches!*, holds a bachelor's in English and a master's in special education. A freelance writer, speaker, and retired teacher, she lives in Kingwood, Texas, with her husband, Charles. Two of her articles are in the When Miracles Happen books by Guideposts. www.published-authors.net/charlotteholt.

Lora J. Homan (7-12) teaches at the university level in northwest Pennsylvania. A teaching artist in poetry and creative writing with the Pennsylvania Council on the Arts, she directs a writers' conference, edits a poetry magazine, and speaks at writers' workshops. Her award-winning work has been published widely. timesing@zoominternet.net.

Judy Howard (6-10), Oklahoma City, Oklahoma, has owned Buckboard Antique Quilts (www.Buckboard-Quilts.com) since 1976. Sample stories of her award-winning *Heavenly Patchwork—Quilt Stories Stitched with Love, Heavenly Patchwork II* and *Centennial Stitches—Oklahoma History in Quilts* are available at www.HeavenlyPatchwork.com.

Kimmy Howard (8-31) is an early childhood teacher at Des Moines (Iowa) Christian School. She graduated from Taylor University with ministry and early childhood degrees. She has written for and been spotlighted in articles in *Christian Early Education*. She is married to Tim, a medical student.

Michele T. Huey (5-4, 8-11, 9-29) of Glen Campbell, Pennsylvania, writes a newspaper column and produces a daily radio program, "God, Me & a Cup of Tea." She published two meditations books, has written for magazines and anthologies, teaches writing workshops, and is a writing mentor and speaker. michele-huey@yahoo.com; www.michelehuey.com.

Pamela Humphreys (9-14) is a freelance writer, Bible teacher, and registered dietitian. She has written patient education materials for the Oklahoma Medical Center and the Oklahoma Diet Manual. She enjoys writing devotions, poetry, and short stories, several of which have been published. Pamela resides in Edmond, Oklahoma. DelandPam1@sbcglobal.net.

Robbie Iobst (6-11) of Centennial, Colorado, has been published in *Today's Christian*, *Chicken Soup for the Tea Lover's Soul*, and *Laundry Tales to Lighten the Load*. She and her husband, John, are the proud parents of Noah. robbieiobst@hotmail.com; www.robbieiobst.blogspot.com.

Brenda Kay Jackson (3-25), Mesa, Arizona, is a devotional/screenwriter, Western novelist and member of American Christian Fiction Writers. Her coauthored screenplay was a quarterfinalist in the national Fade In Awards. She established the East Valley Christian Writers group. arizonawriterbj@yahoo.com.

Gloria Jackson (8-7) and her late husband were missionaries in Africa and Europe, then worked with a media ministry producing videos for worldwide distribution. Gloria lives in Lakeland, Florida, and ministers to missionaries around the world. gjackso3@tampabay.rr.com.

Sally Jadlow (4-14, 6-19, 8-18) from Overland Park, Kansas, is a wife, mother, and grandmother who serves as a chaplain to corporations in the greater Kansas City area. Her latest books are *The Late Sooner*, historical fiction, and *Sonflower Seeds*, a collection of poetry and inspirational short stories. www.SallyJadlow.com.

Nancy E. James (2-1, 4-13, 6-3, 9-10, 11-4, 12-28), a retired English teacher from Pittsburgh, Pennsylvania, leads workshops in creative writing and journaling. Most of her published work is poetry. She is a past director of The Writing Academy, the current newsletter editor for St. Davids Christian Writers Association, and an encourager of other writers.

Sherri Wilson Johnson (8-30) lives with her husband and children in Dallas, Georgia. She is a home-schooling mom, writer, and speaker. Sherri writes fiction, Bible studies, and home-schooling helps. www.sherri-johnsonministries.com.

Louise Tucker Jones (2-10, 5-23) is an inspirational speaker and author and coauthor of three books, including *Extraordinary Kids*. She's been published in numerous magazines and anthologies including *Guideposts* and Chicken Soup for the Soul books. Louise resides in Edmond, Oklahoma. LouiseTJ@cox.net; www.LouiseTucker-Jones.com.

Deb Kalmbach (7-7) is the coauthor of *Because I Said Forever: Embracing Hope in a Not-So-Perfect Marriage*. Deb's speaking gives hope and help to those in difficult relationships. She and her husband, Randy, live Winthrop, Washington. debkalmbach@centurytel.net; www.debkalmbach.com.

Heather Kendall (11-20) is a Sunday school teacher and a women's Bible study leader. She is also a speaker and the author of *A Tale of Two Kingdoms*. Heather lives in Innisfil, Ontario, Canada, with her husband, Barry. They have three grown children. www.tale2k.com.

Virelle Kidder (1-10) a full-time writer and conference speaker, has been speaking and writing for over twenty-five years about the love of Christ. Moody Publishers released her fifth book, *Meet Me at the Well,* in January 2008. Virelle has four grown children and eight grandchildren. She lives in Sebastian, Florida. www.virellekidder.com.

Betty King (2-23, 9-2) is an author of four books, a lifestyle and devotional newspaper columnist and speaker who lives with multiple sclerosis. She is a frequent contributor to the Chicken Soup for the Soul series and other anthologies. Betty lives in Mount Vernon, Illinois. Baking2@charter.net; www.bettyking.net.

Sharon King, Ph.D. (8-20) has an M.A. in anthropology and a Ph.D. in sociology. She researches religion and aging at Georgia State University in Atlanta. Her writing background is mainly academic, but she is exploring God's call to do more inspirational writing. svking@msn.com; www.faithwriters.com/memberprofile.php?id=30473.

Jami Kirkbride (2-22, 4-27, 6-29, 9-19) has a master's degree in counseling. She's a freelance writer, speaker, and personality trainer. She lives on a ranch in Meriden, Wyoming where her husband, Jeff, and four children inspire her. Jami is a contributing author to *When God Steps In* and *Laundry Tales*. www.jamikirkbride.com.

Mary A. Koepke (1-24, 6-22, 10-11) lives in the Passavant retirement community at Zelienople, Pennsylvania. She is a freelance illustrator and writer and belongs to several writing and poetry groups. Taking photos to use as reference for her artwork is a favorite pastime. makoepke@zoominternet.net.

Nancy Julien Kopp (6-18) has published stories, articles, essays, children's stories and poetry in magazines, newspapers, e-zines, and anthologies, including six Chicken Soup for the Soul books. A former teacher, she still enjoys teaching through the written word. Nancy lives in the Flint Hills of Kansas with her husband. kopp@networksplus.net.

Rev. Marlys Korman (1-17), Outing, Minnesota, is a pastor in the Evangelical Lutheran Church in America at Faith Lutheran church, Swanburg, in Pine River. She is also treasurer of The Writing Academy. marlysk@brainerd.net.

Dale Kueter (12-16) is a retired newspaper writer. He and his wife, Helen, have five daughters, thirteen grandchildren, and live in Cedar Rapids, Iowa. He is the author of a nonfiction book, *Vietnam Sons* (2007) and a children's picture book, *Hide the Daddy* (2005). dhkueter5@msn.com.

Helene Clare Kuoni (2-9, 9-5, 12-18) enjoys writing Christian devotions and short stories, especially at her vacation home in Lake Pleasant, New York. She and her husband, John, have also coauthored a book: *Her Pen for His Glory: The 1860s Verse of Isabella Stiles Mead*. helloheleneK@hotmail.com.

Rev. Percy L. Kvitne (6-13) of Grimes, Iowa, graduated from North Dakota State Teachers College. He received a master's in education from Drake University, Des Moines, Iowa, and a master's of divinity from Luther Seminary, St. Paul, Minnesota. He was a public school teacher while serving Lutheran parishes in Paullina, Grimes, and Fredericka, Iowa.

Patty Kyrlach (1-20, 6-16, 8-29, 9-16) is a children's writer who lives in southwestern Ohio near Winchester. She is a founding editor of *Cookies & Milk,* a young readers feature in several Ohio newspapers. patty.kyrlach@gmail.com.

Lonnie Lane (5-21) of Jacksonville, Florida, is author of *Because They Never Asked* as well as numerous articles, stories, and poems. She writes a weekly Web article for Messianic Vision Ministries (www.sidroth.org) on the Hebrew roots of Christianity. As radio and TV producer for Messianic Vision, she also writes scripts.

Bonnie Lanthripe (8-3) and husband, parents of four grown children, reside in Edmond, Oklahoma. Bonnie holds a master's degree in creative writing and a bachelor's in theatre. She has authored stage plays and short stories. Her devotionals have appeared in books published for her church. She is working on a novel. jim-bonnie@prodigy.net.

Kay Laughlin (4-2), mother of two grown children, lives in St. Louis, Missouri, with her husband, Jim. She participates in a women's Prayer and Share group and is one of a group of rotating writers who contribute to the Spread the Word feature in the local newspaper. laugh14642@mindspring.com.

Agnes Lawless (4-18), Snohomish, Washington, is the author/coauthor of seven books, including *The Drift into Deception* (Kregel) and *God's Character* (Gospel Light). She's published many articles and copyedits books. A graduate of Seattle Pacific University, she did graduate work in journalism at Syracuse University. agneslaw@aol.com.

Yvonne Lehman (4-11, 8-12, 12-20), Black Mountain, North Carolina, is an award-winning, best-selling author of forty-five novels. She directs the Blue Ridge Mountains

Christian Writers Conference and the Blue Ridge Autumn in the Mountains Novel Retreat. www.yvonnelehman.com; www.lifeway.com/christianwriters.

Tommie Lenox (1-14, 3-22, 5-19, 7-18, 9-18, 11-7, 12-24) is a retired teacher and principal from El Cajon, California. She is currently writing and producing videos with the San Diego County Office of Education. Tommie is also a poet and author of *Crying in the Wilderness, a Voice for America's Children.* tsdlenox@sbcglobal.net

Patricia Lorenz (1-3, 2-29, 4-23, 6-14, 8-5, 10-26, 12-26) is an art-of-living, inspirational writer and speaker, the author/coauthor of eleven books; over four hundred articles, essays and stories; and one of the top contributing writers for the Chicken Soup for the Soul books. She lives in Largo, Florida. patricialorenz@juno.com; www.PatriciaLorenz.com.

Nancy Lucas (4-21) lives in the Florida Keys with her husband and children. She is an author, speaker, and business consultant. Nancy is a contributing author to *Everyday Grace, Everyday Miracle* and writes devotionals. www.giftedquill.com.

Kimberly Lytle (7-31) lives in St. Charles, Missouri, with her husband, Matthew, and two sons, Joseph and Jason. She graduated from Creighton University with a B.A. in English and received her master's in teaching from Webster University. She's a lifelong member of Immanuel United Church of Christ in Ferguson, Missouri. lytle_kimberly@yahoo.com.

Lea Mack (2-15) is a music therapist, speaker, song writer, and author of *God's Healing Hand Bible Study, Personal Presentation Skills for Pageants,* and devotionals for *Daily Transformations.* Winner of the Alma K. Weber award at the 2007 St. Davids Christian Writers' Conference, she lives in Myrtle Beach, South Carolina. www.LeaMack.com.

Denise May (6-26) is a freelance writer, business consultant and creative writing instructor. On her ranch in Shawnee, Oklahoma, she also hosts life enrichment classes and teaches the art of horse whispering.

maymrktng@aol.com; denisemayhorses@aol.com.

Rose McCauley (7-4), Cynthiana, Kentucky, has been married for forty years to her farmer husband. A retired teacher, Rose has been published in five nonfiction anthologies. Her goal is to be published in fiction. crmcc@setel.com; www.rosemccauley.com; www.rosemccauley.blogspot.com.

Vicki Talley McCollum (7-19) lives with her husband and three children in Tulsa, Oklahoma. She writes book reviews, author interviews, and the Grammar & Style column for www.Dabblingmum.com. jvmccnfam@gmail.com; www.vickitalleymccollum.blogspot.com/.

Donna McCormick (9-25), an Irish/German western Oklahoman, lived through the Dust Bowl and World War II. After college, she married a minister and had three children. Donna belongs to Wordwrights, a monthly Christian writers' group. She lives in Weatherford, Oklahoma.

Carolyn Meagher (7-1, 10-5, 12-7), Okanogan, Washington, writes articles, essays, devotionals, short stories, and a writing contests column for the *Northwest Christian Author*. She's the author of *Seasoned With Love: Heart-healthy Recipes & Reflections about Food, Family, Faith, & Friends* (SpringBoard). carolynmeagher@yahoo.com.

Lissa Merriman (8-22), an Amarillo, Texas native, has been published by greeting card companies Oatmeal Studios and Dayspring Blessings, *From the Asylum* magazine, and *The Amarillo-Globe News*. She was a finalist in novel-writing contests and is working on a book about life on the Texas Plains. Mrsrgm @randym.com.

Ginnie Mesibov (6-24, 9-22) of Philadelphia, Pennsylvania, is the author of *Outer Strength, Inner Strength*. She is a member of the International Women's Writing Guild and a popular Bible study leader and motivational speaker. ginnie@mesibov.net; www.outerstrengthinnerstrength.com.

Ann Michels (11-8) graduated from Colorado State University and now lives in Fremont, California. Ann was published in the e-book *Beyond the Closet Door* and has published a travelogue at www.Edenglory.com. She has also been published in the *San Francisco Chronicle*.

Jane Miller (7-14) from Pittsburgh, Pennsylvania, writes Heart Tales columns for newspapers and also writes for *Pittsburgh Professional* magazine. Jane and Sally (Oberdick)'s Heart Stories at the Children's Museum of Pittsburgh teaches the RRRuff way to write: Respect, Reading & 'Riting Using Fact and Fiction. rkmjam3@comcast.net.

Jet Moore (9-7) spent the last two decades collecting words from the Deep South and Mid-Atlantic. He writes from the greater Columbus, Ohio area with his dogs, Nikita and Midnite. screamingpen@yahoo.com.

Peggy Morris (3-28, 11-16) is a CLASS graduate, writer, pastor's wife, and mom. She's written hundreds of greeting cards and is published in *Chicken Soup for the Chocolate Lover's Soul, The Heart of A Mother, Marriage Partnership, and Woman's World*. Peggy lives in Largo, Florida. peggymorris@htcog.net.

Julie Morrison (4-9, 7-29, 10-25, 12-22) writes essays, poetry and short stories from Sunbury, Ohio. She's been published in *Hurricane Blues: Poetry of Katrina and Rita, Why You're the Best Friend in the World*, and *The Best Dad in the World*. TheRadicalWrite.blogspot.com.

Mary Englund Murphy (1-31, 10-30) is the author of *Winning the Battle of the Bulge: It's Not Just About the Weight* and is a popular speaker. She and her husband, Bill, live in Tulsa, Oklahoma. www.winningthebattleof-thebulge.com.

Sally Murtagh's (5-3, 8-23) passions have led her into reporting, writing and performing music, mentoring a MOPS chapter, and cofounding several local women's ministries. She and her husband are recent empty nesters and reside in Metuchen, New Jersey. sallymurtagh@durhamave.com.

Judith Nembhard (12-17), a retired college and university English professor and administrator, writing workshop presenter, and women's retreat speaker, is now an adjunct instructor and freelance writer in Chattanooga, Tennessee. Jpnemb5@aol.com,

Carol Nilles (6-6) lives and writes in Thiensville, Wisconsin. She belongs to a weekly group called Writing for Publication. In her youth, Carol taught language arts to Iowa middle-school children. She is now retired after years of easier jobs in Milwaukee offices and real estate sales. nillescaapple@yahoo.com.

Marilyn Marsh Noll (5-8, 10-9) has an MFA in creative writing from American University and has been published in newspapers. Her *Thirteen Ways of Looking at Bones* won the 2007 Pennsylvania Poetry Society Chapbook Award. Marilyn is a member of the Madwomen in the Attic writing workshop and lives in Pittsburgh, Pennsylvania. grammyskip@yahoo.com.

Pam O'Brien (12-25) is the associate director of public and professional writing at the University of Pittsburgh, a member of the Mount Lebanon Christian Writers' Group and the Squirrel Hill Poetry Workshop. She has one husband, three children, and two grandchildren and lives in Pittsburgh, Pennsylvania. redactor7@aol.com.

Karen O'Connor (4-8), Watsonville, California, is an award-winning author of more than fifty-five books, a speaker, and a writing mentor for Jerry B. Jenkins' Christian Writers Guild. karen@karenoconnor.com; www.karenoconnor.com.

Ruth J. Otto (5-11) is a charter member of The Writing Academy, a Bethel teacher, and a graduate of Western Seminary. She was a curriculum writer for *Celebrate* and *Being God's Covenant People, Then And Now* produced by The Writing Academy. Ruth is a music educator and church musician in Grimes, Iowa. horo17@aol.com.

Barbara Parentini (5-18, 7-26) lives near Chapel Hill, North Carolina. She writes devotions, creative nonfiction, and fiction. Recent publications include *Soaring Hearts Cards*, and *Living Letters: Letters from the Heart, Letters that Heal,* and a journal available in 2008. www.barbaraparentini.com; barbara@barbaraparentini.com.

Frances Gregory Pasch (11-28) is a freelance writer and poet. She and her husband live in Washington, New Jersey. They have five sons and eight grandchildren. Frances has had several hundred poems, devotions, and articles published. She creates her own greeting cards incorporating her poetry. paschf@comcast.net.

Diane C. Perrone (11-15) has a master of arts in advertising/education. Between grandbabies, she writes from Franklin, Wisconsin. She has been published in *Redbook, Exclusively Yours, Girl Talk, Catholic Digest, Family Digest,* aviation periodicals, *Marquette University Magazine, Catholic Herald, The Milwaukee Journal,* and two Chicken Soup books.

Trish Perry (2-8, 12-14) lives in Northern Virginia with her hilarious teenage son. She discovered her love of writing while earning a degree in psychology. Her novels include *The Guy I'm Not Dating* and *Too Good to Be True.* www.trishperrybooks.com.

William Elof Peterson (5-30), a fifteen-year member of The Writing Academy, has authored *BILL,* a children's book, and four poetry books. Bill and his wife live in Douglasville, Georgia, and have six children, nineteen grandchildren, and eight great grandchildren. BillOnsite@aol.com.

Karen H. Phillips (3-27) of Flintstone, Georgia, kicked off her call to write with a paid published review of the first writers' conference she attended. A year later, she traveled to Mount Hermon Christian Writers' Conference via a Cecil Murphey scholarship. kphillipso@aol.com; sky-highview.blogspot.com/.

Kathy Pride (3-31) is a wife, mother, writer, speaker, parent educator, and encourager. She lives in Danville, Pennsylvania, with her physician husband, two daughters, and menagerie of pets. She also has two grown sons. Kathy@www.kathypride.com; www.kathypride.com.

Roy Proctor (7-22, 11-14) is a freelance writer who resides in Middleburg, Florida. He writes devotionals under the title *Words for Kingdom Living* and is authoring a book with TLC Ministries to help new Christians to become grounded in faith.

Margaret "Maggie" Arnold Register (4-5) and her husband Joe's missionary careers spanned thirty-seven years in Mexico, Chile, Paraguay, Ecuador, and Colombia. They produced a television program for children, *El Lugar Secreto* (The Secret Place). Maggie and Joe retired in Lakeland, Florida, and she is now writing their memoirs. Maggie6@tampabay.rr.com.

Carol McAdoo Rehme (3-29, 5-22, 7-13, 9-8, 11-24, 12-27) is the coauthor of five gift books as well as a ghostwriter and editor. Her second Chicken Soup book, *Empty Nester's Soul,* will be released in 2008. Carol lives in Loveland, Colorado carol@rehme.com; www.rehme.com.

Nancy Remmert (1-11, 5-14), St. Louis, Missouri, is a charter member of The Writing Academy; a trained Bethel Bible teacher; an active member of Immanuel United Church of Christ, Church Women United, and Interfaith Partnership/Faith Beyond Walls; and the mother of four and grandmother of six. NRemm10335@aol.com.

Rosa Lee Richards (10-24) lives in western Pennsylvania with her husband, Jack. She was born in New York and has lived in Latin America, the Philippines and Europe. A retired lawyer, she teaches Hebrew at an Episcopal seminary. Her true vocation, however, is grandparenting her four grandchildren. richardsrosale@access995.com.

Melanie Rigney (3-11, 6-21, 10-17, 11-25) is a St. Davids Christian Writers' Association board member. Her business, www.editorforyou.com, has helped hundreds of authors, publishers, and agents. Her memoir is titled *What to Wear on Your Way to Hell...and Other Detours to Heaven.* The former editor of *Writer's Digest,* Melanie lives in Arlington, Virginia.

Nan Rinella (8-1), Amarillo, Texas, is a late bloomer: married at twenty-seven; mother at thirty-eight; college at forty-eight; Washington, D.C., Humans Events fellow at fifty; and author at fifty-nine. She has served as president and publicity chair of Panhandle Professional Writers and conference director of Frontiers in Writing. ndrinella@gmail.com.

Sandra Robbins (11-2) is a full-time writer and adjunct college professor from Martin, Tennessee. She and her husband have four children and five grandchildren. Her cozy mystery, *Pedigreed Bloodlines*, (2008) is set in the Smoky Mountains. sandra@sandrarobbins.net; sandrarobbins.net.

Cindy Rooy (11-10) is a wife; mother of three adult children; and inspirational writer and speaker. She enjoys writing and teaching women's Bible studies. Cindy is a fan of the Chicago Cubs, NASCAR, and solving the newspaper's daily puzzles. She lives in Kingsport, Tennessee. jcrooy@mail.com.

Marcia A. Russotto (9-26) lives in Gibsonia, Pennsylvania, with her husband, Sam. They have three grown children and one grandson. Creative writing was a hobby until her first magazine article was published. Now it's a passion, and she just finished her first book, a memoir. marcia451@hotmail.com.

Jan Sady (2-28, 5-29, 9-4, 11-29), Mayport, Pennsylvania, is an author, speaker, lay minister, and editor of *The Path Leads*, a writers' group publication. She's published hundreds of stories, articles, devotions, poetry, as well as two devotionals: *God's Lessons from Nature* and *Gods Parables & Lessons 2*, and historical fiction, *The Bird Woman*. janfran@alltel.net.

Joy Salyers (8-21) is a folklorist, writer, consultant, and anti-racism educator in Durham, North Carolina. She believes in the power of stories and writing to connect and to heal.

Connie Scharlau (1-13, 3-15, 4-30, 6-12, 8-8, 10-22, 12-15) lives in the hills of west central Wisconsin. She loves to read, do Sudoku puzzles, walk, knit, read, write, paint watercolors, ride motorcycles, bake bread, read, tell stories, volunteer, learn new things, eat, play with grandchildren, and read. conschar@triwest.net.

Ruth Schlesser (4-25) was born and raised in Arcadia, Wisconsin, and still lives there. She's the proud mother of five grown children, three boys and two girls. Ruth has written Ruth's Garden column since 2003 in the *Arcadia News Leader*. ruthschlesser@yahoo.com.

Kate E. Schmelzer (4-4, 8-25) graduates from Taylor University in Fort Wayne, Indiana, in 2008 with majors in professional writing and counseling and a minor in Christian education. She was the book review columnist for *Ignite Your Faith* magazine in 2006 and 2007 and writes for numerous Christian magazines. kateeliseschmelzer@gmail.com.

Kathy Scott (1-28) has had more than six hundred articles published in more than sixty-five publications. She is a correspondent for Lancaster, Pennsylvania, newspapers. She served on the board of St. Davids Christian Writers' Association and the staff of Sandy Cove Christian Communicators. bobscott@supernet.com

Barbara Seaborn (10-27) has been a newspaper columnist and freelance writer in Augusta, Georgia, for nearly twenty-five years. She is also a church organist, which led to further writing assignments including music commentary for four piano and organ magazines. She has two sons and five grandchildren. seabara@aol.com.

Elizabeth Sebek (3-13, 5-1, 10-15) lives in Woodbine, Maryland, with her husband, George, the pastor of Oakridge Community church in Clarksville. They have six children with two married daughters and two grandchildren. bethseb@hotmail.com.

Julie Sevig (6-1) is an associate editor at *The Lutheran* magazine in Chicago, Illinois. Her 2007 releases are: *Peanut Butter and Jelly Prayers* (Morehouse), and a story, "An Expensive Pound of Coffee," in *Chicken Soup for the Coffee Lover's Soul*. Julie.Sevig@thelutheran.org; www.thelutheran.org.

Doris Jean Shaw (8-13), De Ridder, Louisiana, is a retired educator, writer and member of The Ink Blots. She loves to write about her travels along with children's stories and devotionals. Doris presents a workshop, titled Reclaiming Me, that helps women find direction for their futures.

dj_shorty40@hotmail.com; www.reclaimingme.com.

Dayle Allen Shockley's (3-16, 5-28, 12-6) articles and essays have appeared in dozens of publications. A Houston, Texas, resident, she's a special contributor to *The Dallas Morning News*, author of three books, and a contributing writer to other works. dayle@dayle-shockley.com; www.dayleshockley.com.

Anne Siegrist (2-13, 6-17, 11-3) lives on a farm in Jasper in upstate New York where she and her husband raised six children. She is a volunteer for Compeer, Faith in Action, and Jasper-Troupsburg Elementary School, where she reads weekly to kindergartners. asiegrist@frontiernet.net.

Gloria Tietgens Sladek (4-22, 10-23) is a charter member of The Writing Academy. She and husband Dean reside in Chagrin Falls, Ohio. They have two children, eight grand-children and three great-grandchildren. gdsladek@windstream.net.

Barbara Smith (5-24) is a freelance writer/editor and medical ethicist. She's an emerita professor in literature and writing, and former chair of the Division of the Humanities at Alderson-Broaddus College in Philippi, West Virginia. smith_b@ab.edu.

Sonia C. Solomonson (1-23, 9-13) is managing editor for *The Lutheran* magazine and executive editor for *The Little Lutheran*, a toddler magazine she helped launch in 2007. She has been with *The Lutheran* for twenty years and lives in Streamwood, Illinois. sonia.solomonson@thelutheran.org.

Kathryn Spurgeon (3-7), a writer, counselor, and CPA, publishes articles for Back40 magazines and has written several Bible studies. On the writing team at Henderson Hills Baptist Church, she and her husband have six children and reside in Oklahoma. www.risein-truth.org.

Margaret Steinacker (1-6, 2-14, 3-5, 5-2, 7-2, 8-10) is a Writing Academy worship leader and plays keyboards for a vibrant United Methodist Church. She and her husband, Gerry, live in Winamac, Indiana, and have two sons and seven grandchildren. steinmag@gmail.com.

Ethel Jensen Stenzel (2-27, 5-7, 8-17, 11-12) and her husband, Norman, live in Egg Harbor, Wisconsin, and winter in Dunedin, Florida. She is a speaker for Stonecroft Ministries and has authored and published *Connections of the Heart, A Door County, Wisconsin Girl's Journey of Faith*. ethelstenzel@hotmail.com.

Shirley Stevens (3-14, 5-6, 7-30, 10-10, 12-10) serves as Poet in Person for the International Poetry Forum. She has been published in magazines from *Poet Lore* to *English Journal.* Shirley writes a poetry column and teaches workshops at several writers' conferences. She lives in Pittsburgh, Pennsylvania. poetcat@comcast.net.

Jean Fritz Stewart (8-28), North Versailles, Pennsylvania, is vice president of St. Davids Christian Writers Association. Her passion is to help people develop and use their talents. She is working on a book to help Christians be more creative. Jean_Stewart@verizon.net.

Jackie Strange (8-14, 11-5), a retired university teacher from Bogalusa, Louisiana, directed a Christian association with a radio and television ministry. She has written three novels and fifteen short stories, some prize winning and published in small presses. She now has an editor as she tries to place a novel about forgiveness. strangetosay4@aol.com.

Ellen Strickland (11-13) spent four years in France, four in Scotland, and twenty-eight in New Zealand. A retired nature photographer and poet, she's been published in *Christianity Today.* A member of the Pittsburgh Poetry Society and Madwomen in the Attic, she lives in Pittsburgh, Pennsylvania. ellenstrick@yahoo.com.

Linda Strong (4-15, 10-14) lives near Birmingham, Alabama, with her husband of thirty-two years. Linda has written articles for the newsletter of a local retirement facility and has been published in *The Birmingham News*. meow2133@aol.com.

Marcia Swearingen (2-11), a former newspaper

editor and columnist, now freelances full time. Her stories have appeared in *Guideposts*, Chicken Soup for the Soul books, Cup of Comfort books, and numerous local publications. She and her husband, Jim, have been married thirty-six years and live in Hixson, Tennessee. mswearingen@comcast.net.

Chiara Talluto (7-21) is a freelance writer with a background in instructional design. She writes inspirational, spiritual, and contemporary mainstream essays, and recently completed her first novel. Chiara lives in Chicago, Illinois. ctalluto18@hotmail.com.

Nanette Thorsen-Snipes (10-2) has had articles and columns in over forty publications and forty-five compilation books including: Guideposts *Miracles and Prayer, New Women's Devotional Bible, Grace Givers*, and the God's Way series. She lives in north Georgia with her husband, Jim. They have four grown children and four grandchildren. www.nanettesnipes.com.

James R. Tozer, Ph.D. (1-2) founded and served a church near Purdue University for forty years and wrote *Glen Arbor Pioneers* and *Tales of Manitou*. On October 13, 2007, Jim died after a battle with lung cancer. He was a gift to The Writing Academy for thirty years.

Claudia N. Tynes (10-4) of Clinton, Maryland, is a freelance writer, teacher, and columnist. She has written two books and over two hundred articles, devotionals, short stories, poems, and greeting cards for print and online publications. Claudiatynes.com/.

Elizabeth Mary Van Hook (4-7, 6-20) is retired and lives in Clifton, New Jersey. She is a regular contributor to *Penned from the Heart* and has been published in *Time of Singing*. She is active at the Calvary Baptist Church in Clifton. koekjie@optonline.net.

Sheryl Van Weelden (1-8, 3-10, 7-3, 8-27, 11-19) is a Christian school administrator. She has been published in *Christian Early Education* and recently coauthored *Under the Tea Leaves* with her daughter. She lives in Des Moines, Iowa, where she is a wife, mother of many, and grandmother to more. jsvw@mchsi.com.

Dorissa J. "Prissy" Vanover (2-12, 7-25), Amarillo, Texas, is an award-winning author who has written for *The Amarillo Globe News* and *The Quanah Tribune-Chief.* A member of Panhandle Professional Writers and Inspirational Writers Alive!, she is working on a series of nonfiction Christian books titled *Let's Visit, Lord.* prissy@sablerealty.com.

June Varnum (11-17) is the author of numerous articles, devotions, and short stories. She has taught Sunday school and vacation Bible school, and led women's retreat workshops. June lives in Loyalton, California. jvarnum@psln.com.

Stacy Voss (3-30) of Highlands Ranch, Colorado, writes on topics such as parenting and overcoming obstacles. She cofounded www.meetmeattheintersection.com and is a member of Words for the Journey Christian Writers Guild. stacy_voss@comcast.net.

Susan Huey Wales (2-19) is a storyteller, author, coauthor, and producer. She's the author of *A Keepsake Christmas* with Alice Gray, and coauthor of the Match Made in Heaven series. Susan is the executive producer of the annual Movieguide Awards. She and her husband, Ken, live in California. susan.wales@verizon.net.

Pam Wanzer (7-5, 10-29) left her career of twenty-five years in the financial industry to pursue a ministry in writing. She is writing her life experiences and founding a ministry to help women transition through the many seasons of their life. Pam resides in Edmond, Oklahoma. pamwanzer@cox.net.

Gail Welborn (7-23), Sedro-Woolley, Washington, writes monthly book review columns for *Christian News Northwest* and *Montgomery's Journey;* audio reviews for *AudioFile Magazine;* and book reviews for *The Christian Suspense Zone.* gail.d.welborn@verizon.net; www.gail-welborn.com.

Kathy Whirity (2-16, 4-12, 5-5, 7-17, 9-15, 12-11) a newspaper columnist from Chicago, Illinois, shares her sentimental musings on family life. Her book is titled *Life Is a Kaleidoscope.* kathywhirity@yahoo.com; www.kathywhirity.com.

Robyn Whitlock (10-13, 12-8) lives in Naperville, Illinois, and has been married to her best friend, Paul, for ten years. She is the mother of three boys, Bryce, Andrew, and Benjamin. When she's not chasing after the boys, doing laundry, or running to carpool, she writes. robyn_whitlock@mac.com.

Emily Tipton Williams (5-16, 7-28, 10-19) is a freelance writer and violinist. She serves as a lay minister and spiritual director in the Episcopal Church in Fort Worth, Texas. Emily's novel, *Restless Soul,* is set in the UK, one of her frequent travel destinations. emilywilliams@aol.com; www.members.aol.com\emilywilliams.

Olga M. Williams (5-12, 9-9, 12-1), honorary lifetime member of The Writing Academy, lives with her husband in her hometown of Republic, Michigan. She retired from teaching college in Alabama. Her current writing project is a compilation of family stories. oldow@up.net.

Scott Williams (2-24), Amarillo, Texas, is an insurance agent, writer, member of Panhandle Professional Writers, water colorist, and quilter. He writes mysteries for young adults and adults. scottlite@amaonline.com.

Shannon Wine (2-4, 7-16) is a freelance writer who lives outside Orlando, West Virginia. She writes fiction and nonfiction and has received awards for her writing. She's on the board of directors for St. Davids Christian Writers' Association. nshannonsworld@hotmail.com.

Danny Woodall (3-2, 9-20) lives in Port Neches, Texas. He and his wife have three children. Danny has worked for the postal service for over twenty-six years. He enjoys writing and chess. He has written articles for *Christian Online Magazine* and for LifeWay's *Essential Connections* and *Bible Express* magazines. dannywoodall500@hotmail.com.

Drew Zahn (1-26, 7-11), former editor of *Christianity Today,* writes in rural Iowa, surrounded by his eleven children and all their delightful distractions. He offers writing, speaking, and editorial services through his company, Storycraft Communications. drew@storycraftcommunications.com; www.storycraftcommunications.com.

Beth Ann Ziarnik (1-26, 7-11), Oshkosh, Wisconsin, wrote for twelve years before seeing her first published-for-pay article in print. The author of numerous articles, anthology pieces, and her own monthly inspirational column, Beth also speaks at women's and writers' events. www.bethziarnik.com.

Jeanne Zornes (2-25, 4-19, 7-27, 10-20), Wenatchee, Washington, has written hundreds of articles and short stories and seven books, including *When I Prayed for Patience...God Let Me Have It!* She's worked for newspapers, magazines, and book publishers and has taught writing at conferences and colleges and by correspondence.

Daily Devotions for Writers is a fundraiser for The Writing Academy, a not-for-profit organization 501(c)(3). You may order copies of this book for yourself or your church, club, organization or writers group by visiting www.buybookson-theweb.com or calling Infinity Publishing at 1-877-BUY-BOOK (1-877-289-2665). You will receive a 40 percent discount on all orders of five or more ($11.97) each). On all orders of twenty or more, you receive free shipping and handling from Infinity Publishing. If you order bulk copies of the book and resell them at the retail price of $19.95, we ask that you consider sending $7.98 per copy as a donation to The Writing Academy. You may do this by clicking on Dues & Donations at www.wams.org, using PayPal or a credit or debit card, or by mailing a check or money order payable to The Writing Academy to the treasurer's address posted on the Web site.

Thank you for helping to promote good writing by helping us market this book. May you and your writing be blessed tremendously.

Gratefully,
The Writing Academy members